A Whirlwind Swirling

BOOK 3 of the SUPERSTARS TRILOGY

A Whirlwind Swirling

BOOK 3 of the SUPERSTARS TRILOGY

SIG KRIEBEL

REDEMPTION PRESS

Published by Redemption Press, PO Box 427, Enumclaw, WA 98022.
Toll Free (844) 2REDEEM (273-3336)

Redemption Press is honored to present this title in partnership with the author. The views expressed or implied in this work are those of the author. Redemption Press provides our imprint seal representing design excellence, creative content, and high quality production.

Unless otherwise noted, all Scriptures are taken from the Holy Bible, New International Version, Copyright © 1973, 1978, 1984 by the International Bible Society. Used by permission of Zondervan Publishing House. The "NIV" and "New International Version" trademarks are registered in the United States Patent and Trademark Office by International Bible Society.

This is a work of fiction. All of the characters, names, incidents, organizations, and dialogue in this novel are either the products of the author's imagination or are used fictitiously.

ISBN 13: 978-1-68314-484-7 (Print)
978-1-68314-485-4 (ePub)
978-1-68314-486-1 (Mobi)

Library of Congress Catalog Card Number: 2017952560

See, the storm of the Lord
will burst out in wrath,
a whirlwind swirling down
on the heads of the wicked.

—Jeremiah 23:19

Sparks Fly Upward

BOOK ONE OF THE *SUPERSTARS* TRILOGY

AS THE FALL semester begins routinely at a small-town high school in north-central Indiana, the lives of two teachers and one student intertwine in the widening shadow of a scandal. Brad McCauley, a penny-pinching bachelor and part-time history teacher who is finishing a doctoral degree at nearby Riverside University, hopes to make a professional splash with his controversial research thesis. Robin Hillis, a veteran English teacher and longtime resident of the town, struggles to find meaning in a marriage to a husband who spends too much time traveling as part of his job. Erin Delaney, an intelligent but introverted senior, can't wait to escape the suffocating pressure of her parents and friends to be someone other than herself.

Year after year, Brookstone High School wins state and national accolades for its academic achievements. However, all three characters soon come face-to-face with evidence that the school's excellence is just a façade, and that students—as well as faculty, administrators, parents, and community members—have created a system that props up the school's reputation, lines the pockets of participants, and helps students land lucrative scholarships and gain admission to the most prestigious colleges in the country. One school official in particular, assistant principal Tolan Myers, stands out as suspicious with his Guidance Department access to all student records and his ownership of a local restaurant where dozens of students work.

Plodding toward his Ph.D. finish line, McCauley writes his dissertation, whose thesis itself turns out to be a masterpiece of academic plagiarism that has enmeshed him in a blackmail scheme with a professor who knows his dark secret. Moreover, McCauley is hiding something else from his past, an incident in which he was wrongfully accused of inappropriate conduct with a female student. When he and Robin Hillis begin a romantic affair—which blossoms from their discussions about Brad's research and their major philosophical differences about the character of God—Robin must deal with her own hypocrisy. After all, she is cheating on her husband of twenty-five years at the same time she longs to battle the school's integrity crisis. Erin, too, hides truths from her parents about her school performance and her dreams for college, dreams that stray far from their expectations. To make them happy, she begins dating a brash, risk-taking classmate who recently won a huge lottery prize, but the relationship proves to be a new crucible of stress. Her best times come when she withdraws by herself, alone with nature, or when she visits her grandfather at his home in a retirement village.

The precarious, illicit relationship between Brad and Robin is imperiled by wise and loving neighbors, by an apparent change of heart in Robin's husband Zeb, and by the simple fact that McCauley's days at Brookstone are numbered. Nevertheless, Robin suffers from a divided heart, unable to fully let go of Brad's gratifying attention. Late in the semester, Erin gets so far behind on a major project in her history class that she caves into pressure from her family and friends and—having badly misinterpreted words from both teachers—goes to McCauley's apartment intending to work out a higher grade, whatever the personal cost.

By the end of the semester, all three characters have been tainted by the culture of dishonesty but also contributed to it. With no idea how pervasive the deceit truly might be, they must decide whether to run from it to preserve their names, or jeopardize their futures by trying to expose it.

Above All Things

BOOK TWO OF THE *SUPERSTARS* TRILOGY

WHEN THE NEW semester begins at Brookstone High School, relationships deepen through stress and vulnerability. Erin Delaney develops enough trust in Robin Hillis to tell her about her New Year's Eve misadventure with Brad McCauley. Robin herself, wavering between guilt over her infidelity and anger at her husband, dives headlong into her affair with Brad. As their affair turns physical, Brad confides in her the two tremendous secrets from his past—the wrongful accusations of misconduct against him and his plagiarized thesis.

Meanwhile, McCauley debates whether to intensify his efforts to oppose the rampant cheating at Brookstone High School after the failing grades he gives six students are overturned by the school's administrators, who cast further doubt about their integrity when they offer to pay him for his cooperation. Erin stumbles into a nest of cheating at an SAT test and informs Robin, one of the test monitors. Gradually, the three characters join forces to investigate the academic dishonesty in a more intentional and systematic way, gathering evidence from current and past students.

Erin strives to live for herself instead of always pleasing others. Her stalled history research becomes a blessing in disguise when McCauley encourages her to transform it into an "oral history" project, which allows her to pursue her real passion and interact personally with the senior citizens at her grandfather's retirement village. Moreover, Grandpa Dee helps her hone her skills at the board game of Risk so that she defeats her boyfriend Matt in a scary challenge match and keeps him at arms' length; however, his claim that Myers is blackmailing him for his lottery winnings keeps her worried about his well-being and prevents her from dumping him altogether. Erin's home life continues to suffer because her father refuses to see that his plans for her life are crushing her spirit. She even begins to wonder about his own involvement in what seems to be systematic corruption in the school system.

Eventually, Robin's marriage woes lead her repentant husband Zeb to seek out the help of their neighbor, a professional marriage therapist. Unable to justify her own cheating any longer, she agrees to begin weekly counseling sessions—but in her selfish stubbornness she conceals the true depth of her unfaithfulness.

Growing more despondent and reckless, Matt tells Erin about evidence implicating Myers in the death of a student a year earlier; as for Myers, he begins to focus on the activity of McCauley and Robin with mounting uneasiness, aware that they have raised questions about cheating.

During Spring Break, the trio learn that a local newspaper reporter is also looking into the allegations of impropriety at Brookstone and believes the scandal extends much deeper and wider. About the same time, McCauley is contacted by the school superintendent and agrees to turn over their information and let him handle the issue from his official position. McCauley is pleased with this development since it will let him concentrate on his first priority, finishing his doctoral dissertation. Then he is lured to a secret meeting with Robin on the railroad tracks south of town, but she never appears—and he gets ambushed by two athletic thugs, tied to the tracks while a locomotive rumbles past, and warned to steer clear of Myers. Fearing further pressure, McCauley feels justified in deciding to step back from his visible opposition to the cheating.

Robin, however, is livid with his spineless response to the attack. She goes to his apartment to confront him, but instead she witnesses two burglars make off with Brad's safe and a flash drive, which contain important personal documents as well as the current draft of his dissertation. The brazen theft leaves him even more entrenched in his decision to abandon the cheating investigation—but leaves Robin enraged and bent on further action.

April

1

WHEN ERIN DELANEY and her classmates were finishing fifth grade, balancing nervously on the threshold of middle school, Jessica Southard had thrown her first sleepover, inviting a handful of girlfriends for a night whose entertainment consisted of grilling hamburgers and hot dogs, playing board games like Scattergories and Pictionary, and watching a scary movie till their two o'clock curfew. That deadline had been strictly enforced by Jess's mom, Erin's Aunt Jennifer, the sister of Erin's mom, Cathy. And afterward, seeing what fun the event had been, Jen Southard gave in to Jess's wish to make the sleepover an annual event—having no idea what an elaborate production it would become. Over the years, the Annual Southard Sleepover, despite its unfortunate acronym, evolved into an April ritual that drew as many as two dozen teenagers, employed Russ Southard as the proud grill master, added dozens of games that came and went with waxing and waning fads, and, as the girls matured, dropped its curfew altogether. The previous year, every girl who had come pulled an all-nighter.

This year's sleepover might well be the last. All the girls in attendance recognized that in twelve months they would be scattered to the winds, most of them having already accepted admission to colleges and universities hundreds or even thousands of miles away. Whether the sleepover would survive in some new form or terminate entirely was impossible to predict. The girls recognized the uncertainty of their future together, which tinged the atmosphere in the Southard residence with a somber cast as the sun set and the last few guests straggled through the front door on the first Friday in April.

Uncle Russ was already presiding over the giant Weber grill on the back patio when Erin arrived. Smoke wafted upward into the dusk, and the aroma of beef and bratwurst drifted in through the sliding screen doors. The weather was comfortable—sweatshirt weather, not so cold that the patio doors must be kept shut. Erin's cousin Jeremy, fourteen years old, was standing next to Russ, bouncing a basketball on the concrete while his hopeful eyes flitted among the bevy of older girls mingling inside. As he had grown up, he had taken a greater interest in the spring sleepovers.

Erin said hi to Aunt Jen and passed along a message from her mom. Jen was fiddling with a video camera and explained that she was hoping to shoot lots of footage and burn copies of a DVD the girls could take with them to college. She was learning to edit video as part of her web design class at Ivy Tech, where she was working on an associate degree with hopes of someday starting a business. Erin and Jen talked for a few minutes about Grandpa Dee, for everyone now accepted—with guilty gratitude—that among all his local descendants, Erin had become his favorite thanks to the time she was investing in his life. Sadly, most of his relatives now regarded him as a necessary burden in their lives.

Next, Erin sought out Sally Richards, her best friend among the seniors who would stay the night. Secretly, she was pleased to see Sally wearing neon-yellow gym shorts that did not try to hide her legs, which were still skinny but clearly adding mass after her struggles with anorexia. All the girls knew about it but nobody talked about it. Sally had been dating Cody Summers since October, and because of their relationship Erin too had gotten to know Cody as a friend and not merely a classmate. Baseball season started in a week, and Sally wanted to talk about that, for she was a team manager who this year would keep the scorebook, allowing her the privilege of sitting in the dugout for every game. When Erin's interest in that topic flagged, Sally wandered off. The back of her yellow shorts were emblazoned with a logo Erin had seem somewhere before, a logo with shapes that looked like the letters *Y* and *L*.

When Uncle Russ and Jeremy brought in a metal pan full of steaming burgers and brats, many of the girls formed an assembly line to pick up paper plates, plastic dinnerware, and napkins, and to begin putting together their dinner. Each girl had contributed a snack, side dish, or dessert item. Erin had brought a potato salad she had made herself, which now sat on a separate table with other sides—baked beans, green beans, several pasta salads and fruit salads. The desserts not requiring refrigeration occupied another table, larger and covered with a thin protective sheet of teal-colored plastic. Amid the usual variations on brownies and cookies, Erin saw that Sally (or probably Cody, she was sure) had donated three cans of weird new flavors of Pringles, including one called "Jalapeno Taco." Jen had ordered a single-layer slab cake whose frosting showed a color photograph of the Southard home, produced by some high-tech process Erin did not understand. Above the tables, Jen had printed, laminated, and hung a banner announcing LAST (?) ANNUAL SOUTHARD SLEEPOVER; Erin realized that her aunt was using this night as a warm-up for Jess's graduation party two months in the future. That explained the color-coordinated napkins, dinnerware, and plastic cups, too.

Within the next hour all of the expected "party-party"—that's the term they had adopted for themselves a couple of years earlier—had arrived, eaten, and settled into the inevitable cliques that would shift and merge into numerous combinations through the night. Erin had grown to appreciate the sleepover for its unmatched potential for what Cody called "intelligence gathering and information processing." Gossip ran rampant. That quality of the party had also evolved over time as regular party-partiers accepted and enforced an unwritten rule that what was shared at the sleepover stayed at the sleepover. Erin tended to listen rather than gab; however, the events of her senior year had stocked her with ample ammunition should she choose to open her mouth for something other than food. She was actually excited about the evening.

And so, hour by hour, the sleepover unfolded with a life of its own. Having popped several large bowls of popcorn, six or seven girls retreated to the basement to watch and poke fun at a vampire movie. Erin drifted into and out of their company long enough to hear them debating the pros and cons of other movies currently in the theaters while keeping close enough watch on their vampire flick to toss out sarcastic comments when warranted. Laurie Fritz amused Erin. Every comment from Laurie's lips followed the same pattern: "I heard it's really *dumb*" was her contribution to the assessment of every movie.

In the living room Erin plopped onto a couch next to Lauren Lancaster and Terri Harlow and joined their laments about Mr. Hostetter's annoying penchant for puns. Terri especially was a noted complainer, but Erin agreed that Mr. Hostetter's jokes were tiresome.

"I think he knows everybody thinks they're stupid, but he just wants kids to like him," suggested Lauren.

"How many times has he called Amanda Leer 'Chanda'?" Erin asked with affected irritation. "He always acts like it's the first time he's said it."

"'Chanda Leer, get it, get it?'" mimicked Terri. "He sounds like such a moron. Yes, we get it, Bob. Go make babies with Michelle."

Earlier in the school year, Mr. Hostetter's rumored dalliance with another math teacher, Michelle Newman, had spawned rich speculation. Hostetter's skin was pale and Newman was of Indian descent, so students often joked about the skin color of their future family. Cody had even constructed a chart showing genetic possibilities.

When Terri and Lauren's target shifted to other senior girls—not at the sleepover—Erin politely excused herself.

She sidled in among a circle of giggling girls watching Jeremy Southard shoot baskets outside, under the arc of two floodlights. Soon she gathered that the girls were aware that Jeremy was aware of their interest. They were flirting, essentially, with the sliding glass doors between them.

"Give him two, three more years and he'll be a hunk," predicted Julie Straley, authoritatively.

"His feet are puny," offered Mora Partridge, and after a suitable pause, the tittering began.

"I heard he wants to be a Marine," Julie added. "We need to ask Jess."

Their talk turned to the future plans of dozens of other seniors. Rosie Osborn was expected to have her baby and go to Ivy Tech, at least for now. Juan Melendez—presumed to be the father—would be settling for Riverside after failing to get into the University of Illinois.

The girls agreed that it was best for him to be close to Rosie. Jill Henry had not yet chosen between Stanford and Cal-Berkeley but was leaning toward Stanford because she had an aunt who lived in the San Francisco area. Knowing that eventually the spotlight would fall on her, Erin grew uncomfortable. She *did* want to talk about college, or rather her indecision, but not with these girls. With whom? Jess, perhaps, since she might understand Erin's silent conflict with her dad. Sally Richards, maybe, since she had talked some to Cody about her dilemma. But most of all, Erin knew, she wanted to talk to Mrs. Hillis. Well, that would not happen at the sleepover.

Erin studiously avoided Uncle Russ, fearing that he had been in touch with her father and would want to talk about her college plans. She wished just one person would side with her, would not surrender to the notion that the bigger and more famous school was always better.

Around 11:30 the movie critics took a break and a large group began playing Scattergories. Erin played a few rounds, less for the friendly competition than for the amusement at the arguments that arose over whether or not to accept certain answers. Diminutive Kelly Bennett, always vying for attention, learned she could get it by stringing multiple adjectives onto the front of her answers. She tried to use "wet, wild, wonderful wafers" for THINGS FOUND AT A BEACH, which earned her a unanimous thumbs-down. The game's instructions were nowhere to be found, though, so nobody could prove that her adjectives were illegal. Pleased with the controversy she was generating, Kelly proceeded to answer "laughing little lion lozenges" for THINGS IN A SOUVENIR SHOP and "cold, clammy, ceramic, catcher's cup" for SPORTS EQUIPMENT. At that point, several girls threw down their answer pads and the game split up in a raucous cacophony of laughter and irritation.

Sue Fisher and Sheena Straley, both Dairy Queen employees for Mr. Myers, debated the merits and shortcomings of different DQ Blizzards. Sheena proposed they make a DQ run, but the majority of the party-party voted to stay put, so the mission never materialized.

"We could always have J.J. bring us Blizzards when they close," Sheena suggested, unwilling to give up. J.J. Weaver was working that night till close. But the idea of a boy crashing their party, even to deliver ice cream, was off-limits according to the sleepover tradition.

A lot of kids were trying to unravel a mystery that was also perplexing Erin—the appearance on the hallway walls and classroom doors at school of signs and posters bearing the message *1-2-3-4*: ARE YOU READY? Teachers were tight-lipped, everyone agreed. But Sue Fisher claimed that Mrs. Newman's student teacher in math class had let slip that the signs would be just the first of many and that the faculty were "kind of cynical about it."

Close to midnight, Cara Eberle began showing off photographs of her prom dress on her iPhone. Everyone who already had a prom date (or hoped for one) joined in around the snack table, producing similar photos and jabbering about plans for dinners and limousines, and for the following day, when the school tradition was for seniors to drive in a cavalcade to Cincinnati for a day at King's Island. Erin had no plans to go to Prom—unless Nate Dyer surprised her with an invitation—but she was mildly envious of the fancy dresses her friends were buying, borrowing, or renting.

"If I had a famous parent, I would want them to be a country singer," Molly Traxton remarked to Julie Straley, and that stray comment started an impromptu half hour in which most of the girls weighed in on Molly's hypothetical issue and invented their own. Jess asked, "Of all the senior guys, which one has the cutest nose?" After they had taken turns responding, a consensus was reached: Jim McHeaton was the winner. Next, Lauren Lancaster asked, "If you were going to spend a year on a desert island, what TV series would you take on DVD?" A number of candidates were proposed, but the game fizzled when Sally Richards suggested *Man vs. Wild* and Jess related that on a recent episode she had watched Bear Grylls eat a pair of goat testicles, calling them a "delicacy," and Jill Henry asked, "I wonder where he got those?" By this point, fatigue was settling into the party, lowering inhibitions, and Jill's comment sparked uproarious laughter that carried on for five minutes.

Erin remembered the same pattern of degeneration at previous sleepovers. Once weariness set in, the focus and moral quality of the conversations spiraled downward until the girls who remained awake were reduced to judging classmates and teachers and generally unveiling the darkness seething within them. Only the vigilance of Aunt Jen and Uncle Russ kept the parties free of alcohol and drugs.

At least one of her fears was apparently not going to materialize: the raid from the boys. Despite the rumors and threats, it was late enough now that no boys were going to crash the party. Uncle Russ and Aunt Jen were still awake, even though they were keeping their distance from their guests.

During the first hours of the sleepover, the possibility of boys not only showing up but actually joining the girls had seemed likely and seemed to energize most of the girls. Not Erin. When she protested with trepidation and attempted diplomacy that adding boys to their mixture would be dangerous, she was teased for being a prude. Jess herself stated for all to hear that Erin needed to join the new century. After that, Erin kept her misgivings to herself. Throughout the evening, however, she kept thinking about the source of her scruples. Why would a boy-girl sleepover be so wrong? There might be unwanted consequences, surely, but was something right or wrong depending only on its results? Likewise, she could not make such a judgment based only on *her* convenience or preference, could she? She let her conscience experiment with different moral hypotheses, just as she had been doing with the school cheating. What troubled her most was that she knew that the cheating, and boys at the party, were wrong, yet she could form no coherent argument to explain why. Trying to do so left her thrashing like a drowning swimmer. She just *knew* some things were wrong. And she knew that such a moral struggle was also part of her growing up. That's what Mrs. Hillis continually reminded her—Mrs. Hillis, who because of her relationship with Mr. McCauley also had said, "I'm the last person to ask about right and wrong right now." Regardless, when no boys appeared, Erin was pleased. She really needed a few days away from Matt, whose behavior had become so erratic and frightening ever since he had come back early from his Spring Break trip to Florida without giving her any clear reason and had gotten angry when she tried to pry the reason from his tight lips.

Back in the basement, a few girls were dozing on the couch or in chairs, so last year's perfect record of no sleep would not be equaled. A fire was blazing in the hearth, and Jeremy, still hoping to get his foot inside the older-girls door, was jabbing at the flames with a poker. The girls were debating whether the Islamic promise for heroes was seventy-*two* or seventy-*six* virgins.

"Whichever, it doesn't make any sense," argued Laurie Fritz. "It's all so dumb."

"How long would they be virgins, is what I want to know," Molly Traxton said, yawning prodigiously.

"Right!" agreed Laurie. "And once they aren't virgins any more, then what happens? Is the hero stuck with them forever? Or does he get a whole new batch of seventy-two?"

"Seventy-six."

"Whatever..."

"It's seventy-two," Julie Straley said, waving her smart phone. "I just googled it."

"What if a girl is the hero? What does she get?"

"It's all so dumb."

Erin noticed Jess hovering at the perimeter of the conversation—an unaccustomed spot for her. When their eyes met, Jess gestured with a nod for Erin to follow. They went to Jess's bedroom. Jess locked the door behind them.

"Can you believe all that?" Jess asked. "About the virgins?"

Erin could sense where this was headed, so she steeled herself.

"Why do you ask?"

"Well, I don't know. It's just that you and Matt, and ..." Jess was nervous almost to the point of stuttering. What did she want to say?

"I just wanted to tell you that ..." Her eyes seemed suddenly mesmerized by the hanging philodendron in the corner of the room. "Well, Matt and I ..."

For a split second Erin thought that Jess wanted to say that she and Matt were getting back together, and she rejoiced—but then the incongruity of the idea made her laugh, and something like jealousy began pounding in her chest. Jess, newly bold, finished: "Matt wanted me to tell you ... Well, I just want you to know that Matt never ... that me and Matt never slept together."

It took a moment for the statement to register in Erin's mind.

"So, all your little comments ever since school started? What were they all about?" Anger was supplanting her jealousy. Then she realized the truth and whispered, "You were trying to help Matt win that stupid bet, weren't you?" She shoved her cousin sharply and Jess fell backward onto her bed.

"Erin, I didn't even know about that until …"

"You mean you didn't know that *I* knew about it! That's what you meant. But Matt told me before Spring Break. I can't believe you would do that to me!"

"It wasn't really doing it *to you*," Jess said defensively, apologetically. "It was more *for Matt*."

"Whatever," Erin said, unlocking the door. "You and your drama—all of your drama and everyone else's drama. It makes me sick. You know what? It's weird. Everyone is so excited about going off to college, and that's all anyone talks about, it seems like. And I don't really want to go, because …" She stopped. She didn't want to talk to Jess about Riverside and Nate Dyer and her dad. She didn't trust Jess at all right now. "Well, it's just weird, because I think I'm more ready for college than everybody else with all their immature drama."

Without waiting to hear Jess's response, she walked out. Nothing her cousin had said surprised her. She had long suspected that Jess's boasting about her exploits with boys was all hot air—and Matt's confession about the bet confirmed it. Although Jess had not exactly said so, Erin concluded that her cousin and her boyfriend had not only never slept together, but they had never been with anyone else, either. Who cared, anyway? At least Matt had finally respected her enough to tell her the truth. If it weren't already two o'clock in the morning, she might try to go find him.

Instead, she returned to the living room. Several girls had started watching another movie, a suspense flick that Cara Eberle said was called *I Know Where You Live*. It featured a teenage girl baby-sitting in a home where the power went out during a lightning storm with an escaped stalker/killer on the loose.

Erin plopped down on the sofa beside Sally Richards, who was actually munching on a snickerdoodle and sucking milkshake through a straw. Erin felt compelled to say something encouraging, so she whispered, "I meant to tell you earlier, Sally: You're looking great!"

Sally smiled drowsily, evidently still self-conscious. She held out the cookie toward Erin, who shook her head and said, "No thanks. I'm trying to *lose* weight"—then realized the careless insensitivity of her comment. But Sally chuckled.

"Really," Erin went on, "what you've done is just amazing." She didn't want to say that she and dozens of other girls had done a lot of their own research into eating disorders when Sally had become ill. The hallways at school were full of experts, now.

"Not really," Sally said. "I mean, I don't deserve the credit. I had a ton of help."

Erin studied Sally's face.

"A ton of prayers," she added.

That seemed like a strange thing to say, but before Erin could ask or even indicate her confusion, Sally said, "I've got a lot of new friends."

"You do?"

"Yeah."

Erin looked at the other girls on the couch, their eyes all glued to the TV screen. The teenage baby-sitter in the horror movie was on the phone looking out an open window, the stalker hiding in the shadowed shrubbery just a few feet below her. Any moment now she would see him and scream—and so would all the girls on the couch.

"Not these guys," Sally said. "I mean, they're my friends, but I'm talking about my friends at Young Life."

"Young Life?" Then Erin remembered where she had seen the logo on Sally's shorts before. YL—that was the group she had been invited to by the wife of Mr. McCauley's friend from ¿Que Pasa?

"They've stuck with me all the way," Sally continued. "They helped me keep to my *purpose*. I feel like I have a purpose every day now, from when I wake up in the morning to when I go to bed at night."

To Erin, Sally's words sounded like something she was reading from note cards or a teleprompter, as if she were auditioning for a commercial. But Erin didn't dare say something so rude to someone who had battled back from someplace as dark and dangerous as Sally had been a few months before. And even if the words sounded fake, they were full of hope. What Erin herself wouldn't give to feel a sense of purpose with her life!

"That sounds great," she finally said.

The TV baby-sitter reached to shut the window, the stalker rose from his hiding place, and the basement couch erupted in screams.

"Hey Erin," said a boy's voice behind her. She looked up and saw Jeremy's face, upside down.

"Hey, Jeremy. What are you still doing up?"

"I don't know."

"Looking for action?"

He chuckled and admitted, "You guys *are* fun to be around."

"I've watched you, watching us. Scouting."

"I like all the nice smells," he joked. "Yours best of all." He sniffed. "Lilac, right?"

She nodded.

"I can say that to you because you're my cousin and you won't think I'm hitting on you. Want to shoot some baskets?"

"Sure. Why not?"

She pulled on her sweatshirt and followed Jeremy onto the patio, where he turned on the floodlights. The scent of grease hovered thickly in the air.

After a few minutes of shooting, Jeremy asked, "So, how's Nate Dyer doing? Mom said that Aunt Cathy said you were with him the other night."

Did she really want to spill her guts to this freshman? Okay, so he was her cousin. Still, he might be spying for Jess, or even for Matt.

"It was just a coincidence, a chance meeting," she explained. Which was true. Her mom had called her at home, having forgotten two boxes of supplies for a catering job, and begged Erin to bring them to a building on the Riverside campus. When Erin made the delivery, she found that Nate was attending the event, a banquet for a club. She stuck around. They spent nearly an hour talking in the corner, not leaving until custodians began running their brooms along the floors and shutting out the lights. At first Erin had felt uneasy, but when Nate said he was thinking of switching his major to forestry, her spirits rallied. She ransacked her memory: Never had she shared with Nate her own interest in that field. She wanted to interpret their conversation as a sign that she should not give up on him. The next day in her psychology class, though, she learned about wish fulfillment and wondered whether her new interest in forestry might be just a projection of a subconscious desire to be together again with Nate. Totally confused, she imagined herself reeling in the turbulent vortex of a whirlwind, like the one she had seen at the Junction, crying out for someone to reach into her chaos and save her—and she wanted that someone to be Nate.

But she did not dare tell any of this to Jeremy Southard.

"Lemme ask you something, Erin," Jeremy began tentatively. "There's this girl I like, and I was wondering if it's a good thing to buy her a gift certificate to a hair place or a spa or someplace like that."

"Wow, I'm impressed," Erin countered teasingly.

"I remember how *hot* you looked during Christmas, and Jess said you had gone to that new place at the mall."

"Well, thanks," she said warily, "I guess."

Aware that he was waiting for her to finish, she said, "You don't know the whole story about that." And he wasn't about to find out now. After Christmas Break, when she returned to school, the remnants of her visit to Looking Good! at the mall had drawn raves from guys and questions from girls, yet she couldn't tell anyone the whole truth. She had gone to Hot Shots on New Year's Eve, just hours before her fateful visit to Mr. McCauley's. Her outfit, if you could call it that, she had chosen herself—but she wanted her face done professionally. Later she told her girlfriends all about her experience at the mall but withheld her reason for going there.

"My other idea," Jeremy went on, "was to buy her some perfume. What do you think?"

"Like I'm the expert?"

"More than *me*! I would ask Jess, but she would just make fun of me and try to find out who the girl is. I don't want to tell her, not yet."

"You're so loveable, Jeremy!" She reached up and patted his cheek. She wondered whether everyone in the family had the same one-track mind. She could excuse Jeremy, though, for he was a guy.

"So? Would you like it if a guy gave you perfume? If Matt did?"

"Well, I guess so. But it would have to be a perfume I liked. Do you know what she likes?" By now Erin had gotten off the couch and was face-to-face with her cousin. At her question, his countenance fell.

"I never thought of it that way," he said dolefully.

"You little cheat!" she joshed. "You were going to get her a smell that *you* liked."

"Yeah, but …" His voice trailed off in embarrassment and defeat.

"Find out what she likes first."

"How?"

"Hmm. That isn't easy for me to say without knowing who she is. You could ask her sister, if she has one, or her best friends."

"Okay. I can try that."

He was so transparent! Erin could see that all he really wanted was for this mysterious girl to smell like he wanted her to smell. Boys were so selfish!

"What's the perfume you like so much, anyway?" she asked.

"Well," he said sheepishly, "whatever it is that you have on right now."

Erin laughed.

"It's called Spring Lilac," she answered. "And you can get it at Kohl's at the Bridgebury Mall. But don't get it until you find a girl who likes it, too. Promise me!"

The movie reached a particularly scary part that drew screams—some genuine, most faked—from the girls on the couch. The two sleepers shifted but did not awaken. Jeremy inched toward the stairs, heading to bed.

Erin mused. Something about her perfume was igniting unusual interest. At school both Mrs. Hillis and Mr. McCauley had asked about it, too. Why were they so curious? They had nearly gotten her to confess that she had been with Matt—who had come home early from Spring Break, blaming and breathing threats against "that bastard" Myers again—on both Wednesday and Sunday nights. So far, she had kept his secret.

2

J. BRADFORD MCCAULEY was drunk, or close to it. For two hours he had huddled alone in a booth at ¿Que Pasa? with a plate of mostly untouched nachos and a collection of empty beer glasses, a collection that kept growing because the server was too rushed to clear them away, though not too rushed to bring him new drinks when he ran dry every ten or fifteen minutes. He had come here hoping that a change of venue might bring a change in his attitude toward his dissertation, which for several days he had been painstakingly reassembling from fragments and memory after losing his flash drive—which not-so-mysteriously had reappeared a few hours ago. Only the editing of his final chapter, plus a general final read-through, remained before he could officially deposit the completed manuscript with his committee for a preliminary interview that should be the last hurdle before his actual defense. Yet he was having trouble summoning the wherewithal to chip away at the tedious editing.

For several minutes his focus had been fixed on his wristwatch, which lay on the table next to the nachos. Even though he could not hear its quiet ticking in the noisy bar, his imagination magnified the absent sound to the point that he could almost hear the louder tick-tock that filled his apartment when he sat for hours writing and revising.

Over the past ten days he had battled a steady restlessness, and he knew why. His decision to back out of the investigation of the cheating at Brookstone High School simply refused to sit well with him. On the face of it, he had made the right choice, the best choice, the only smart choice. His energies ought to be directed toward his future, which meant toward his work at Riverside University (and beyond) as opposed to his part-time high school teaching, which really represented a backward glance at the past that he must overcome. Thanks to Mary Ann Childress, his career as a high school teacher was history, no pun intended. He needed to let it go—like he needed to let Robin Hillis go. By now their relationship probably would have ended entirely if not for their work together researching the cheating. Besides, her husband Zeb was back in the picture. Yes, he needed to let it go.

He smiled wryly. Ironically, "let it go" was the phrase Robin kept using when she urged him to jettison his life's philosophy.

And that philosophy found its most perfect expression, its most fitting symbol, in the wristwatch sitting in front of him, its second hand sweeping him moment by moment into his future. McCauley basked in his sense of the austerity and simplicity and beauty of his belief that the Universal Clock, his true god, had ordained a future of scholarly recognition and reward.

And yet …

He felt restless. Why? He had made the right choice—there could be no question about that. After catching several of his high school students cheating on a major first-semester project, and then discovering a possible—probable—cheating conspiracy involving school officials and community, he had gone too far by taking the first swings in a fight that should not be his. And when the powers that be had figuratively counterpunched and bloodied his nose a couple of weeks earlier, he had seen the stupendous stupidity of his ways. He would never be able to forget the frightening shriek and the fearsome roar of the freight train as it bore down on him that night. Even thinking of it now made his heart race. So, when opportunity knocked in the form of the school superintendent offering to take the evidence and press the battle that he and Robin and Erin Delaney had begun, McCauley was more than willing to cut his losses and save his skin. It was best to let the proper authorities handle it.

That was his state of mind—let the proper authorities handle it—as he stared at the wristwatch.

And yet … he felt restless. Robin would throw up her hands at his decision and throw his wristwatch across the bar.

Sipping meditatively, he acknowledged that whatever their unusual relationship was all about, it was unquestionably forcing him to rethink many of his beliefs. Perhaps that was *why* they had met—but no! That very idea threw him into a mental maelstrom, for where did the sense of purpose come from if not from the Universal Clock? Yet such a purpose, if true, cut the legs out from under the source of that purpose! The logical quandary made him glad he had not chosen philosophy as his major.

The instrumental track of a Bruce Springsteen song called "Jungleland" played in the background, too muffled to hear clearly, but McCauley knew the lyrics by heart and fast-forwarded to lines that seemed apropos to his perplexed state, lines that juxtaposed images of churches and jails and pronounced them equally impotent in the lives of real people living real lives.

Jungleland! What could better describe his confusion? He should have chosen English as his graduate field, for then he could have done his thesis on Springsteen's lyrics as contemporary poetry. Across the room he saw two English Ph.D. students, whose names now escaped him, who were doing just that—writing their dissertations, one on the song lyrics of Bob Dylan, focusing on their connection to the American Dream, and the other on the interpretation of European history in the lyrics of British singer/songwriter Al Stewart. McCauley felt a bit jealous. Whatever was brewing in the English Department smelled way more pleasant than the tedious sweat of his dissertation editing.

A fleeting image of dead ivy, crackly and brown, passed through his mind—the dead ivy clinging to the walls of some of the engineering buildings that he walked past every day near his graduate office. Lately he had found the sight of that ivy painfully emblematic of his lack of motivation.

"Want another one, sailor?" the server asked sardonically. "Let me get the rest of these out of your way." She began to remove the empty glasses.

"Actually, I've had about one too many already," he said. "Just bring me some coffee, please. And you can get rid of the chips, too. I wasn't in the mood."

He certainly wasn't in the mood for editing. His hope of a refreshed outlook from the break at ¿Que Pasa? had not materialized.

Okay, for ten days he had been restless. By every reasonable measure he had done the right thing—yet something kept nagging at his conscience, something surely but uncomfortably linked to his philosophy. Yes, he, J. Bradford McCauley, was by nature a passive person, though he would prefer to call himself *careful*, or *cautious*, or *circumspect*. Those words were less judgmental. Every time Robin mentioned his passivity, he shrank from her tone of condemnation, even when she spoke with playful sarcasm. He felt convicted. He became defensive. Was he reading into it more than she intended? Suppose he was. Did that mean he was having second thoughts about himself? He could not deny one thing, try as he might—he was the type of man who always backed down, avoided confrontation, took the easy road. He would love to be the type of man who was *less* passive, who didn't shy away from a fight that was justified and necessary. That's not who he was, but that's who he *wished* he was, who he really *wanted* to be. And Robin had zeroed in on that deep desire, saying at one point that she believed every man really wanted to be that way and was made to be that way. Even if her own beliefs were coloring her claims, she had hit the mark squarely in his case.

"J. Bradford McCauley!"

He felt a clap on his back that jerked his eyes from the wristwatch.

Turning, he looked into the dark complexion of Manny Sarks, whose broad forehead and wide smile transported him far above and beyond his worries about Brookstone High School's cheating scandal and his dissolving relationship with Robin Hillis and even his ever-present fear of Gregory Travis. Whenever he ran into Sarks he felt the same weird effect, the same inexplicable sense of freedom.

Without any invitation, Sarks sat down opposite McCauley.

"You look like a man taking a break from his dissertation," he said. "Am I right?"

McCauley felt his cheeks pull upward into a smile.

"Spot on," he replied.

"Want company?"

McCauley shrugged and said, "I'm about ready to get back to work. If you'd been a few minutes earlier you could have had some free nachos."

Sarks leaned forward as if in conspiracy and said, "I thought of you this week. Did you know Riverside University has a Deism Club? An actual *official organization*, for crying out loud. Deists or Deism, one or the other."

"I checked them out once."

"I thought you'd be camped out on their doorstep waiting to get in," said Sarks.

"I checked them out. They seemed too … politically oriented for my taste."

"*Too* political. I see. That's sort of ironic, isn't it? Considering your dissertation?"

"They were talking about all the causes they should support, on campus or in Washington. My interest is in the philosophy itself, and in how it affected the men whose ideas shaped the founding of the nation. Those men were shaped by the philosophy, and they shaped the nation. But I myself, two hundred years after that, am not particularly interested in politics. Even if I find deism personally meaningful, I don't have an agenda. I'm not trying to shove it down people's throats."

Sarks nodded, but McCauley could tell he was dubious.

"Anyway," Sarks said, "I thought of you."

"I'm touched," McCauley joked, aware that he was just tipsy enough that he needed to check his impulse toward sarcasm. "What are you doing here?"

Now it was Sarks's turn to shrug.

"Just … browsing among the Crazies," he explained. "There's a guy over there I've been getting to know." He nodded toward a corner where a middle-aged man with a Riverside jacket and horn-rimmed glasses scribbled feverishly onto a legal pad. "He has what I guess I would call a get-rich scheme. Sooner or later he's bound to strike it rich, if he doesn't go bankrupt first. See, he sits around and thinks of common phrases that he can try to get the internet domain rights for. So he has a list that keeps growing bigger and bigger. Right now he has about two thousand phrases. He says it costs ten bucks per name to buy. And he's looking for investors."

"How does that work? How can he ever make any money?"

"Here's what *he* says. Suppose he has the rights to a phrase like, say, *cautiously optimistic* or *under the hood*. Then if some business comes along and uses the name, he can sue for copyright infringement or something like that. Or ask the company to buy the rights from him. Or maybe a music group, a band, or maybe a new TV show tries to use his words. Same idea."

Based on that description, McCauley could see no way the enterprise could ever be profitable—unless this particular "Crazy" figured out a way to get gullible idiots to fork over money as investment. Maybe it was some kind of pyramid scheme. Thinking about it, he wondered whether the Brookstone cheating scandal and possible interstate cheating network that the journalist Pete Doty talked about might be the same kind of racket.

"Every time I think of a phrase now, I jot it down to pass on to him next time I see him," Sarks finished. "I think of stuff all the time. *Bald spot. Crowning achievement. Coming of age. Tuition increase.* Once you start playing the game, it grabs hold of your mind and doesn't let go. *Tragic irony.*"

In the gale of the verbal onslaught, McCauley had to make a concerted effort not to start thinking of phrases himself. He flagged down the server and asked again for a cup of coffee, Sarks shaking his head no to the server's request to get him something.

Sarks was a bit of a character himself, McCauley thought. He was always working Jesus into conversations—a tendency that McCauley generally tolerated but secretly hated in anyone, especially the so-called "One-Tracks" at Brookstone High School, the religious kids who wore that nickname with pride even though it had been invented and slapped on them in contempt. Yes, Manny Sarks was a grown-up One-Track—yet McCauley had liked this man from first meeting him here at ¿Que Pasa? back in November.

As though reading his mind, Sarks asked, "I've heard it said that at the time of the Revolutionary War, not everybody favored fighting for independence. Only about a third of the colonists wanted to fight, and a third wanted to keep loyal to England, and a third were undecided. Is that right?"

"That's probably about right," McCauley said.

"Which means," Sarks went on, picking up steam, "that the war was really a gigantic *risk*, right? I mean, not only because the Americans were big underdogs, but also because the ones who really were passionate about the fight were in a minority, right?"

"You could say that," McCauley conceded. He had the uneasy feeling that he was being coaxed along a path he would not have taken otherwise, like one of Socrates' naïve students being taken by the hand and led into wider pastures of truth. Nevertheless, he was curious as to where Sarks was going.

"And look what that risk got us!"

"Right," McCauley remarked in a droll tone. "No War for Independence, and no place like ¿Que Pasa? would ever exist, no place for the Crazies to feel like they belonged ..."

"Exactly!" Sarks seemed delighted by the conclusion.

McCauley opened his mouth to ask, "What is your point, anyway?" when Sarks suddenly leaned forward again, his grin spreading ear to ear, and whispered, "You wanna know the greatest risk anybody ever took?"

"Okay. What?"

"No guesses?"

"I'm not in the mood."

Where was that coffee?

"Fair enough."

"I didn't say I wasn't curious."

"The greatest risk ever was Jesus."

I should have known, McCauley thought.

"How so?"

"Just think about it," Sarks said, rising to go.

"I'm not in the mood for that, either."

"Fair enough. Maybe some other time. I gotta go find Rachel. Good luck on that dissertation. When do you defend?"

"April. May. Not sure exactly."

McCauley watched Sarks make his way back to the Phrase Collector, whisper some contributions into the man's ear, and leave ¿Que Pasa? with a visible bounce in his step.

Four months before, when they first met, Sarks had introduced himself as *Emmanuel*, but his wife Rachel always called him *Manny*, so McCauley carefully avoided calling him either. After they had bumped into each other three or four times, McCauley began to wonder about the reason Sarks was in his life, just as he had once wondered the same about Robin—that is, what purpose in the Universal Clock's scheme of things those people were fulfilling. Then, as if by coincidence, Sarks himself raised that question, spinning it from his Jesus perspective, saying he didn't believe their frequently crossing paths was random circumstance. "I don't believe in accidents," he claimed. McCauley remembered rolling his eyes and thinking that the high school kids would categorize Sarks as a One-Track.

However, try as he might, McCauley couldn't help but respect Sarks, the most level-headed person he knew among the regulars at ¿Que Pasa?

His coffee arrived, bitter but bracing, clearing his head quickly. He wished he had a donut or some other pastry, some cake or a muffin, but ¿Que Pasa? offered no such morning fare. It was not a morning place, but suddenly McCauley felt like morning.

Most of what Sarks had said he could easily dismiss. But that part about *risk*—that was clinging to him. He could not shake it off. If the American colonists had never taken their risk, they would never have won their reward, their freedom. That was beyond dispute. But what did that mean for him, for J. Bradford McCauley, in the here and now?

Without him, Robin and Erin Delaney's work on the cheating had come to a standstill. His leadership in that effort was indispensable, evidently. Early on in the investigation, he had noticed their looking to him, and it troubled him, for he didn't want to ruffle any feathers with higher-ups. Or did he? Which was the *real* J. Bradford McCauley? Or—perhaps more critically—which was the J. Bradford McCauley he would *choose* to be?

Did he really have a choice?

He looked at the watch again. Tick-tock.

One week after Spring Break ended, he had met with Robin and Erin after school, informally, he sitting on his motorcycle and the two of them standing to the side, shading their faces under the sun-splashed sky. He laid out his reasons for deciding to quit their investigation, explaining calmly and rationally, but then Erin began to shudder and sob. Robin immediately threw her arms around their young friend and took her to a metal bench near the parking lot. At that point, McCauley realized in retrospect, he should have ridden away, making a clean break with them. However, something compelled him to stay. Over the next half hour, as passersby eyed them awkwardly, Erin told them through fitful tears how worried she was about Matt Rademacher. She thought he was suicidal. He was acting inconsistently, carelessly. At last she burst into a fresh paroxysm of weeping, bellowing about how she had lied to them when they asked her about her perfume, admitting that she had been with Matt on both the nights they had asked about—the night McCauley had been attacked on the railroad tracks, and the night his apartment had been broken into and his safe stolen while Robin cowered under his bed. Yet Erin insisted that nothing that happened was Matt's fault, that he was merely a victim. Mr. Myers had put him up to it.

Listening to her story, McCauley could only shake his head in reluctant respect for Myers's power. Both he and Robin had known without any hard proof that Myers was in back of the railroad scare and the apartment burglary. Now they had three bits of corroborating if circumstantial evidence.

First, the scent of Erin's perfume at both scenes connected her to Matt and Matt to the railroad attack and the theft of the safe. Second, McCauley's discovery that the cords used to tie him to the tracks were in fact bungee cords, the same kind used at the kids' Junction operation, further pointed to Matt.

The third piece of evidence had come earlier that very day and was admittedly more subjective: the galling manner in which McCauley had recovered his flash drive. Myers had sent word—through Robin, of all people—that "something" was in his school mailbox, the same box that had remained empty since Myers's forged note, supposedly from Robin, had lured him to the railroad ambush. Everything was covered with Myers's figurative fingerprints. The note wrapped around the flash drive said that Bragley had found it on the floor near McCauley's desk. Right! The truth was not hard to figure: Myers had combed through every file on the stolen storage device, found nothing that implicated him in the cheating network, and decided to give the flash drive back—not because he wanted McCauley to have his dissertation files, nor because he feared the brazen theft might spur McCauley to challenge him, but because he knew that McCauley knew he was the culprit but would do nothing or could do nothing to stop him. In his pride, Myers did not even think he needed to hold on to the dissertation files as leverage. He was rubbing everything in McCauley's face.

These facts paralyzed McCauley with rage. He looked around ¿Que Pasa? and it occurred to him that most of his grad school colleagues were just as passive as he was in their relationships to the outside world, the world beyond their tightly circumscribed areas of study, where they rested in contentment and their own degree of arrogance. He was no different from the rest of them. Rather than take comfort in the company, though, he realized that he was just making an excuse for his inaction. He was blaming his passivity on his environment, and, by extension, on the Universal Clock, which was responsible for his surroundings and his lack of freedom.

Nonetheless, he was genuinely livid about Tolan Myers. And he knew that he had to choose between paralysis and action, between shrinking back and fighting back.

If not for the shadow of Gregory Travis's blackmail payments darkening his calculations, he could simply quit the job at Brookstone. But no, he had to have that paycheck or else jeopardize his entire future ...

He got another coffee refill and for the millionth time, it seemed, reviewed his situation.

For several months he had let his life run along parallel passions, parallel tracks, when only one was right for him. He had let his passion for the cheating investigation challenge what ought to be his sole priority—finishing his Ph.D. As for a *third* passion, Robin, well, his passion for her had slipped to the back burner, understandably. With her husband back in the picture, McCauley doubted that anything would rekindle between him and Robin, even though she kept wavering between him and Zeb.

All that made sense, and yet ... he was still restless.

He simply could not ignore the cheating. Or Myers.

His fingers squeezing the coffee cup, he allowed his anger to simmer. He began to plot a campaign of new action. Gradually his thoughts circled back to his old idea, which would now serve as a bold counterstrike to recover his safe and find the necessary written or electronic records that would destroy Myers and bring down the cheating network.

With or without the help of Robin and Erin, he had to do it. He *would* do it. He would break into LaGrange's and Myers's office.

3

ROBIN HILLIS SHOULD have felt hurried, but she didn't. Or, looked at from a different point of view, she should have felt comfortable and justified in taking her sweet time, but she didn't. Those two attitudes were colliding in her heart as she exited from Interstate 65, rounded the off ramp in a graceful curve north, and glided to a stop before the YIELD sign at the entrance to Highway 53. After a Sunday afternoon shopping in Bridgebury, she would be a few minutes late to her appointment with Howard Roost.

And therein lay the inner conflict. She ought to step on the gas and hurry home on time for the counseling session—yet she dreaded what might take place there, what *would* take place there some evening, what would *have* to take place there, ultimately, if there were any justice in life. Eventually, she knew, either Howard or Zeb would ask the question that she never wanted to answer. Sooner or later, one of them would raise the issue she hoped she would never have to face.

Just north of the intersection with the McDonalds on one side and the State Police post on the other, the highway narrowed to two lanes of two-way traffic. According to Zeb, funding was in place to widen the road to four lanes from the stop light all the way to Doc's Corner, two miles north; until then, however, drivers in a hurry were at the mercy of the traffic fates.

Tonight, Robin was in no hurry, the impulse to dawdle having conquered her desire to be punctual. She was in no hurry—but somebody else was, somebody in a silver compact car behind her, somebody who was stuck there because of the long line of cars in the single southbound lane that made passing her impossible for the next two miles. In her rearview mirror, Robin could see the driver gesticulating. She was about to accelerate but caught herself in time. To speed up would be to admit that she was driving too slowly, which she was not, legally. She was humming along at forty miles per hour, the posted speed limit. True, she often hit sixty through this stretch, and the police didn't monitor it too closely. Still, Robin did not want to send any signal to the guy tailgating her that she was in the wrong. He could just be patient. Anyway, she was in no rush to get back to Brookstone.

What happened over the next seven or eight minutes was comical and sad and fearful and finally surprising.

As soon as the opposing flow of traffic thinned enough to allow the Flailing Tailgater to pass, a change in the terrain interfered. Slight hills rose up and made passing unsafe (and illegal). For the rest of the trip into Brookstone, every time the Tailgater might have safely passed her, southbound traffic stopped him from trying. And every time that oncoming traffic disappeared, the Flailer's frustration mounted in yet another DO NOT PASS zone. Robin laughed, at first; then she began to sympathize with his plight, one she herself had suffered through hundreds of times over two decades of the Bridgebury-to-Brookstone commute. Closer to town, passing was not permitted because of Highway 53's intersections with county roads and the access to and from truck-heavy construction businesses. Reaching that part of the route, Robin saw in her rearview mirror that the Tailgater was not merely waving madly but screaming and shouting. His head bobbed and jerked this way and that, his curses rang east and west, and his hands waved wildly and stabbed the air, even out his driver-side window. Her windows cracked, Robin could hear his angry noise competing with the whoosh of wind in her own car. She could almost imagine hot breath bellowing from his nostrils as he waited for the chance not to pass her—no, he would long ago have given up on that—but to vent his fury at her for her lousy driving, her inconsiderate granny-speed nonchalance, her refusal to just get out of his way.

She probably deserved it.

Then, when she went through the gentle curve west into Brookstone, real panic rose—fear that the traffic light ahead, at the intersection of 53 and 22, would be red, red as the Tailgater's frustrated face. She feared what he would say or do, for she was turning right at a NO TURN ON RED corner, and until the light turned green he would be idling alongside her, free to glare at her and exhaust his pent-up wrath and who knows what else? Even worse, suppose he stayed behind her, following her east on Highway 22? What if he followed her all the way to Dogwood Street, all the way to her house or to the Roosts? Looking backward now, she regretted that she had not just gone off onto the emergency shoulder of the highway when she first noticed him wanting to pass her. Had she inadvertently caused an episode of road rage?

The signal turned red! Too late, she thought of staying in the straight lane, of changing her course to ensure that he would not pull up next to her. The idea of damage control kicked in: She rolled down her window all the way to apologize to him before he began to yell at her ...

But his attention did not shift toward her when his vehicle, which she saw now was, like hers, a Honda *Civic*—oh, the irony!—rolled to a stop. His arms shook as though suffering from an epileptic frenzy. Then they clapped repeatedly and beat on the steering wheel in rhythm with the drumbeat. Music! The driver was listening to music, and singing with abandon—screaming words like *joy* and *love* and *freedom*—and her impotent apology was swallowed up in the sheer power of the song, and she felt tears on her cheeks and did not realize why.

"Why do you look at your hands so much?"

Howard Roost's question froze Robin with fear. She had always suspected that Howard could see more than average people. Either he was expert at reading body language and interpreting similar signals, or else God told him things directly. She did not know which.

"I wasn't aware that I did that," she replied evenly, ransacking her memory of college psychology classes. What did hands represent? In Shakespeare, Lady Macbeth's *washing* her hands signified guilt. But what about simply *looking* at your hands?

"People should look *up* more," Howard remarked, and she could tell from his tone of voice that he was making a general comment about human nature, like many similar pronouncements he had made at the Roosts' Sunday brunches that she and Zeb used to attend.

Tonight, though, she was all alone on the couch where she and her husband had sat for two months of Sunday evening counseling sessions. Zeb was gone on a business trip. For all Robin's complaining about his loving his work more than he loved her, she had to admit that since Christmas, that pattern had changed. She would not have believed it possible, so deep had the roots of her bitterness grown, but he was winning back her beleaguered affections.

Still, tonight was awkward. She knew—and she believed that Howard knew—that she had yet to deal with the elephant in the room of Howard's elegant library. For eight weeks Zeb had been fully forthcoming about his many faults as a husband, his surprising candor slowly disarming her. He never defended himself, even when she fabricated exaggerated charges just to vent her frustration. Whenever she did that, Howard came to Zeb's rescue, gently, and she felt obliged to tone down her accusations. Because she trusted Howard, she had come to recognize that she was not seeing her situation clearly. Zeb had gone astray, yes, and she was not to blame for that. But she had been reluctant to extend him any grace whatsoever.

The real Zeb was not the selfish man who had abandoned her, but the repentant man who was trying to love her. He was a good man, a good husband, and their marriage could be good again.

And in the matter of her messy relationships, when she truly sought her own heart—as she was forever encouraging Erin Delaney to do—she knew that beneath all the layers of deceit she had let accumulate, she was yearning for Zeb, not for Brad.

She waited for Howard to explain why people should look up more, although she could guess what he was thinking. Looking up meant recognizing and submitting to the will of heaven; looking down meant focusing on yourself and the world.

Finally she said, "My hands have done some terrible things."

"So have mine."

Why would he say such a thing? Didn't he see that she was trying to open up?

"I was just thinking," she went on, "that when Zeb and I were in college, he would have me cut his hair to save money for the barber. He would always tell me how good it felt, my fingers running through his hair."

"That's a beautiful thing, Robin," Howard said warmly. "Your marriage has hundreds of special things like that."

She had come to the threshold. With her next words she would take a step forward that she could never take back. Did she really want to confess without Zeb there? Or would it be easier this way, and leave her no escape route with Zeb?

She took a deep breath, momentous, and ran her tongue over her top lip.

"But my hands have run through somebody else's hair," she began. Before she could finish, a deep wave of shame and sorrow rippled through her, convulsively, shaking her on the couch. She forced out the next words: "Another man's hair."

She could not stop her tears, nor did she want to. They overwhelmed her with relief and liberation. As they flooded forth she felt Howard pushing tissues into her palm; she was aware that Jerri had come into the den and sat down next to her, embracing her; and in bizarre testimony to the strange way her mind operated, she recalled another Shakespeare snippet, Juliet's father calling his weeping daughter "a conduit." That set Robin to laughing amid her weeping, at which point she surrendered any hope of control or understanding and turned to Jerri, holding on for dear life. When Robin opened her eyes, Howard had left the room.

She took several deep breaths to compose herself. Jerri was crying, too, and when Howard came back in and took his seat, his eyes were swollen and red.

Robin wondered what would happen next. She needed to tell the whole truth—that she had gone a lot further than simply cutting Brad McCauley's hair. She ought to say so, explicitly, although perhaps it was already obvious.

Whatever the case, Howard spared her the trouble of deciding.

"This is a good stopping point tonight," he said. She saw that he was debating whether to make another comment, so she prompted him, asking, "And?"

"And you need to talk to Zeb."

"Yes," she said confidently, sniffling. "I do."

But Zeb would not be available to talk over the phone until his plane to Houston landed in another hour, maybe two. Even then, she did not want to tell him about Brad long distance. Something that important, Zeb deserved to hear face-to-face. Part Two of her confession would have to wait twenty-four hours.

Another impulse now seized her—to see Brad, to shut the door with him. Robin was not naïve. She knew the way a man's heart worked. No matter what he said, Brad might be hoping even subconsciously for a revival of their affair, just as she caught herself wondering about, and, when her guard was down, even longing for. Well, what had happened, had happened. And though it lay technically in their past, it had left them forever vulnerable to its memories and the treacherous hope that such memories would forever engender.

They met at the newest landmark on the Riverside University campus, the center of the Engineering Mall, where four massive granite spires surrounded the fountain illuminated by floodlights.

Robin allowed him to give her a brief hug, then both of them blurted out simultaneously, "Before you say anything—" which sparked an awkward shared chuckle. Then Brad gestured toward one of the benches arranged in a sweeping circle around the fountain, and they sat down on its cold surface, metal mesh covered by some kind of polymer probably developed by the school's materials engineers.

"You first," he said. Robin perceived that he was excited about something. The last time she had seen him, he was mired in despondency over his missing flash drive and the added burden it had dumped on top of the existing pressure from his impending dissertation deadline. He had not even been at school on Friday, having called in sick.

"No," she said confidently. "You first. You seem in better spirits."

"Okay," he replied. The air was cool with a slight breeze, the area empty except for occasional undergrads walking past in pairs or small groups, their voices low. The colored lights played on the fountains. That was the weird thing about college—the environment appeared so serene, when the lives of thousands of young men and women were roiling with personal pressures and passions.

"I've changed my mind," Brad said.

Robin felt dizzy. What did he mean? For a moment she forgot that she had called him and asked to see him for one purpose only, to say she had let out the secret of their affair, so they didn't need to worry or hide it any longer, and it was all right if they stopped trying to figure out the great Brookstone Cheating Scandal because she had to get on with the rest of her life.

She had not considered that Brad too had something important to say.

So she listened as he related "a bit of a personal crisis" that had come to a head as he drank himself into a mild stupor a few nights before. He said he had decided to resume the battle against Myers and the war against the cheating. He laid emphasis on the fact of his *decision* and claimed to see now that he had been underestimating the role of choice in his life for a long time. He said that she, Robin had been right all along in arguing that his philosophy, for all its austere elegance, did not really account for human freedom, or even God's freedom. He wasn't ready to abandon his Universal Clock entirely, for he still believed it explained a lot of early American political discourse, but he was willing to concede that he had let his love of the idea captivate and enslave him.

Robin could not believe what she was hearing. More so than during their weeks of illicit lust, she wanted to kiss him—to cradle his head, her fingers once more swimming in those dark, rich locks of hair, and plant a happy smack of victory on his lips. How could this be? How could her immorality—her sin—have led to this? It made no sense, the world made no sense sometimes.

Then, looking at his hair, another realization floored her. She was thinking of him as a little boy who needed to be encouraged and rewarded! Had she always thought of him that way—as someone to mother? Was that the foundation of her attraction to him? Was this what Howard Roost meant when he kept drilling home the point that we are all victims—of the world, of the devil, of our own weakness and blindness? Up to now, Robin had portrayed herself as an innocent victim of Zeb's obsession with work, not considering that Zeb himself might be a victim of social and professional pressures he could not see or overcome. That's why forgiveness was so important, according to Howard.

His ideas were actually making sense. They usually did, in retrospect.

Then Brad said, "Anyway, I know what we have to do next. Do you want to hear about it?"

"Sure." She wanted to go along for this ride, to see where the new Brad McCauley would take the renewed Robin Hillis.

He had it all mapped out. They would get Erin to get Matt to get Bragley's keys. Then they would sneak into Myers's office, recover the stolen safe, get into Myers's filing cabinet, find all the proof they needed about the cheating network, and either steal the documents or make copies—"on his copier, even, for good measure."

Robin felt her own excitement surging.

"What about his computer?" she asked. "Everyone says Cody Summers is a genius at programming code. We could get him to hack into—"

"No, no," Brad said, shaking his head. "I thought about that, really I did. But the fewer people who are involved, the better. Just you and me."

"And Erin?"

"Well, maybe."

"Maybe Cody could still hack Myers's computer without having to be there."

"From a remote location? Maybe. It's worth a try."

"When?" she asked.

"I don't know. We can decide that later. I just wanted to tell you that I haven't given up after all."

"I'm so glad!"

"Okay, then." A lull ensued, then Brad said, "So, what did you want to tell me?"

Her story, weighed in the balance against his, sounded anticlimactic. As she spoke, she could sense Brad's enthusiasm waning, but she assured him that she was still on board with him as far as the cheating investigation. She just insisted that they meet no more alone but only in public places.

"Look," she said, laying her hand on his knee. "We already knew we were finished, and if you look at it honestly, don't you think we could *both* say it never should have happened? I know I can say that. It was nice while it lasted, but it was … wrong. We made choices, and they were the wrong choices."

He stared into the fountain, its color changing from green to blue.

She might still call Zeb tonight, she thought. Then she turned to look at the enormous clock housed in the top of the tower at the other end of the lawn—and she saw that it was broken.

"Am I right?" she asked Brad. "We made wrong choices. But with the cheating, the school cheating, we are making the right choice. And this is really weird to say, but I'm having more fun with you and Erin and our crusade than I ever did with you last fall. No offense intended."

Brad laughed half-heartedly.

"None taken," he said.

4

GREGORY TRAVIS LOOKED like *death warmed over.*

Almost automatically, that phrase rose in the mind of J. Bradford McCauley as he stared at the prone, pallid body of his dying university professor. However, the influence of Robin Hillis—her influence as his *editor*, that is—checked his impulse to let that description settle securely into his brain. For several weeks Robin had been closely reading through his thesis manuscript, giving it a final proofreading that was not technically necessary but that McCauley hoped would … would *what?* He had gotten beyond the immature belief that Robin might be impressed or swayed or wowed by the lucidity of his thinking or the magnificence of his expression. Or *had* he? Sometimes he caught glimpses of his own character that sickened him.

But the real sickness, the literal, non-metaphorical sickness, lay before him.

Travis was breathing on his own, but barely. A loop of clear plastic tubing ran around his face, supplying regular puffs of oxygen to his nostrils. Separate networks of tubes were connected to IVs into the back of both his hands, which curled impotently at his sides. McCauley studied the bags of colored liquids suspended from aluminum poles on either side of the bed. Different machines with baffling displays and beeping signals rose in back of the professor.

"If you say something to him, he might say something back," came the calm voice of Emma Travis, the professor's wife, who a few moments earlier had ushered McCauley into the room. "He hears everything, he says, but he just doesn't have enough energy to say much."

McCauley nodded absently, his face assuming the same vacant look as the professor's, his mind fumbling with ideas he never much considered—ideas about death.

"Go ahead," Emma insisted. She seemed preternaturally calm, touching the bun of grey-white hair atop her head. "I'll go outside."

Good, thought McCauley. If he *does* say anything, I don't want you to hear it.

Once they were alone, McCauley slumped into the comfortable armchair beside the bed, a chair obviously intended to sustain somebody sleeping, keeping a vigil.

Travis's eyes were shut. His lips were shut. Whatever breathing he was doing went through his nose, where half the time, McCauley calculated, it would be operating against the flow of oxygen from the tubes. He hated hospitals.

"Professor?" he asked. He repeated himself, a little louder, and added, "It's Brad. Brad McCauley."

Travis's eyelids fluttered but did not open. His lips parted and his tongue ran along them. McCauley searched the room in vain for a pitcher of water, or even a cup, to offer. He noticed that the digital clocks on the different machines showed different times.

When Travis tried to speak, all McCauley heard was a harsh, agonizing rasp.

The professor cleared his throat and then croaked, "Looks like I'll miss your *tri*umph."

"Yes, sir," McCauley answered, nodding humbly. He felt obliged to give the man his utmost respect. Travis liked to use that word—*triumph*—when talking about McCauley's dissertation and bright future. Every time McCauley indicated any uncertainty about their secret agreement, Travis assured him that his *triumph* was close at hand.

Now, Travis's demise was even closer.

"He could go any time," Emma Travis had said, conveying the doctors' prognosis.

McCauley's drive down to the Columbus, Indiana hospital from West Bridgebury had taken just less than two hours, time tense with back-and-forth conflict raging in his heart. He wanted to know whether Gregory Travis had told anyone else their secret. He was hoping that the old man, sensing the end was near and wanting to "tie up every loose end" and "get his affairs in order"—more sayings that Robin would frown upon—would tell him that everything was square between them, that McCauley had made good on his part of their agreement and that Travis had told nobody else and would take to the grave the truth about McCauley's plagiarism of James West. But what if Travis would not say, or *could* not say? Should McCauley raise the question? What was proper etiquette when you were talking to a man who might die before another sentence rolled off his tongue?

Travis hacked and swallowed. The great irony of his death, as his wife had noted, was that despite his decades of heavy cigarette smoking, his lungs were as clear as a sunny sky. His cough was from pneumonia. Congestive heart failure—not cancer—was doing him in.

"West," Travis began before stopping to take a breath. "West blew it."

What did *that* mean? At least McCauley could tell that Travis, regardless of any pain-killing drugs in his system, was alert and lucid enough to recognize his visitor. Moreover, the enigmatic sentence convinced McCauley that he could safely ask about their secret.

"How so?" McCauley asked, succinctly, unconsciously imitating the professor.

"He never crowed." Every word sounded strained, painful. "You know … you have to *crow*." He emphasized the last word by raising one of his taped, tubed hands six inches off the tight white linen bed sheet.

McCauley managed a smile. That was another one of Travis's pet words—*crow*, as a verb. He was always urging his students to *crow*, to trumpet their literary opinions, to shout them out loud from the rooftops of the academic village. Waiting for the professor to elaborate, McCauley leaned back in the soft chair.

Thirty seconds of silence passed.

"So, what are you saying?" McCauley asked. "That I need to make the case that James West never made?"

Travis grunted and his head moved up and down slightly in what might have been a nod.

It's now or never, McCauley decided. He leaned toward the professor so that his mouth was a few inches from Travis's closest ear.

As soon as he opened his mouth, the door swung open and a nurse came in, crisp and efficient, followed by Emma Travis.

"I think you'll have to go now," Mrs. Travis said apologetically. "They have to check some things." She waved vaguely, helplessly, at the beeping, humming machines.

McCauley stood and thanked her.

"I'm so sorry," he said. "Maybe I'll be able to visit him again, if ..." He let his sentence trail off, not sure how to finish it with sensitivity.

"Don't feel like you have to," she said, shaking her head. "It was nice of you to come all this way today."

After grabbing lunch at the McDonalds near the hospital, McCauley wandered into a used book store called Between the Lines half a block away. The name of the business elicited a chuckle that once more he stifled when he remembered that Robin would disapprove, her reading of his dissertation leading her to complain about his overuse of clichés, trite expressions, and other informal language.

"Sometimes you try to be too clever by half," she said, an ironic twinkle in her eyes. For years, laboring over his Ph.D. project, he had persuaded himself that not only his original thesis but also his innovative writing style would turn heads in scholarly circles. Thus, her criticism bruised his feelings.

Their relationship had transformed. Nowadays it was all business, at least compared to the heady days of the fall and winter, not that the business was unimportant—his dissertation, and their collaboration to expose and eradicate the cheating at Brookstone High School.

McCauley found a couple of potentially promising paperbacks. The bookstore had a nook with a pair of blanketed sofas and a coffee table where he sat and read while he finished his drink from McDonalds. A cat that evidently lived in the store rubbed against his legs. He stretched contentedly. All things being equal, he was living a pretty good life these days, living on a shoestring but comfortable and happy in his element, content with the trappings of his graduate student world, where everyone accepted him for who he was. That would all change in the next year. He would become a full-fledged professional. One time before, he had started down that road—until Mary Ann Childress and her lying, greedy lawyers forced him off.

Strange, how things worked. Over the past month or so, supervising Erin Delaney's oral history project with the residents of her grandfather's elder-care facility in Orange Stone, McCauley had been caught by surprise, caught by a wistful tug from the past, from that road not taken. Working with Erin had revived something in his blood. Really he was just keeping out of her way, making a suggestion here and there in what was evolving into a textbook independent study effort. Erin was a joy to mentor—she was fresh, energetic, original, always thinking of new directions to take her research and its presentation. The last time they consulted, she was breathless with excitement, having sweet-talked her annoying classmate Tyler Batta into editing and splicing together her numerous video interviews into a single fifteen-minute clip and even to do the overall narration. This was true education. This was what McCauley had once longed for. This was how he once envisioned his career as a high school teacher—sparking young people's interest in the past and working with them as they pursued their own passions that intersected the study of history.

Erin's enthusiasm had resuscitated his own, revitalized that old dream destroyed seven years ago. And even as he reveled in the whiff of exhilaration, he knew he must tamp down his feelings, for that dream was dead in the dust of his own history.

A cheap cuckoo clock pinched between two bookcases squawked the time: one o'clock. His watch said it was four minutes later.

McCauley sighed and set the books in a stack on the coffee table, squaring their edges. His once-proud philosophy was disintegrating, the conflicting clocks and his changed relationship with Robin both grim emblems of that fact. During their happier times together, she had challenged his worldview, half in jest, half in candor. And now he saw that she was right, or at least that he was wrong. His belief in the Universal Clock, deism's great symbol of ultimate reality, was crashing down. Life was not as predictable and programmed as clockwork, no matter how valiantly and vehemently he argued that it was. Often, defending his philosophy with Robin, he had babbled on and on about the complexity of the program, its intricate beauty and magnificent glory. Well, he was only fooling himself. Based on all the unexpected, inexplicable twists his life had taken lately, it made more sense to think that a personal, hands-on God was not only interested in his life but actively interfering in it with a whimsical, alternating sense of comedy and tragedy.

This trip to visit Travis was just the latest example. Who could have predicted that the sly old blackmailer would escape lung cancer, which he deserved, which would have been fair and just, which would have made sense? And in a few minutes, McCauley would start home no wiser about what his future held, whether he ought to be confident about his dissertation defense and job prospects or fearful that at any moment the rug might be pulled from under him when somebody raised the question of why his thesis borrowed so heavily from James West, deceased. No longer could he reconcile the topsy-turvy uncertainty of his life with the notion of a clockwork god and a clockwork universe. Still—the cat leapt nimbly into his lap and he stroked its thick fur—he would miss a lot of the simple comforts of the past several years. He would miss being a graduate student.

The weather was gorgeous. A trifle cool, still, but the sunshine pouring onto the flat fields along Interstate 65 as he rumbled north toward Indianapolis hinted at even lovelier days ahead. What if he wound up taking a job in a part of the country where the seasons didn't change much, like southern California or Arizona or Florida? He would miss spring, and fall. Sooner or later he would probably need to get a car.

The pleasant day was conducive to thinking, and he had plenty to think about. Even though he recognized that his life at Brookstone High School was essentially over, he wanted to finish strong with his one class and its students as well as with Robin. Not Myers and LaGrange—he could care less about them or what they thought of him. They had threatened to kill him, maybe even tried to kill him already, or surely tried to scare him into quitting his job. He didn't owe them anything. His students were another matter. Neither his part-time status nor his higher-priority work at Riverside had weakened his commitment to be the best high school teacher he could be. This semester, the kids were taking him more seriously, no doubt because word had gotten around about his refusal to back down from administration and parental pressure about his opposition to the cheating. He had stood his ground, and somehow in the crazy calculus of teenage logic, that position had earned him some grudging credit. The grade appeals of the six students remained officially unresolved. But those six had buckled down this semester and, though not technically admitting their guilt, had by their improved behavior as much as admitted their guilt—at least that was how McCauley interpreted things. He felt vindicated.

However, he felt uneasy about where he stood with Walter Patingale, the school superintendent. After turning over a copy of the information that he and Robin and Erin had gathered—but pointedly keeping a copy for himself, in blatant disregard for his boss's clear request—he expected some kind of reprisal. So far, none had come. Perhaps he was living on borrowed time and his dismissal was imminent; or, perhaps Patingale had figured that ignoring McCauley and letting him finish the semester and fade into the sunset was the wisest response to his insubordination. Either way, McCauley was convinced that Patingale was in communication with Myers and LaGrange, even if not in league with them. He would hear from Patingale again, directly or indirectly.

To the east a freight train appeared, moving south from Indianapolis, silently, its distant din swallowed up by the noise of the motorcycle and the muffling effect of his helmet. Every train he saw, now, reminded him of the one that almost killed him outside Brookstone a few weeks ago. Never again would he be able to watch a train with the innocence of a child counting cars or a baby lulled to sleep. No, from now on trains would be the stuff of nightmares for him. And for the next six weeks or so, he would always worry about being on the "right track," as Myers's thugs had warned him.

Thinking of the train turned his attention once more to the mystery of whether Matt Rademacher had been one of his attackers that night—Matt, one of the first-semester cheaters he had caught; Matt, who had frequently hinted at his entanglement with Tolan Myers; Matt, whose girlfriend Erin wore the lilac perfume whose scent still clung to his memory of the horrific night. At some point he would have to ask

Matt, face to face. Whenever it happened, that would be a difficult conversation.

McCauley wished he could talk to Robin about confronting Matt, but he was reluctant to raise any topics with her outside those that were part of their cheating investigation or his thesis. For weeks she had seemed unconvinced that he was through waffling with respect to the first issue. As for her help with his dissertation, she had the last chapter in her hands—as soon as she offered her feedback and he made necessary changes, he would deposit the manuscript and wait to defend it. The last several weeks had taken him on a roller-coaster ride between despair and elation. After the break-in at his apartment, when his flash drive with the only up-to-date version of the dissertation had been stolen, he had literally groaned in anguish at the thought of having to reconstruct his argument, in particular its elaborate expression. He thought he might have to ask for an extension from his Ph.D. committee while he rushed to rewrite the lost chapters. Then, in the most ironic twist of all, *Myers* returned the flash drive in an act of brazen arrogance (or stupidity, if Robin was right), saving McCauley the frustrating work of recreating what he had already produced with months of mental sweat.

A flock of birds wheeled in majestic formation over a corn field. He thought of Travis's remark about *crowing*, and then his remark about *triumph*—and suddenly a new thought occurred to him—a thought pregnant with promise but also mystery. What if the professor meant that his death would mean that McCauley would triumph *over him*? He had said he would miss the triumph. Yes, he would, if he was dead. ... Was this the old man's way of saying McCauley was now free of their agreement? Oh, the timing! If only Emma and the nurse had waited a minute more before coming into the hospital room, then McCauley might have heard the whole truth straight from Travis's mouth. Now, he would have to live in the throes of uncertainty that would pile on the stress until he defended his dissertation, if not indefinitely longer.

Back in West Bridgebury, he went to the blood center, where he had made an appointment to donate. As the nurse took his blood pressure, he took stock of the many physical problems that had plagued him over the past couple of years. Every single one was real—yet in the excitement of the past months he had forgotten many of them. He was no healthier now than then. And the ailments had not been psychosomatic. Still, while his mind had been occupied with his relationship with Robin, and his anger at the injustice of the cheating, and his fear for his job and life at separate points in time, and now his joy at Erin's progress and his confusion about his secret with Travis—while his mind had been focused on so many different problems, his physical aches and pains hardly mattered. He wanted to tell Robin about that, too. She would probably credit Dr. Vance, the chiropractor.

When the nurse squeezed his finger to prick it for the drops of blood they always took to check your type—why didn't they ever believe you when you told them you were O-positive?—he stared at his finger, swollen and red, and he could think of nothing else besides the perpetually red face of Tolan Myers tugging at his tight collar as if struggling to breathe.

Finished donating, he sat at a round plastic table and munched on cookies and drank two cups of orange juice. A discarded newspaper sat folded on the next table, which made him think of Pete Doty, the Bridgebury *Courier* reporter who was investigating the school cheating from his journalistic perspective. The last message Doty had left for Robin had hinted at "progress" and "some major findings." More mystery. McCauley felt utterly out of control, just like Erin Delaney, who had complained to him and Robin about her home life, her hopes for college, and her relationship with Matt Rademacher. He chuckled—when Erin had told them she felt blown this way and that and that her life was "like a whirlwind," Robin had nodded gravely, as though she would offer some consoling comment. But instead of giving some adult advice, some motherly word of wisdom, as the moment called for, she had replied, "'Like a whirlwind.' That's a good simile." And they had all laughed wildly in their Dairy Queen booth.

Even though half the clocks in his life were broken and the other half disagreed about the exact time, McCauley's day proceeded on schedule. A half hour after his visit to the blood center, he met Kelly Graham at ¿Que Pasa? His classmate, slightly ahead of McCauley on the path to dissertation defense, had gotten word that his day of reckoning would be May 8. In the meantime, he was job-hunting and had actually received two offers, both from colleges in his home state of Tennessee. Graham loved to talk, loved to process out loud, and that was his point in asking for McCauley to meet him at the bar. He simply wanted a listening ear. McCauley was happy to provide one—he was in no mood to talk shop, to talk about his own shop, that is. Once Graham had talked through his options, running through the pros and cons of each school, he offered to buy McCauley a drink.

"I shouldn't," McCauley said, holding up his palms. "I just gave blood. I think that somewhere on the list of post-donation instructions they gave me is a warning not to drink any alcohol for x number of hours."

"Rain check, then?"

"Rain check. Once you take a real job."

Rain check, McCauley thought. *Blood money. Circular reasoning.* Every time he went into ¿Que Pasa? now, he automatically started conjuring up two-word phrases.

When they got up to leave, a familiar voice called McCauley's name, and he said good-bye to Graham.

Unlike Brad McCauley and his slavery to schedule and clocks, Manny Sarks appeared to operate outside of time. He blew around like wind, like Erin Delaney's whirlwind. If he had any schedule to keep, any agenda to follow, he never allowed it to show. Increasingly, McCauley was fascinated, enthralled really, by Sarks's gradual insinuation into his life. Their relationship in some ways mirrored his relationship with Robin, particularly in that it had blossomed wholly unexpectedly and left McCauley constantly questioning where it was headed.

Sarks inspired uncanny confidence. For no apparent reason, McCauley over the past few weeks had admitted Sarks into parts of his life that he previously had fenced off to everyone except Robin. He had confided to Sarks, for example, that he had gotten involved with a married woman—without mentioning Robin by name—and that his dissertation, for all its strengths, had one potentially fatal defect—without identifying that defect. And he had told Sarks about being ensnared in an imbroglio at Brookstone High School that sooner or later would explode, with serious consequences. Sarks was more than politely interested in that last confession and soon explained why—he and his wife were involved in a ministry to students in the Harrison County schools, and he wondered whether any of their kids were involved. McCauley had not so far explained the exact nature of the situation, but he felt certain that soon he would, for he felt connected to Sarks by an invisible thread of sympathy.

And as they sat and talked for the next hour—McCauley now ignoring the blood center's warning about alcohol—that thread gently tugged him into dropping hints about his daring plan to retrieve "a piece of stolen property." Having learned that Myers and LaGrange both would be absent from school in ten days, and fearing that Myers might be spooked by McCauley's unflagging pursuit of the truth and move any incriminating documents from his office, McCauley now had a date circled on his calendar to attempt to execute his plan. With Sarks, he was circumspect about details. Avoiding the term *burglary*, he drew a word portrait of a conjectural break-and-enter operation whose setting was the office of "executives" of an unnamed organization. His goal in describing everything to Sarks was basic: He hoped his friend, who was a good listener, would point out possible flaws in his plan.

What he got was something else.

"So, what am I missing?" he asked Sarks after he had outlined the scenario. "I'm sure I have blind spots. Help me see what I'm not seeing."

Blind spots, he thought. *Fire sale. Island paradise.* Had he not been so interested in Sarks's opinion, McCauley would have surveyed the room in search of the patron fixed on two-word combinations.

"Seriously?" Sarks asked, as if he could not believe the question, as if the answer was as obvious as the half-full glasses of Heineken on the table in front of them.

"Seriously."

Sarks fixed McCauley with a stare that lasted just long enough to make him feel stupid, a stare that suggested the question, "Where do I begin?"

Then he said it, rhetorically: "Where do I begin?"

McCauley thought of replying, in self-defense, that he was not an experienced criminal. Sarks obviously saw through the "hypothetical" smokescreen. He knew that McCauley was referring to something he himself was thinking about.

Rumor mill. Job security. Window dressing.

Sarks spared him further embarrassment by telling a story about his own reckless behavior in college, a story about him and a girlfriend breaking into the university *library*, of all places, and "leaving reminders" in room after room. What these "reminders" were, he did not specify, and McCauley did not ask. Sarks related the incident not with the affected bombast typical of many wistful graduates but rather with a sheepish penitence that left McCauley wondering, What was the point? He was accustomed to listening to Sarks refer back to his hell-raising days, always in regretful tones, always trumpeting his past guilt and present innocence—all because of Jesus, of course.

And that pattern held true once again.

His eyes glued on his beer, Sarks said ruefully—no matter how hard McCauley tried to discern whether the humility was false, he could not tell—"Some of those things I did in those days, so many of those things …" He shook his head as though truly sorry. "I should not be here today talking to you. I should be dead, or in jail somewhere. What I have now, with a great marriage and a good job …" He shook his head again. "It's more than I could have ever hoped for. That's what grace is like, too much to ever hope for. Not too good to be true—too good *not* to be true."

The funny thing was that these carefully recounted stories with the same well-worn morals never left McCauley feeling manipulated as so many sinner-saved-by-God tales did. That was curious, but not inexplicable. Sarks was just a good storyteller; that was the reason. He sometimes talked about his father, a retired journalist who lived in Bridgebury, who impressed upon him at an early age that everybody has stories to tell, and every one of those stories teaches us something not only about the story-teller but also about ourselves.

5

"THIS IS WHAT I hate about these games in April," Erin Delaney muttered. "It's always about twenty degrees wind chill, and raining half the time."

She pulled her blanket tighter and leaned closer to Matt Rademacher, whose attention was riveted to the baseball field, where Cody Summers, Brookstone's shortstop, was advancing toward home plate for his first at bat of the season. Matt shouted, "It's Summers Time!" and even from their top-row seat in the cold aluminum bleachers, they could see Cody smile just before he spat with determination and stepped into the batter's box.

The first pitch he saw struck him on his left shoulder, and he flung his bat toward the home dugout and trotted toward first base. Matt shouted, "Way to take one for the team, Cody!"

Matt's good mood managed to coax a smile from Erin, but it was only half-hearted. She had become increasingly certain about her ability to look beyond Matt's demeanor and discern the deeper, true condition of whatever lay beneath—his heart, his soul, the real Matt. What she saw now troubled her. She was convinced that all Matt's outward serenity and good humor were concealing a buildup of pressure that would ultimately explode. Exactly how, she could not imagine. Occasionally he mumbled threats against Mr. Myers, but much of that rhetoric she attributed to typical male teenage testosterone-induced bravado that you couldn't take seriously. Still, ever since that embarrassing blow-up at DQ, Matt had retreated emotionally, adopting a sense of unspoken confidence that hinted at a fixed purpose—a purpose he had not shared with Erin.

Tyler Batta was in mid-season form. Sitting on a quilt two rows beneath Erin and Matt, he was "broadcasting" the game into his cell phone's voice recorder. Erin had observed throughout the year that people sitting near Tyler as he plied his future craft either loved him or hated him. He could be either immensely entertaining or embarrassingly annoying. As Jake "Tripper" Sondgerath came to the plate, accompanied by a few lines from his chosen walk-up song, Tyler's voice rang out in the silence: "Fans, here's Jake Sondgerath making his first plate appearance of this young season. That music you hear in the background, by the way, is 'I'll Take my Chances' by folk artist Mary Chapin Carpenter, which also happens to be the senior song for Brookstone High School's graduating class. Jake, of course, is a senior. And with a runner on base, Delphi will be taking *its* chances with Sondgerath. The first pitch catches the outside corner for strike one.

"Fans, Jake's nickname is 'Tripper,' and there's an interesting story to how he acquired it. As a toddler, Jake was known for tripping over toys and whatnot, so his siblings took to calling him 'Trip.' As he grew up, his friends also adopted that nickname and eventually added the *–er* ending as teenagers do to almost all names. So today most people know Jake simply as 'Tripper.'"

Listening, Erin could only giggle. Tyler was nothing if not amusing.

In fact, his unflagging *desire* to be entertaining had nearly kept her from seeking his help with her history research project. Mr. McCauley had urged her to think about matching her original *material*—the interviews with the nursing home residents, which he called "oral history"—with some equally fresh *form* of presenting it. As great as that sounded, and as optimistic as Mr. McCauley tried to be, she could not think of anything beyond the routine written paper. A day after she happened to mention her dead end to Tyler, he suggested she shoot some video clips of the residents going about their daily routines and then merge it with the audio she had already recorded. That plan also sounded great, but Erin grumbled that she had no equipment or experience shooting video. Then Tyler volunteered to help. He would shoot new video and put together the footage with the existing interview audio, on one condition—that he be given "rights" to use the material in the future. In particular, he was interested in adding it to his current portfolio of work, which was an important component of his application to all the colleges where he was applying for admission.

Even though she was a bit baffled by the idea of "rights" (especially after hearing Mr. McCauley complain so much about lawyers), she trusted Tyler and said she would agree to anything as long as she finished her research project on time.

Their partnership blossomed quickly. Whatever ideas Tyler proposed met with Erin's immediate approval. The only thing that slowed them down was Tyler's frequent second-guessing and fine-tuning, for he was a perfectionist both behind the camera and across the table from her when they planned. Even when they went to Lake Haven to shoot video, he often thought up new ideas on the spot. At his behest they actually *re*-interviewed several residents so that the finished presentation would have more variety. Erin nearly balked at that suggestion, fearing that the residents might grouse at having to repeat themselves. However, she was pleasantly mistaken, for not only were they happy to talk to her as many times as she liked, but many of them in various stages of senility had forgotten the earlier interviews. Asked the exact same questions, some of them gave different responses.

Tyler's neatest idea was to use what he called "B-roll footage" for the "segues" or transitions between the interviews. Those were places where Erin's interpretation and summary of the interviews should be inserted in the form of "voiceovers." For this material, he said, they should use the background of the Lake Haven fountain and pool with the statues of dancing children. The contrasting imagery—the children and the old folks—would "create a poignant tone" and help reinforce the themes that emerged in Erin's research into the changes in elder care. Listening to Tyler's suggestions, Erin nodded in a perfunctory way. She understood only about half of what he said, yet his enthusiasm mesmerized her and carried her along. She felt proud to learn the vocabulary of the videography profession. She felt special.

And her biggest fear never materialized. Tyler never took over the project, never tried to rewrite the "script" in his own inimitable voice, never let his penchant for theatrics overshadow Erin's plainer vision for the project. Only one time did she overrule him, when he tried to sneak in the Brookstone High School *1-2-3-4* motif, the latest fad, which made Erin cringe but evidently had found in Tyler a receptive heart.

All in all, his work at Lake Haven had been splendid. A baseball game, though, was more Tyler's preferred element. Expounding on the trivia of Jake Sondgerath's name, he continued: "Of course, Brookstone baseball fans are hoping that nickname becomes prophetic and that soon they will be calling him 'Round Tripper' for his many home runs."

At the climax of all of Tyler's bombastic buildup, Sondgerath struck out.

What made Erin's worry about Matt all the more thorny, morally, was that she had decided (again) to break up with him. Today, in fact. By the end of the seven innings of chilly baseball, she would tell him. Although she felt somewhat responsible for Matt and what the pressure in his life might bring, she had finally summoned the wherewithal to throw off that self-imposed burden. It was unrealistic. Mrs. Hillis and others were right—in the end, she had to do what was best for herself first. Matt was mature enough to take care of himself.

Or so she hoped.

Cody came around to score on a line-drive single to center off the bat of a sophomore, Tristan Phillips, whom Matt called "a phenom." Matt himself had quit playing baseball as a freshman, choosing to focus on football and wrestling. Then funding had dried up and the school had cut its wrestling program.

One other issue complicated Erin's intentions with Matt. Actually, it involved Cody, but since Matt was Cody's best friend, she might need Matt's help—which she might not get once she dumped him. At her urging, Mr. McCauley and Mrs. Hillis had agreed that they should ask Cody for help in hacking into Mr. Myers's computer to search for incriminating evidence about cheating. Erin didn't know whether Cody would agree, if she asked him directly. She might need Matt's help. Like a true gambler, though, she was holding onto a hidden trump card: She knew Matt would help if he believed Mr. Myers was involved.

In the third inning, Matt went to the concession stand and returned with a steaming cardboard cup of hot chocolate for Erin.

"You didn't need to do that," she asked. Inadvertently, unknowingly, he was making everything she must do harder.

"How long since you've seen Nathan?" he asked, surprising her. She had never told him about their chance meeting weeks before.

"I don't know. Why?"

"I just wondered."

Erin sensed an opening.

"Do you ever think about ... what's happening between you and me?"

"You mean after this year?"

"Yeah. Or just, you know, in general."

"Not really. I'm just taking things one day at a time right now. How about you?"

"Well ..." She tried to indicate by her tone that she had given the subject plenty of thought. Matt turned to her and said, "Well, what?"

"To be honest, Matt, I never understood why you wanted me to be your girlfriend back in the fall. And I still don't. Can you explain that?"

Like most guys, she knew, he would stumble trying to express an answer to that question. That was part of her strategy—to talk him into a corner from which the only reasonable escape was for him to concede that she was right.

"I just like being with you, I guess."

"Why?"

"I don't know. We have fun. Don't we?"

"Sometimes." She couldn't lie about that. "But, you want to know what I think?"

"I don't know. Do I?" He was clearly on the defensive now.

Behind the backstop, several farmer dads had gathered in their usual spot. People were such creatures of habit. The same types of baseball fathers who farmed for a living congregated behind the same backstop year after year to talk seamlessly about two worlds—pitch counts and bat speeds as well as per-acre-yields and machinery repairs and upkeep. They wore battered caps that advertised agricultural products with an arcane vernacular every bit as undecipherable to outsiders as that of baseball. Mr. Tillson's cap, for instance, bore the insignia DAWSON'S XY HYBRID. Erin had no idea what that meant, and would be embarrassed to ask anyone other than Grandpa Dee, who, in his day as a young dad, would have been part of the backstop gang from April through June. Then, like the rest, he would shift his preferred meeting site to the perimeter of the bed of somebody's pickup truck.

Erin turned on the cold metal seat to face Matt squarely.

"There are two things I need to tell you," she began falteringly.

"Shoot," he said.

"Okay. Should I start with the good or the bad?"

"The bad. The good. I don't care."

"Okay, the good." She shifted as if priming herself. "After all these months, I just want to thank you that you quit putting pressure on me."

"You mean, about …?"

"Yes."

"Aw, that's okay. I told you it was all a joke anyway, just a stupid bet."

"Yes, maybe so, but still, I think it showed who you really are that you told me the truth and all. If you want to know the truth, it surprised me when you changed so much. About that, I mean."

Matt seemed embarrassed. He said, "Aw, Erin." He threw up his hands, uncomprehending. "There's nothing I can say now that won't hurt your feelings one way or the other. The fact is, even if I still wanted to … even if that was still a big deal to me, the fact is, I have more important things to worry about right now."

"Like what?"

"Never mind. Maybe later. What's the *bad* thing?"

She mentally composed herself, inhaled deeply, and said, "I think it would be best if we stopped going together." She let her eyes wander to the diamond, averting his gaze, hoping for a reaction somewhere short of fury. After all, Matt might reasonably feel like he had wasted most of his senior year on her.

"Yeah," he said softly. "I thought so."

"That's all you're going to say?"

"I don't know. Maybe I'll have more to say later. It's like I said, I have other fish to fry right now. That's what Steve always used to say. I always got such a kick out of that, since he loved to fish so much. Did I ever tell you about the last time we were ever together? Fishing at the Junction?"

"No," Erin replied, caught between the rock of not wanting to talk about Steve and the hard place of not wanting to discuss their break-up. Thankfully, Matt did not pursue the thought.

An uncomfortable silence followed, broken only when they both heard Tyler Batta remark into his recorder: "Fans, just a reminder that any rebroadcast, reproduction, or other use of the pictures and accounts of this game without the express written consent of the Indiana High School Athletic Association and Brookstone High School, Inc. is strictly prohibited"—at which they and other nearby fans broke into laughter.

In the fifth inning, Brookstone pushed across two runs without a base hit. Cody laid down a sacrifice bunt that advanced two base runners, who each scored on successive wild pitches.

Matt brought Erin another cup of hot chocolate. Handing it to her, he asked, "Even though we aren't going to be together any more, I still have one favor to ask you."

"I don't know," she said with hesitation.

"Come on, Erin. Just to thank me for being so good to you."

"Okay. I might have one more favor to ask you, too."

"I can't really say what mine is, yet," he said. "I just might need your help with something. Before the end of the semester."

"Do I get any hints?"

"Naw. Not yet, anyway. It's an *assignment*, that's all I'll say. Something I have to do. I don't even know all the details yet. So what's your favor?"

"Well, I don't want to say yet, either. It depends on what happens when I talk to Cody." Then she felt an upsurge of good will compelling her to ask, "But there is one other favor. This will sound funny, I guess, but it's serious. Will you go with me to Prom?"

He chuckled.

"Sure. It's probably too late to get another decent date anyway!"

Pitch by pitch, Matt shouted encouragement and exhortation to the Brookstone players. He loved any environment where he could show off his people skills—not *show off*, really, that was not fair. He just thrived in any setting where his natural bubbly personality could roam free. She and Matt were a good pair, in that respect, if you believed that opposites attracted.

Erin was studying the pattern of tiny light bulbs that formed the numbers on the scoreboard when Matt suddenly fell silent. His change of mood was stark, and it pulled her attention away from the lights to his face, whose countenance had taken on a brooding cast, his eyes fixed on the ticket booth behind the first-base dugout. Erin followed his icy glare—Mr. Myers was standing there, speaking to the ticket-sellers. She looked back to Matt, whose nostrils were flaring.

"Hey," she said, tugging on the leathery arm of his letterman's jacket. "Hey, the game's over here."

Tyler Batta's voice crackled below them: "Fans, just a reminder: This game is being simulcast in Spanish where available. Tune your radio dial to 98.4 FM."

Nursing a 4-3 lead in the seventh inning, Brookstone's coach, Mr. Noonan, brought in Cody to pitch. While Cody took his warm-ups, Tyler fabricated a "Trivia Question" for his listeners: "Which member of the Brookstone roster was once voted, based on his name alone, 'Most Likely to Become a Lawyer'? Text your answers to star-5664. Usual messaging rates will apply. The answer will come sometime during the next game."

"Aw, Tyler, you snoot!" Matt called. "You can't do that, leave your audience hanging! Who is it?"

Tyler turned his cell phone toward the field, turned his head toward Matt and Erin, and mouthed: "Roderick Pittinger."

Cody walked the first batter he faced but then induced a pop-up and a weak grounder to second base. With two out, Delphi's best hitter strode brashly toward the plate, tapped his bat against his spikes to knock off the clinging dirt, and stepped in. On Cody's first pitch he smacked a long foul fly. Then he took two straight called strikes to end the game, his shoulders slumping in disappointment at the umpire's final call. In celebration the Brookstone players spilled out of the dugout to congratulate Cody and the fielders, after which both teams lined up to shake hands at home plate.

Erin watched in a state of fascination—of *epiphany*, to use a word she had learned in English class. Her fingers and toes felt numb with freezing but her heart felt buoyant and free and newly expectant. What a strange and glorious afternoon this had turned out to be! The fallout that might have come from jilting Matt had turned into a warm afterglow she never could have foreseen, in whose halo she sensed something emerging, something truly herself, genuine and strong. She felt suddenly ready to tell her parents what *she* wanted and what *she* was going to do about her future. She was through submerging her hopes and desires and wishes. All the incisive observations she had made over the months about Matt's false front had blinded her to recognizing the lie of herself—of her own lifelong mask that kept evolving through the seasons of her life. Of all the cheating she abhorred, what could be more ugly and vile than the way she was cheating herself?

Matt clambered down the clanging aluminum steps and with other fans waited at the fence between the backstop and the home dugout. As the players came through the gate, he high-fived them and chattered encouragement. He was such a people-pleaser too, in his own way. Just a little boy looking for a place to belong, a circle of friends to love him for who he was. But he didn't know who he was—Erin knew him better than he himself did, maybe. All that outward joy was false. Underneath it beat a heart seething with turbulence that more than any other characteristic really defined his day-to-day existence.

Erin kept patient. She caught Cody's eye and waved. A few moments later, when most of the fans had dispersed to their heating cars, she tapped him on the shoulder of his pinstriped uniform and said, "Cody, I need to ask you a favor."

6

THE DRIVE TO Indianapolis for the play was quiet and cordial but tense—at least from Robin's perspective ensconced in the plush, heated passenger seat of Zeb's well-equipped Ford Taurus. Quiet and cordial, because except for small talk about their kids and the weather, only a few polite, safe words passed between husband and wife. Tense, because Robin felt more pressure than ever to tell Zeb the whole truth about Brad McCauley, to finally crawl out from under that terrible burden as she knew that sooner or later she must.

She watched the passing scenery with feigned interest. A few farmers were plowing and seeding land that any day now would show the first tinges of light green. Even though most of the grass was still brown, signs of spring were everywhere—dogs romping in large lawns, homeowners starting spring cleaning, and runners in brilliant attire logging outdoor miles along country roads. Her interest was feigned because she still suspected that Zeb suspected her. That nagging fear occupied her focus, intruded on almost every thought, clouded her outlook. Until she confessed her infidelity to him, she knew, her secret would continue to press her down.

If it even *was* a secret.

Way back at Christmas, when Zeb had bought the season tickets to the plays at the Tarkington, tonight's title had stuck in her mind. *Inherit the Wind.* All its connotations were negative, convicting. She was well aware of the title's allusion to a Bible verse about judgment. Just to be sure, she checked it out before they started their one-hour drive, and there it was, Proverbs 11:29. *Whoever troubles his own household will inherit the wind.* How could she read that and not think about herself, her sin, the trouble she had brought to her own household? The connection could not be more obvious ...

Passing through the city of Lebanon, Robin noticed a flickering sign atop a tall pole at a truck stop, and her eyes fixed on its red gasoline prices flashing back and forth between CASH and CREDIT, alternating every five seconds or so. Just like her mind, she thought. Jumping back and forth between facing the fact that she must tell the truth to Zeb and avoiding that fact by paying attention to some detail out the window, acting as though it mattered, investing it with some false significance—anything to keep the truth at arms' length. Some of her attempts at escape were ludicrous, she had to admit.

Like when she saw a digital bank clock's time of 12:34 and immediately felt her mind sucked to the silly *1-2-3-4* public relations campaign that Tolan Myers was pushing at school, trying to build up momentum for it as though it were a new Dairy Queen menu item. Robin had respectfully pointed out that all the rules and experience of rhetoric called for a three-step structure, but Myers was sold on four. He had thought it up and no one could talk him out of it. For a month or so he had been trying to ratchet up enthusiasm for his promotional plan, putting flyers in teachers' mailboxes with ideas, asking for everyone to think up ways to invite school athletic teams and academic clubs and even local businesses to climb on board the *1-2-3-4* train. As a fad it had started out harmless enough. At the latest faculty meeting, however, Robin had noticed a shift in emphasis that felt like coercion, a rising sense of discomfort about how their building and individual classrooms and teaching styles were being subtly ... compromised? Molded? Myers wanted them to try to incorporate the *1-2-3-4* theme into their lesson plans. "Look for anything in your curriculum or unit plans or daily plans that can be grouped into fours," he had urged. "And then figure out a way to connect it to the *1-2-3-4* plan." She wasn't sure exactly how to characterize the change. Moreover, she wondered why any such PR gimmick was necessary. Everyone in government, in education, and in business and industry in the northern part of the state of Indiana knew about Brookstone's reputation and ongoing excellence. *1-2-3-4* seemed like an utter waste of time, energy, and probably money.

"What do you think the title means?" asked Zeb, shaking her from her contemplation. *"Inherit the Wind?"*

He was just trying to make conversation by asking a question tailor-made for her English-teacher expertise. Or was he? Maybe he already knew the answer and was trying to lay a guilt trip on her. Not quite sure how to wriggle out of her corner, she sighed as if considering her reply, then said, "It's an allusion." Prudently, scrupulously, she avoided identifying the source of the allusion. But in the silence that followed she knew that Zeb was waiting for more.

"I've heard that there are a lot of historical inaccuracies in the play," she went on, irrelevantly. "It takes liberties with the historical facts." She thought of Brad McCauley.

"Like what?"

Good, he apparently hadn't noticed her evasion ...

"I'm not sure. I don't remember."

They were seated early. Robin opened her program and began to devour its contents—mostly to avoid talking to Zeb.

When the curtain rose on the opening scene, she sighed in secret satisfaction, expecting the action of the play to provide a refuge. Instead, it provided a surprise, and a distraction. The actress playing the role of Melinda Loomis, who came onstage to talk to a boy digging for worms in the soil, looked like a younger version of Erin Delaney, with long, straight brown hair, a hint of freckles, and big brown eyes. The similarity was so strong in Robin's mind that for several minutes of dialogue she could only stare at Melinda's pretty face.

Then she remembered Erin's whirlwind. She remembered the wonderful, inspiring description of what Erin had witnessed one day at the Junction, all by herself, communing with nature, just minding her own business, she said, when from out of the sky came the miniature tornado that sucked up leaves and dirt and twigs in its spinning spiral fury. She remembered that Erin's account ended with her amazement at how the whirlwind with its astonishing power had cleaned the bank and bridge, how it had swept away everything but the ground and concrete. That was a type of judgment, Robin thought. And she remembered that two hours earlier, looking for the Bible reference from the play's title, she had mistakenly looked for the word *whirlwind* rather than *wind* in her concordance and found another verse, Hosea 8:7, where the prophet thundered: *They sow the wind and reap the whirlwind.* Then she found another wrong verse, Jeremiah 29:13: *See, the storm of the Lord will burst out in wrath, a whirlwind swirling down on the heads of the wicked.*

Robin fought to ignore the memories, to escape the associations with Erin's whirlwind. But soon after she succeeded in fixing her mind back on the play came another jolt of surprise in the shape of the unkempt mop of hair on the character of Bertram Cates, the jailed teacher accused of illegally teaching evolution. When the bailiff escorted Cates from his cell to talk to Rachel Brown, his love interest, Cates appeared wearing a befuddled expression beneath an unruly shock of hair that begged to be trimmed.

That hair! It sent Robin through a flashback more agonizing than the one landing in Erin's whirlwind. A few days earlier, she had taken an intentional step toward Zeb—a step far short of admitting her affair with Brad, but a step nevertheless. Digging into the back of their bedroom closet, she unearthed a cardboard shoe box with a relic from the early years of their marriage, the hair-grooming kit Zeb had bought at a garage sale so that she could cut his hair to save them the expense of regular visits to a barber. So many years had passed! She plugged in the cracked cord of the clippers and was surprised that they still worked, their vibrations throbbing along her forearm, pulsing with memories ... Convincing Zack to sit for a trim was not difficult; he too was captivated by the nostalgia. Robin truly hoped the gesture would revive something between them. But no. While she ran her fingers through her husband's thinning hair, there was no spark, not even a hint of a spark. Still, she knew she should not give up. These things took time. Rekindling a flame took time. What pushed her closer to despair were the thoughts of Brad's younger, thicker hair that kept intruding and corrupting her new hopes. Then, merging with the memory of her hands in his hair came images of *his* hands, a scholar's hands and fingers, white, well-manicured, his bumpy knuckles, the small scar on the back of his ring finger, the calouses on his palms from gripping the motorcycle handles, the prominent veins (or arteries, she always confused those two) crisscrossing the back of his hands. What saved her from succumbing to the seductive pull of those ideas was Zeb suddenly shifting in the seat before her and remarking, "I have always loved your hands." That was all. He did not elaborate. He did not need to. So many times over the years he had complimented her hands, saying that their real beauty was not in how they looked but in what they did—they cleaned laundry, they planted flowers, they fixed meals, they soothed aches, and in a million other ways they loved everyone around her.

Robin struggled to shift her attention back to the play, where the bailiff was saying that having a teacher in the jail might "improve the writin' on the walls."

Robin cringed.

The first part of the play was set in front of the town courthouse; the next scene moved indoors for the jury selection. Robin chafed at the selection of jurors, who squirmed during their interrogation by the attorneys and even the judge. They all asked so many personal questions, even questions about people's religious faith and practices. All the trappings of justice in the set and props exacerbated Robin's own sense of being examined, of being put on trial. There was an objection and discussion about one lawyer's using the word *conform*. Robin recalled how Brad hated lawyers—oh! What would it take to get free of him? Then, as if the heavens were laughing at her plight, the lawyer named Drummond said he was afraid that "clock-stoppers" would rewrite the Constitution with their religious beliefs. *Clock-stoppers!* She simply could not escape Brad McCauley!

Act 2 began back outside the courthouse. By this time, Robin had surrendered all hope of a pleasant, peaceful evening with Zeb. That was evidently too much to ask for, she reasoned, considering all her sins against her marriage. God was out to even the score, hounding her through her conscience and through every creative coincidence that He could muster in His infinite power and wisdom. Up there on His throne, He must be doubling over in side-splitting laughter as line after line of the play stabbed at Robin's guilt. She began to twist every innocuous gesture and word from the players on stage into accusing fingers pointed in her direction. Soon she quit grimacing and actually began to chuckle sarcastically at the craziness of what was happening. Next to her, Zeb was engrossed in the story line, caught up in the tug-of-war between Clarence Darrow and William Jennings Bryan, between science and faith—while she was buffeted this way and that by words and phrases whose literal meaning was merely a masquerade for a subtext that had already tried and convicted her. She fell into a trance, almost senseless, oblivious. During a prayer meeting scene, when the Bryan character uttered the title line—"He that troubleth his own house shall inherit the wind"—the words made no impression on her, she had grown so numb. The one sentence that *should* have bothered her had no more effect than the lazy current of Boots Creek running through Brookstone had on the huge rock that gave the town its name.

Surrendering to her fate, as she imagined it, she accepted that either in fact or through her warped perceptions, the events of the day were collaborating to judge her—or that God was manipulating them, orchestrating them to the same end. She surrendered to that notion—then a strange thing occurred. The passion of the two sides in the drama on stage began to energize her to fight back against *her* fate. Job had fought against God, hadn't he? And in the end, wasn't he justified? Yes, but he had not been guilty to start with … Nonetheless, she decided she would not merely sit and be a passive puppet in the hands of … of whoever or whatever was harassing her. On stage, the Bryan character confronted his friend-turned-foe about his change of heart: "Why is it, my old friend, that you have moved so far away from me?" To which the witty Darrow character retorted, "All motion is relative … Perhaps it is you who have moved away …" Hearing the words, feeling accused once more, Robin leaned toward Zeb.

And a spell was broken, somehow. For the rest of the play she heard not a peep from her conscience.

For dinner they went to a swanky steak-and-seafood restaurant overlooking a lake on the northwest side of the city. Zeb insisted they sit outside, despite the cool weather, where the gas-lit torches not only kept them comfortable but added intimacy as darkness fell. Robin took a long time to decide on her order after she vetoed Zeb's suggestion that they get the "Pick 4" special on the menu insert. Those numbers 1, 2, 3, and 4, with their echoes of Tolan Myers's silly schemes, repelled her.

Their appetizer arrived, steaming, a combination of stuffed mushrooms and fried dill pickle slices, all covered with a drizzle of cheese. They compared impressions about the play. Zeb thought the anti-fundamentalist rhetoric was overdone; he wished the overall treatment of the historical conflict had been more balanced. Robin nodded as he argued his point. His mention of history naturally made her think of Brad—but she was pleased at how easy it was for her to suppress his mental image. A few months earlier, sharing a dinner with Zeb, she would have felt powerless to resist imagining Brad sitting across from her … She felt proud of her progress. Still, she would not be satisfied until she was completely free of his influence. Looking out over the lake, its rippling waves reflecting lights from the other side, she thought of her involvement with him as *entanglement*, and she remembered Erin Delaney's explanation of that physics property called quantum entanglement, one of the most bizarre things she had ever heard about the universe …

The clam chowder was delicious, the salad so-so. Robin recalled a soup-and-bread community dinner and party that the Roosts had thrown some years back. Then Zeb steered the conversation to their counseling sessions with Howard Roost. When he did so, Robin expected to grow anxious; instead she noticed a change in *his* demeanor. He looked away, fiddled with his napkin, and shifted in his seat. From her experience in coaxing reluctant students to share in class, she could tell that he *wanted* to say something but didn't know how to start. Well, she could certainly identify with that! And she was not about to encourage him.

Their server came and went, apologizing for the delay in bringing their entrees.

Finally, Zeb cupped his hands over his mouth, blew on them, and rubbed them together.

"Okay," he said in prologue. "Okay."

Robin sat back, amused. The only thing that kept her from feeling superior was the burden of her own secret.

Zeb reached across and took her hands.

"Honey," he began, and his eyes locked with hers. Robin could actually feel his hands trembling, which worried her.

"What?" she asked tenderly. "What is it?"

"I just want to tell you that ... that I have failed you."

Once he had stated his thesis, Robin thought later, reviewing the evening, he became downright voluble. He started to explain—"confess" was his exact word—that over many months he had poured altogether too much time and effort into his work and ignored or neglected her. He called it "a crime." That admission was hardly new; he had said the same thing several times in their counseling. But tonight he was more energetic and passionate in condemning himself. His voice cracked. Tears welled up in his eyes.

"Do you remember our wedding, the sermon?" he asked. "What Pastor Dave said to us?"

"I ..." Robin shrugged, not sure exactly what he had in mind.

Zeb said he remembered in detail.

"He said that in heaven, when we stood before God, that God would say to me, 'Just look at Robin! Look at how wonderful she is, how magnificent and loving and faithful she is—and you deserve credit! Look at her glory! More than anything else, I worked through *you* to make her into this beautiful woman, and look at what you've done for me and for her! *Well done!*' And then God would say the same thing to you about me, that you were the main reason I became such a good, strong, faithful man. Do you remember that?"

"Yes."

Now, Robin felt her own heart stirring, her own tears of mixed joy and sorrow pooling in her eyes. She remembered. She was supposed to be the best way that God would transform her husband into "a creature of unimaginable glory." She had never forgotten *those* words.

"But I've failed, Robin. I let you down. I let God down. Can you ever forgive me?"

She gave his hands a soft squeeze. Something about his words surprised her, yet she could not put her finger on what it was.

Then—as the server returned with their meals and additional apology—her insight came. The surprise lay not in what Zeb was saying, but rather in what he was *not* saying. He was not claiming that he had let his work consume him because he wanted a better life for her or for their family. That would have been an understandable excuse, a reasonable and unassailable explanation that any guilty workaholic husband would fall back on. But in his humility Zeb was not trying to justify himself. He was refusing to say that his good intentions were to blame.

This realization stunned Robin so deeply that she didn't hear a word of his prayer for their meal. Only the pressure of his squeeze on her hands told her he was finished.

She was thankful that the food had arrived when it did, for it gave her an excuse to not respond at once and gave her time to plan her words. That was what she had hoped, anyway. Actually, she could not think of what to say in answer to Zeb because her own guilt crowded out every other thought. She looked at the appetizer dish, congealing in the cool air, its web of cheese strands linking the one remaining mushroom and a cluster of pickles.

Entangled.

She and Zeb were like the little particles, she thought, recalling the mysterious miracle. Just like them! No matter how far apart they had drifted, some power kept them connected. *Some power?*—listen to her! All the time that God was working in her wayward, unfaithful heart, nudging her toward the confession that would seal her repentance, He was also working in her husband!

Her time had come.

"Zeb," she said, gripping his hands tightly. "There's something I have to tell you, I *need* to tell you ... No, no, something I *want* to tell you."

7

ERIN KEPT WATCH. She hovered near the door to Myers's office, where a tall rectangular window looked out into the main lobby of the administrative suite. After breaching the outer door, they had relocked it so that if anyone else entered they would have a few seconds to retreat to the inner office, the back room that connected the fancy main offices of LaGrange and Myers. That room also had a further hiding place of sorts—a deep, narrow closet crammed with a row of filing cabinets and stacks of paper boxes, but no lock.

As planned, Erin had secured the necessary keys through Matt, who had long ago befriended Bragley. The easy-going custodian had given Matt free access to the building all year with a hidden key, and Matt, through numerous late-night forays, had learned where Bragley kept the rest of the keys, and through trial-and-error had discovered the building's master key.

McCauley peered through the eye-holes in his ski mask until he located his safe under Myers's desk. With Robin aiming her flashlight at the lock, he opened the safe, and rustling through its contents, ascertained that no valuable documents were missing.

"Now what?" Robin whispered in the darkness. They had chosen to keep the room lights off and operate using their flashlights. "Do you want to take it out to my car?"

McCauley considered. As amateur criminals, they had not discussed this eventuality.

"If I take it back, then first thing in the morning Myers will know we've been here," he said.

"Maybe just take the stuff from inside it."

Erin whispered from her post, "Do you know if he's even gotten inside it?"

That was a good question. Nothing was missing, but maybe that was because Myers had not yet cracked the combination. If he had, then he would know if McCauley took back the documents. If he had not, then even if and when he did, the safe's contents would not betray their burglary. The possibilities ricocheted inside McCauley's head. He did not know what to do.

"I've got to have these," he said desperately. "But I don't want to leave just yet. If something happens, we might not ever get this chance again."

"I could put your things in my locker," Erin said, stepping silently toward them in her slippers. All three of them were wearing the darkest clothing and quietest footwear they could find, along with thin latex gloves, also black. "You can both stay here. It'll only take me a minute."

Robin added, "There hasn't been a sign of anybody else in here. It's probably okay."

"All right," McCauley said, handing several manila envelopes to Erin. "If everything goes well, we'll pick them up when we leave."

Erin peeked out the window, painstakingly unlocked the door, opened it, and glided out. Earlier they had taped squares of black construction paper over the security cameras in the parts of the building where they would be operating, a precaution McCauley now felt thankful for.

The clock mounted above Myers's desk read 11:45.

McCauley swung the arc of his flashlight beam around the office, its walls plastered with tear sheets bearing ideas, apparently, for various applications of Myers's *1-2-3-4* scheme, which Robin kept disparaging and which he, as a part-timer, had felt safe in ignoring so far. The halo of light moved from page to page, each one headlined with a different department or team written in Myers's slanted scribble—SCIENCE,

Math, Guidance, Special Ed, Basketball, Choir—and crowded with the fruits of brainstorming.

Behind the desk stood a mobile blackboard overflowing with further notes in different colors of chalk. McCauley smirked. That explained the mystery of Myers's chalky ear lobes.

The assistant principal, along with LaGrange, had gone to Indianapolis for two days of meetings, including a planning session with state officials putting together the governor's education tour, whose keynote speech would come at Brookstone in late May.

McCauley looked at Robin, who was ransacking her purse, her flashlight poking from the mouth-hole in her black mask.

"What is it?" he asked.

"Nothing," she said around the flashlight. "Just looking for my mace."

"Your *what?*"

"Mace. Just in case."

They had discussed how to respond if they were caught. Only when Erin suggested rather cavalierly that she could steal her dad's handgun did the two adults comprehend the gravity of their plans; nevertheless, they vetoed Erin's option. In the end, they decided to take their chances. If they got caught, they got caught. Robin would lose her job, both she and McCauley would no doubt be arrested and prosecuted, and Erin would probably escape severe punishment as a minor—yet all three of them were set on carrying their crusade as far as they could.

Still, Robin had brought mace.

McCauley eyed the back room, yet they dared not proceed until Erin came back. The second hand of the clock tick-tocked evenly, but in his anxiety it sounded monstrously loud, as if the ticks and tocks were screeching alarms signaling their crime. It occurred to McCauley that for the first time in years, he was *listening* to a clock and not associating it with his grand philosophy.

Erin returned.

"Quiet as a graveyard out there," she reported.

"Okay," said Brad. "Erin, you keep on watching. Robin and I are going to see about getting into the filing cabinet in the back room. Remember—if anyone is coming, come back to us and we'll hide.

There's no back way out." He added, "Any second thoughts? We can still stop where we are."

Both Robin and Erin shook their heads dimly in the darkness. The flashlight reflected off their eyes; otherwise, they were nearly invisible.

The filing cabinet in question was locked, as they suspected, and they had no key from Bragley to open it. However, they assumed that as in most offices, the keys to such cabinets were kept nearby. Opening the top drawer of the closest desk, they found several small keys and tried them individually until one of them turned smoothly and *click!*—the bolt slid out. McCauley cautiously pulled out the top drawer, more fearful now than ever that a small noise might be magnified by the silence and give them away. Robin's flashlight illuminated the file folders, mostly not labeled, forcing McCauley to take them out to determine their contents.

With the fifth folder he hit pay dirt, dozens of clipped-together pages, including copies of newspaper articles, a few photographs, and what looked like typewritten reports, all with a teacher's name on a Post-It note—McGREW—stuck to the first page.

"Leverage," he whispered. "Jeez, these guys are just like Travis."

"What do you mean?"

"These are documents Myers and LaGrange have found that they use to keep teachers in line, I think," he said. "Look at this—invoices from Drake & Sons."

"Who are they?"

"According to these line items, private investigators, I would guess."

Robin said, "You mean Myers and LaGrange hired detectives?"

"To dig up dirt on teachers. So when any teacher gets too nosy about the cheating, or if a teacher knows about the system and threatens to tell the truth, Myers and LaGrange just pull the skeletons out of the closet."

"Am *I* in there?" Robin asked, her voice verging on hysteria.

"I don't think so. But there are more folders."

He found files labeled HARTMAN, RAY, ST. CLAIR, YOUNG, plus others bearing names he did not know.

"We ought to take them and go somewhere and burn them," said Robin. "And then tell all the teachers that Myers and LaGrange have nothing on them, now."

"Except they probably have other copies."

"What should we do, then?"

McCauley's flashlight swept the room.

"Stick to our plan," he said. "Make copies. We'll have to use the copier in the outside office. There isn't one in here."

Handing Robin the folder, he saw that the front contained a scrawled message: FILE WITH 1234.

"I wonder what that means," he mumbled. "Didn't we see something—" He focused his flashlight on the desktop computer, where its halo fell on another Post-It note occupying the middle of the screen that also bore the cryptic reference: 1234.

"It's everywhere," Robin whispered.

"But how could this be connected to the PR push?" McCauley wondered aloud. Another mystery, one that they could worry about later.

Robin took the folder and left him. A moment later he heard the hum of the machine powering up.

He moved down to the next drawer. As Robin rhythmically copied the documents, he found more labeled folders with information apparently about participants at other schools in Bridgebury and beyond. The names would be valuable, he thought. He didn't know who these people were, but their connection would be something Pete Doty from the newspaper could investigate.

Robin shuttled back and forth, copying more of the evidence. McCauley put it back in the same order he had discovered it.

"What we really need is evidence of money changing hands," he complained. "So far I can't find anything like that."

"I bet it's on the computer," Robin said.

"Yeah," he muttered. "I was afraid of that. Let's go talk to Erin."

During the previous week, as part of their strategy, she had prevailed upon Cody to help her hack an anonymous computer—for a prank, she claimed—and Cody, always up for either a prank or a challenge, said he would lend his expertise. McCauley's fear was that at some point in her persuasion, she would need to tell Cody specifically that Myers was the target, or that Cody would insist on being physically present. However, when Erin said the whole operation was part of a surprise for Matt, Cody said to just call him at any time and he could talk her through a process for finding an unknown password using software they could access online from any computer, including a laptop with Wi-Fi capability.

McCauley now produced his ailing laptop from his black backpack, plugged it in next to Myers's desktop machine, and turned it on. Erin edged toward them, sensing that the execution of their plan had reached the stage where she would be needed.

"Do you remember the website?" McCauley asked. "Or do you need to call Cody?"

"I think I can do it myself," she said. "He told me how to do the connection. Just give me some light."

Erin's tone conveyed that she was enjoying their adventure immensely. Two days before, she had turned in the next-to-last draft of her new research paper—a gem reflecting her passion, well-focused investigation, and solid organization, the last quality assisted by Robin. He had told her tonight that even though he hadn't seen her final version, he knew he would have no qualms about raising her grade on the project to an A and figuring some way to use Myers's policy of "borrowing" to retroactively give her an A for the previous semester. No one in the administration would squawk, especially if, as he expected, they decided to unilaterally raise the grades of his first-semester cheaters.

Erin scanned the back of the tower on Myers's desk and snapped into place the cables Cody had provided. Then she snaked them along the desk to the laptop, found the corresponding slots, and completed the connection.

Once the laptop flashed to life, McCauley logged on and yielded his place to Erin, who stripped off her gloves. Meanwhile, Robin had taken over as the lookout a few steps away. Except for the sound of Erin's fingers tapping keys, nothing disturbed the silence. McCauley began to worry. Things were proceeding too smoothly.

"Okay, here's the software," Erin whispered. "Now turn on the second computer, Cody said. Turn on Mr. Myers's computer."

Brad found the on-off switches on the tower and the monitor and punched them both on.

Soon the log-on screen appeared, prompting them for a user ID and password.

"Okay," Erin said. "You said you knew his ID."

Robin called lightly, "Try T-hyphen-MYERS first."

Erin complied.

"We won't know if that's right until we do the password," McCauley cautioned.

Erin tabbed down to the password box. The cursor blinked, waiting.

"Okay," she said, "now ..." She turned her focus to the laptop, checked a couple of options in its dialog box, pressed ENTER, and sat back. On Myers's screen, a row of dots appeared on the password line, flashing on and off and in between.

"What's happening?" McCauley asked.

"I think it's going through combinations," she said. "This is what Cody said would happen."

"How long will it take?"

"I don't know."

She did not look worried, but the prospect of an uncertain wait filled McCauley with dread.

Many office workers kept lists of passwords in desk drawers, he knew. So he pulled open the one next to him, hoping against hope that they might get lucky and avoid any delay. Instead they got a shock—the drawer contained a shiny revolver! McCauley felt his heart race. He slid the drawer shut, silently.

"Take it!" Erin whispered.

"No way," he said. But her idea had some merit.

His nervousness grew. The clock read 12:15. How was Erin able to remain so cool? She was staring at a photo on a shelf near the clock—a photo showing a young Tolan Myers in a football uniform, holding his helmet, his hairline receding even then. His jersey number was 55.

A few moments passed. Then Erin clapped and whispered, "We're in!"

Robin joined them. They huddled around the glowing screen, their eyes looking for clues among the collection of desktop folders with innocuous labels: GUIDANCE, CONTRACTS, HOME ROOMS, DISCIPLINE, TEACHER EVALUATIONS, and DAIRY QUEEN. Nothing seemed suspicious.

Then McCauley cried, "There!" He shook the mouse to life and pointed to a folder called 1234.

"That's got to be it. We keep coming across that number. It's got to be code for something."

"But what would it have to do with all the *1-2-3-4* stuff we keep hearing about? It doesn't add up."

"Open it," Robin said. "Hurry. I think we're living on borrowed time." She crept back to the door.

McCauley double-clicked on the folder and a new dialog box opened, prompting him for another password. He uttered a curse and immediately apologized.

"Can your software crack this?" he asked Erin.

"I guess," she said. "Let's see."

McCauley joined Robin and said, "This is making me really nervous."

"Me too," she said. "But we're sticking to the plan, right?" Her question underscored her confidence and buoyed his spirits.

Erin started the decryption program, but after hacking into Myers's machine in only a few seconds, it found the password to the 1234 folder a tougher challenge. The waiting only made them all more anxious to finish and get out.

"Can't you speed it up?" McCauley asked.

Robin shrugged. The teenager seemed the coolest of them all, and McCauley marveled before realizing that beneath all her bravado she probably had no way to realistically assess the jeopardy of their situation. She didn't know enough to be afraid. The program ran on.

To battle his worry, McCauley knew he had to do something, to act. So he went back to the inner office and opened the closet. Its filing cabinets were locked, and the drawers had no labels. He tried the smaller keys they had located earlier. They did not work. He shone his light around the small room and finally found a single key dangling from a paper clip taped to a shelf. This key worked on all the cabinets. As soon as he opened the first drawer he could hardly contain his excitement—every folder had a 1234 label. Inside the first folder he found pages of information about someone named Kenson Prather. The next folder was full of documents associated with a Carrie Warren. Every folder dealt with a different person, none of whose names McCauley recognized.

He called in to Erin, "Any luck?"

"Yes!"

He returned to her side. The clock reached 12:30.

The opened folder contained subfolders with names that made no sense to McCauley—except for one that was called 1234 MANUSCRIPT.

"That one," he said, pointing to it. "Open that one."

Erin double-clicked to reveal an array of Word files titled CHAPTER 1, CHAPTER 2, on up to CHAPTER 13. Without further prompting, Erin opened the first file. McCauley skimmed the first paragraph of text and chuckled. He did not need Robin's English expertise to see that the prose was clumsy but direct:

Teaching never earned anybody much money. But as a career teacher, I have learned that switching a few letters makes a difference. Teaching turns into Cheating. All the students and parents do it, so why shouldn't I profit from it? In this book I will tell you my story and show how four simple steps have made me rich.

"Jeez, he wasn't kidding. He *is* writing a book about it ..." He whistled and fished a flash drive from his pocket. "Here, Erin, copy everything."

As he turned away, Robin whispered loudly, "Someone's coming!"

"What?"

"It's Myers!"

He cursed and whispered, "How could that be?" Already he and Robin were scurrying into the back office.

Erin kept her cool while the text files copied. With a fluid sweep of her hands she pulled out the flash drive, shut down the desktop machine, and jerked the cables unplugged. She swept them up with the laptop and rushed into the back room just as they heard a key scraping in the outer door's lock.

A moment passed before they heard two voices, first Myers and then LaGrange. Their flashlights off, they backed into the closet but had no time to pull the door completely closed before the administrators came into the back room, turning on the lights and chuckling.

"Perfect timing," LaGrange said. Through the door, barely ajar, McCauley glimpsed Myers seated at the tiny desk, punching numbers into the telephone keypad. The speaker was turned on, and the digits as they were dialed and the three rings at the other end of the connection sounded sharp against the silence. Above him on the wall the clock read 12:34.

All three of them held their breath.

A scratchy voice answered, "Hello."

"Laverne Cartwright?"

"Yes."

"Laverne, this is Tolan Myers, assistant principal at Brookstone High School in Brookstone, Indiana. You're on speakerphone with William LaGrange, principal."

"Yes, sir. With me are ..."

Following the formal introductions, Myers announced with businesslike air that the "exploratory discussion" about to take place would focus on options for cooperation between the two sets of school administrators. At one point he made a crack about the lateness of the hour, which suggested to McCauley that Cartwright, et al. were perhaps on the West Coast. Myers also made brief mention of the governor's upcoming visit and bragged, "So you see, if this system is run well, secrecy is maintained. We carry on right under the noses of the elected authorities."

McCauley could barely contain his excitement as the conversation continued. Events could not be unfolding with any more promise! At the same time, their chances of avoiding detection were almost nil—especially since they were holed up in what appeared to be ground zero for evidence against Myers and his cohorts.

Erin activated the voice recorder on her cell phone and set it gently on the linoleum floor, close to the opening in the door. Robin was struggling with her purse, probably searching for the mace.

McCauley strained to catch every word. His emotions swirled with fear and anticipation. He wished he could see in the dark, to jot down notes. The unknown officials from the unknown school peppered Myers with questions, which he answered expertly, and McCauley's respect grew even greater. However long Myers had been at this game, he had perfected his tactics and strategy. He carried himself with the air of a consummate professional—a professional *criminal*, but still a professional. LaGrange seldom said a word.

After about twenty minutes, Cartwright said, "All right then. You've definitely given us plenty to think about. How should we leave this? Should I contact you if we choose to proceed?"

Myers answered, "One way or another, contact me within one week. As you consider this proposal, you need to keep two things in mind. First, the entry fee is non-negotiable and non-refundable, and it must be paid by wire to our account. There is no other method of payment accepted. Second, if you choose to not join the program, then you are sworn to secrecy. We would of course deny any communication of the sort that has just taken place."

Cartwright said, "Understood. And the fee is fifty thousand dollars."

"Yes."

The conversation ended. McCauley heard the phone headset being replaced and LaGrange asking, "Comments?"

"This is about what I expected. But this opportunity is critical. If San Jose bites, the door opens to the whole western half of the United States."

"Mmm. Well, it's getting very late. You said you wanted to show me some papers."

McCauley felt his adrenaline spike. Myers's hand reached for the closet door—and suddenly McCauley felt Robin's hand in front of his face, brandishing the tiny cylinder of mace.

"Actually," Myers said, "they're in my briefcase, which is still in my car. They can wait until tomorrow."

8

THE SENSE OF buoyant, extravagant freedom that Robin Hillis hoped would follow in the wake of her confession to her husband never came to pass. She felt relief, nothing more. Her weighty burden lifted, but no corresponding and compensating euphoria took its place. This perplexed her for a day or so, until she decided that since the burden was her own fault, maybe she ought not expect any version of a tingly feeling once she set things right, or once she took steps in that direction.

She floated in an emotional limbo. Zeb now knew about Brad McCauley, and Brad knew that Zeb knew—even though she had not told Brad, not explicitly. During their time together with Erin, stealing secrets from Myers and LaGrange, Robin could feel Brad observing her, studying her. Even if she had not told him, he knew. He knew that Zeb knew.

At home, she waited for Zeb to say something more than he had over that pivotal dinner in Indy, when she finally told him about her affair, something more than, "Well, that's over now, right?" *Yes*, she had assured him, aware that her words might mean nothing to him. Once he understood that Brad would be gone after the current semester, Zeb asked her to limit her interactions with him to school-related matters the rest of the way. *Keep it professional*, he repeated about a dozen times. That was fair enough. Generous, even. In fact, Zeb was so forgiving that his silence about her unfaithfulness rankled her. She wanted him to express at least a hint of anger or hurt or regret. She deserved that.

At work, she waited for Brad to say something acknowledging that her revelation to Zeb marked another step in the sunset of their relationship. Sadly, he did not oblige her. Instead, he grew more obsessed with their research into the school's cheating conspiracy, or network, or epidemic, or culture—his description of choice changed day by day.

Wrestling with her conscience, Robin prevailed in convincing herself that this collaboration with Brad, and with Erin Delaney, fell under Zeb's "professional matters" umbrella. Throughout the late-night hour of crime with him—her adrenaline transporting her into throes of adventure she hadn't felt since she couldn't remember when, while she rushed to copy the secret records knowing that at any moment a light might come on and her career and marriage and life as a free citizen would be over—throughout those minutes of excitement she had kept thinking *keep it professional*, and she actually hushed herself once, whispering those words, when she felt the drugging warmth and firmness of Brad's body as she leaned against him peering through that closet door, slightly ajar, to watch Myers and LaGrange during their phone call with the potential recruits from the West. *Keep it professional.* She had kept her promise to Zeb. And yet … despite the relational ambiguity she felt with the two men in her life, the emotional highlight of the whole past week had been the burglary.

Thanks to a habit that developed when she was closer to Brad—when she was *not* keeping it professional—she still spent her afternoon prep period in the teachers' lounge, though Brad had long ago stopped coming to Brookstone early every day to see her. Why did she continue to haunt the place, then? And *haunt* was the right word to use, for surely she was acting like a ghost tethered to a house or room by some vestige of earthly attraction that not even death could sunder. Howard Roost would probably explain her behavior in terms of the psychology of loss or addiction, she knew. Subconsciously she was still wanting to connect with Brad because their months together had injected her monotonous life with a boost of excitement. Yes, that made more sense. But no, no—Howard would say no such thing. That interpretation was hers, all hers, and it was more a sneaky try at justification than an objective explanation. In any case, whatever the truth, whatever she might be looking for, and whatever motives really impelled her, she needed to stop.

Today she could honestly say that her presence in the lounge was professional. She had asked the only teacher she trusted who shared her prep period—Lydia Knowles from the Art Department—to meet her. Lydia had once been summoned by the school board for violating some policy or another, involving oversight of students, if Robin recalled correctly. With her own hour of reckoning before the board drawing closer, Robin was beginning to feel edgy.

"It was so silly," Lydia said, sipping her coffee, reflecting on her brush with suspension five years earlier. "See, here's the thing, Robin. The administrators decide every year to focus on certain rules they think aren't being enforced. One year it's dress code. Another year it's teachers leaving school before contract time. And another year it might be food in the classrooms. My husband calls them *points of emphasis.* He says referees have them in sports. So every year there's a new *point of emphasis.*"

Lydia, who could be very expressive verbally, was working up a steam of anger.

"What happened to me was, I let students in my ceramics class work out on the patio outside the art room. You know, in the late summer or late spring when the weather's nice. I've done it for years with nobody raising a *stink*, and then—well, they had good reason, I guess, because one day some students who I thought were working outside decided to take a little *field trip.* They took a little stroll around the building. No big deal, right?

"Well, one thing led to another. It was my fault, in retrospect, but … Whatever, a couple of days later the same students got a *little bolder* and decided that just going around the building wasn't cutting it, so they actually walked off campus. I didn't have a clue. I just trusted they were always out on the patio working on their pottery! Turns out they were spending the whole period kicking back in the lawn by the church down the street, just staring at the stained-glass windows and shooting the breeze."

"So, what? What happened to you?"

"I got a letter calling me to school board meeting. I was so mad at the students for getting me in trouble, for betraying my trust! It was a kind of open-and-shut case at the meeting. I admitted I wasn't watching my students as well as I should have been, they read me the riot act and tried to make me feel stupid and ashamed—you know, what if one of the kids had been hit by a car, yada, yada, yada, what if some parent wanted to sue us for negligence, that kind of garbage. It was all true, and I was at fault, but they didn't need to make a federal case out of it."

Lydia leaned close and finished: "But that's the thing. See, *supervision and oversight*"—she made gestures with her fingers to indicate quotation marks—"was the point of emphasis then, and I happened to slip up at the wrong time. I don't know: Timing is everything, I guess."

"But what did they do to you? Were you penalized?"

"No. Yes, I guess so. There was a *letter of reprimand*"—more fingered quote marks—"put in my file. Does that count as a penalty?"

Robin shrugged.

"Why are you asking?" Lydia asked.

"You probably heard. I got a letter."

"For what?"

Robin debated briefly whether to go into more detail.

"That's what troubles me," she said. "I'm not entirely sure, but if it has to do with what I think it does, then it's not really one of those points of emphasis you're talking about."

"Oh?"

"I think it has to do with cheating. Cheating by students, and …" She strategically let her sentence trail off. She wondered how Lydia would respond.

"Yeah. Well, you're right. That wouldn't be the same kind of trouble I was in. That's more of an *ongoing* thing, an *ongoing emphasis*."

"Lydia," Robin began. They were alone in the lounge, yet she felt with absolutely no good reason that whispering was necessary, that the room might be bugged. She actually scanned the room in search of hiding places for bugs! Behind the clock perhaps, or in with the wiring for the fire alarm, or maybe in the electric pencil sharpener.

Shaking off the paranoia, she continued: "Lydia, can kids cheat in art classes?"

"Not really. Most of their work they do in class, right under my nose."

"As long as they don't go out on the patio, or beyond."

"Yeah, right."

"Do you think cheating is a problem at this school? You've been around as long as I have. What do you think?"

Lydia sighed.

"I've seen things, heard things. To be honest, I don't want to kick any hornets' nest. Like you said, it's not really an issue in art classes. But I've noticed things over the years."

Robin replied sullenly, "I think I've kicked a hornets' nest."

Two hours later, she stood on the concrete stoop at Brad's apartment door. He was not home; he had told her earlier that he needed to work in a library most of the afternoon and evening. Recalling the days when such news would have disappointed her, Robin sighed wistfully then just as quickly checked that response. Her whole reason for being here was to further put away those feelings.

She unlocked the door, using his key for what would be the last time.

Inside she saw nothing but mess, bachelor mess. She smiled again with a surge of nostalgia, however, for through all that mess she could make out the vestiges of her impact here and there—the clean curtains, the table cloth, and other hints of order.

Finding a pad of paper and a pen, she scribbled a note, taped the key to it, and hung it on his fridge using a Yippy's Pizza magnet.

There, she thought, that was done. A practical and symbolic act, returning his key. And it was easier than she thought it would be, too.

Then things grew more challenging. Somewhere in the apartment, in all the mess, were a pair of her jeans and a sweatshirt she needed to find. Exactly why those particular articles of clothing were still at Brad's she could not even remember—perhaps that fact alone summed up the depths of her fall with him. No, that was not fair. She couldn't blame him. It was *her* fall, hers alone. Regardless, where were the clothes? As she started to rummage among the piles of laundry in the room, she couldn't help but rearrange things, return things to their proper place—how horribly telling that she even knew the proper places for things in this man's apartment!—and in general clean up the place.

She set a couple of dirty mugs in the sink and filled them with water, remembering Grandma Jane's blanket dishwashing exhortation: "Let 'em soak!" Next, she tossed into the trash can several used paper plates and plastic forks. Then she took a bag of trash out to the garbage bin behind the apartment. Finishing up in the kitchen, she ran a sponge along the counter top. Then she tucked up the hideaway bed and slid the couch cushions back into place.

"There," she whispered to no one but herself. "That should help a little bit."

Next to his computer on the sagging card table she spotted several bulging manila folders. When she went to straighten them, to align their corners, a single word scrawled on the label in Brad's distinct handwriting caught her attention: DOTY.

She opened the folder and flipped through its contents, which consisted entirely of emails and printed attachments from Pete Doty to Brad. Robin moved to the couch and sat there, voraciously devouring the pages. Doty had dug up an astonishing amount of information—so much, in fact, that Robin concluded he must have been doing his research for several months, for a long time before he ever came into contact with her and Brad. Now she saw why Doty had called their suspicions of cheating at Brookstone just the tip of an iceberg. The printouts included summaries of everything he had discovered about an organized cheating network with participants in Indiana's neighbors such as Ohio, Michigan, Illinois, and Kentucky as well as Colorado, Pennsylvania, New York, Washington State, and California. There were lists of schools, people (education officials, faculty, school board members, students, and parents), civic organizations, and businesses. One printout recorded an interview between Doty and a STUDENT X spelling out in elaborate detail how he or she took part in his or her school's system. That eight-page, single-spaced transcript was paper-clipped to a page with three columns of student names, leading Robin to believe that Doty had talked to nearly a hundred students had transcripts available from every interview.

Once again Robin fell into a funk of accusing Brad. Why was he leaving the folder out for anyone to see—especially since his apartment had already been targeted by Myers for burglary? Then she considered that whatever Doty knew and whatever records he had were beyond Myers's reach. Her attitude softened somewhat. Yet she felt left out, too. Why hadn't Brad shared any of this with her? Didn't he trust her? He would say, probably, that he was trying to protect her, or that none of this information was directly related to Brookstone, or, more likely, that he respected her decision to stick with Zeb and thought that sharing Doty's material would be insensitive.

It took an exertion of mental effort for Robin to restrain herself from going any further down the road of self-pity.

She spotted her clothes, folded neatly, atop Brad's safe, which he had restored to *its* proper place beneath the end table next to the couch. The sight of them evoked a long sigh, a sigh full of the sadness of turning her back on a part of her life that would always be special, even if regrettable. A triangle of pink protruded from a hip pocket of her jeans, and she pulled out the construction paper valentine she had kept after it fluttered down from the Atrium ceiling months before.

When she opened the door to leave Brad's apartment, a huge surprise met her—Erin and Tyler Batta sitting on the steps of the porch!

Flustered, she blurted out, "Hi guys!" Did Tyler know about her and Brad? Yes, she quickly remembered, thanks to the *Independent Clause* article that "outed" them. So she didn't need to try to hide anything from Tyler.

"We're supposed to meet Mr. McCauley here," Erin explained. "We're going to work on my project. The video. That's why Tyler's with me."

"Oh, great!"

What was so great about it? Robin wondered. She felt a pinprick of jealousy that Brad was working with Erin after she, Robin, had already spent so many hours helping Erin with the *writing* part of that project … But what worried her more was the wisdom of Brad's course of action. With his history, he shouldn't be meeting at his apartment with students, particularly with a female student, particularly with *this* female student. What would that look like to everyone else? True, there was a legitimate reason for the meeting, and there were still hours of daylight remaining; still, Brad was taking a big chance, considering his history. Robin weighed the pros and cons of his choices—then, gradually, gently, another thought bubbled up amid the cauldron of her ideas and they evaporated. *Butt out*, she said to herself. *He needs no mother. He must live his own life, and you must live yours.*

"Great!" she repeated, more sincerely. "He keeps saying how wonderful your project is. And Tyler, you're a true talent with some of the stuff you do!"

He nodded humbly and muttered an embarrassed thank-you.

Their presence meant Brad could not be far away. Had he lied to her about all the library time he needed to put in? Was he avoiding her? Well, she reasoned, if that were true, she ought to take advantage of his distance and take another step, figuratively speaking, back toward her husband.

Zeb arrived home from work at 7 P.M. but walking in with him through the door from the garage came another surprise—a double surprise—Anyssa and Trevor!

"Katie was spending a few days with an old college roommate," Trevor explained. "I didn't want to play bachelor, so I called Anyssa and … here we are!"

Although she was happy as always to see her kids, Robin knew that Trevor's explanation was hollow, incomplete. He hadn't said *why* he and Anyssa had come—he didn't want to say, because the truth was still too raw a wound for them. They were visiting to show support for their parents' marriage—that was the naked truth—but to say so would be too embarrassing for them, for all of them.

That truth pierced Robin's soul all the more.

Complicating her anguish, Zeb announced, "Dinner is on me." He had ordered fancy steak dinners from the Top Notch, which he would pick up in thirty minutes. "That way, Mom can rest after her long day at work. Instead of slaving over our dinner, she can visit with you"—he indicated Trevor and Anyssa—"while I do the heavy lifting," by which he meant setting the table and going for the food, steaming in its six Styrofoam boxes, two appetizers and four entrees. All the while, Robin caught up with the kids, forcing herself to focus on them, on Anyssa and her studies, on Trevor and his work and marriage, fearing the inevitable question about how she and Zeb were doing, wishing she could retreat to the shelter of the kitchen and let the kids talk to their father alone. She did not deserve to have Top Notch steak; she did not deserve her forgiving husband or terrific children. She did not deserve any of this.

Dinner provided a respite. Once they were all seated, the kids occupying what had been their regular seats when they still lived at home, Robin could more gracefully keep silent. She let Zeb do most of the talking, Zeb and the kids, and thankfully their conversation turned nostalgic. Trevor in particular kept them laughing at his memories of everything from food to board games to household chores to holiday traditions.

When dinner ended, Robin insisted on serving ice cream sundaes, really only to generate a few dirty dishes, so that she would have an excuse to labor afterwards in the kitchen and avoid any prying by Anyssa. Zeb and the kids went back into the living room, their laughter roaring. Robin smiled ruefully. Rather than simply rinsing the bowls and spoons and putting them in the dishwasher, she filled the sink with soapy water and carefully cleaned them all by hand. She worked slowly, engrossed in the sweetness of the minutes, the beauty of the silence, the loving ripple of her family's conversation like soothing background music from the next room. She twirled her fingers through the water, creating a different kind of rippling, a tiny wake whose thought stirred up a swirl of chaotic associations … her ongoing, obsessive, introspective vigil at the death of her relationship with Brad, which was a sick sort of wake … Kate Chopin's novel *The Awakening*, which she had read in college and thought about often during her fling with Brad … and the fact that finally she had awakened and seen the error of her ways …

The doorbell rang. She heard Trevor answer and greet the Roosts, whose voices added to the happy sounds filling the house.

Robin could not help but join everyone then. Howard and Jerri beamed at her when she appeared around the corner. Lena was there, and Philip, and even Jack Kitchell. Robin wondered whether he was helping any, behind the scenes, in the cheating investigation. If Pete Doty had any brains, she thought, he ought to enlist Jack's help in looking for anything suspicious in all that financial data he had uncovered.

She caught Howard's eye, and he winked. That lifted her spirits. After a day and evening of self-flagellation, that wink reminded her of what was true, really true, eternally true. Jeremiah was right about her heart being full of deceit—but Howard had assured her time and time again that the prophet was not talking about her. She had a new heart, and her "fall" had come from sliding back to old ways that were not the real Robin. Thinking about the whole idea of her two selves tied up her mind in confusion. She needed to leave theology to the pros.

The Roosts stayed for ten minutes, wished everyone well, and left.

Robin returned to the kitchen, to the sink, to the cloudy water. She drained it.

Then she looked at her hands—her tired, hard-working hands, her loving hands—recognizing that when it came to her hands and their beauty, Zeb was right.

Later, upstairs, while he was in the bathroom, she took the blank pink valentine, wrote him a love note, and set it on his pillow.

9

JESS HAD DONE it again—gotten into a jam thanks to her big mouth—and as usual she wanted Erin to help her out of it.

"I mean, it was just a stupid bet," she stammered with an air of nonchalance that couldn't be more obviously faked.

"A bet about what?" Erin never failed to find amusement in her cousin's difficulties, or in Jess's feeble attempts to downplay them.

"Oh, nothing. It was stupid. Did you see that *Independent Clause* story about the newspaper reporter from Bridgebury snooping around here?"

"Mmm."

Okay, so Jess did not want to talk about it. Whatever she had done must be really embarrassing. That was fine, Erin thought. Sooner or later she would hear the whole truth, maybe from the *Independent Clause!* More probably from Jess's own lips, though. That was the usual pattern.

"Young Life," Erin repeated. "Isn't that the …?" She tried one more time to pry the details from her squirming cousin. "Jeez, Jess, I never thought you'd get involved with *that* bunch. Are you going all One-Track on us?"

"Oh, stop it! Will you go with me, yes or no?"

"Seven o'clock, you said?"

"Yeah. No. Actually it's exactly 6:57 P.M. They're really weird about times, Sally says. Nothing is ever exactly something o'clock; it's always a few minutes before or after that."

"I wonder why."

"It makes the meeting times easier to remember, they say."

"You seem to know all about them. Is there some *guy* there you're checking out?"

"Stop it! Please! Please go with me."

Erin wanted ask, "What's in it for me?" but resisted. She had tortured Jess long enough. The poor girl was too embarrassed to be seen alone with the One-Tracks. Evidently she had lost a bet with Sally Richards and now had to attend a Young Life meeting.

"Okay, I'll go," Erin answered. "But I can't stay past 8:30. I have to meet Matt."

"Why?"

The nerve of that girl!

"Nothing," Erin replied with strategic vagueness. "Something stupid, probably."

Jess hissed through her nose.

"You can't argue with success," her father often said.

Erin agreed, up to a point. She wondered whether Dad used that motto to justify an overall ends-justifies-the means bottom line. Now that she knew he was at least sympathetic to what he called the "ways of the world"—meaning the system that essentially rewarded cheating, all in the name of helping students speed down the higher education highway—she feared learning more, learning that he was an active participant, and learning what he might have already done without her knowledge to "help" her along.

Anyway, Erin thought his motto applied perfectly to Young Life. Sally Richards had kicked anorexia, or bulimia, whichever. And even though she had been seeing a doctor in Indy, she remained unapologetic in proclaiming that the support of her YL friends had helped her more than the expertise of the specialist in eating disorders at the high-priced clinic in the big city. You couldn't argue with that success, could you?

Erin had helped her mom cater an event for YL in Bridgebury a year earlier, some kind of fund-raising banquet. A bunch of high school kids shared their stories, always crediting YL for helping them turn their lives around. Like Sally, they talked about finding a purpose or direction previously missing from their lives. At the time, Erin regarded the testimonies as the usual feel-good propaganda expected for an event trying to raise money. What stuck in her mind, though, were video clips from the YL meetings projected on big screens around the ballroom. They had struck her as *incongruous*—a vocab word she had learned last week—with what she expected from One-Tracks. The kids were jumping up and down, clapping and dancing and giving one another a variety of high-fives as loud music played, popular music, not the boring church kind with pipe organs and choirs in white robes.

More recently, YL had intersected her life through Mr. McCauley's friend Manny Sarks, and his wife Rachel, whom Erin had met at ¿Que Pasa? earlier in the spring. Every couple of weeks Rachel showed up in the school cafeteria before school handing out donuts or at lunch talking to kids, inviting them to YL, most likely. Erin had never spoken to her at school.

Nonetheless, she was growing more curious about the group. She had her own reasons for agreeing to go with Jess to the meeting that night.

Along with Sally Richards, they reached the church in Tipmont ten minutes early and mingled in the parking lot with Brookstone classmates and students from other schools. For all Jess's trepidation about being seen with the One-Tracks, she seemed to fit in well enough, mostly because the topic of discussion while everyone waited for the leaders to arrive and let them inside was the yearbook's annual Senior Superlatives. Throughout the morning, yearbook members had taped flyers onto the lockers of students who had garnered enough votes to attain "Finalist" status in each Superlative category. Jess's locker sported three such honors: MOST LIKELY TO MARRY MULTIPLE TIMES, MOST SARCASTIC, and MOST LIKELY TO BE TARDY TO GRADUATION. The first was the fruit of her five different boyfriends in the past twelve months; the last recognized her frequent tardies to her first-period class, which she blamed on her bus driver and locker location. She reportedly once whined to Miss Newman, her math teacher, "Fate dealt me a bad hand!"

Erin herself received enough votes for MOST MYSTERIOUS and MOST HUMBLE to earn a pair of locker flyers, which she immediately tore off, wadded up, and tossed into a trash can. The whole idea of Senior Superlatives angered her, yet she understood how the MYSTERIOUS label fit her, considering how quiet she was around school.

By the time Manny and Rachel Sarks wheeled into the parking lot, the horn blaring from their beat-up, dented, rusty Chevy, about thirty kids were on hand.

Erin remarked to Jess, "I didn't know this many high school kids were One-Tracks."

"Anything for free food," Jess muttered, smirking.

Inside the building, the kids all headed through the empty, musty, vaulted sanctuary and took a side door that led down a narrow flight of stairs to a spacious basement. Someone turned on the lights, three rows of fluorescents. A large mobile whiteboard appeared, covered with announcements in colored markers. Speakers hummed, a guitarist began strumming, and a girl tapped and tested the microphones on the stage.

Within five minutes the room was rocking. Erin's memory was accurate—the song lineup was contemporary and popular, songs that all the kids knew, songs overflowing with emotions, with the lyrics projected on a white wall. Erin could hardly stand the volume or believe the energy. To her left and right, in front of her and behind her, all the teenagers were swaying, clapping, stomping, and singing at the top of their lungs, no matter how horrible they might sound. To one side, Manny and Rachel also sang and danced, greeting late-arrivers with hugs or high-fives or handshakes or pats on the back.

After the music, the leaders—the Sarkses plus a couple of college students from Riverside—did a funny skit about job interviews and followed that by organizing a game in which teams of four kids, blindfolded, competed in relay races rolling donuts along a table top using their noses. Erin didn't volunteer to play, but both she and Jess got caught up in the excitement of rooting for their team, the one with Sally, who wound up with a sugary, chocolatey nose and then promptly grabbed the donut she had nudged past the finish line and crammed it into her mouth.

Everyone cheered, and Erin realized these were the friends whose love, Sally claimed, helped nudge her back into the world where people ate.

Next, the kids took their seats and Rachel Sarks stood in front of them, open Bible in hand. Someone shouted, "Preach it, Sister!" and the rest of the kids added encouragement with whoops and hollers and loud cries of "Amen!"

Rachel described an Old Testament prophet, speaking for God, who spent his whole career trying to get the people to turn from their wicked ways. He wrote sixty-six chapters, one whole book of the Bible, according to Rachel.

"And one of the things he said to the people was this: *Come, let us reason together*. That's from Isaiah chapter 1, verse 18."

Erin settled back into her seat, ready for one of two evils: some serious, judgmental Bible-thumping, or some boring intellectual sermon.

She got neither.

Rachel Sarks *closed* her Bible and deliberately dropped it onto the nearest empty folding chair. Then she spent five minutes, six at most, explaining how important *reason* was in following God, in living faithfully. She said that the sentence she had just read came from a courtroom setting and was God's way of saying, "Let's talk this out. Let's communicate. Here's my plan for you and me to get past our past."

That was good, Erin thought. This woman was speaking a language teenagers could follow.

Then Rachel called Jesus the most reasonable man who ever lived, and she talked about some stories in which Jesus debated with people and argued with them using all the same reasoning that anybody uses, the same cause-and-effect logic they as students were learning every day in their math and science and English classes.

Wow! Erin thought. This was not so bad.

Jess, next to her, was examining her nails and paying no attention.

Finally, Rachel got religious, relatively speaking. She explained that God's "plan" involved Jesus dying on the Cross for sinners. Everyone needed to be washed clean, to be made "as white as snow," in the prophet's words.

Erin felt herself dodging that idea. She wasn't perfect, she would be the first to admit. Still, it was people like *Jess* who really needed to clean up their lives. What Erin had nearly done with Mr. McCauley, Jess had probably totally done over and over with enough guys that she might win that MULTIPLE MARRIAGE award in a landslide.

"But you'll never know about that if you won't listen to what God says," Rachel closed. "And what He says is in this book." She picked up her Bible again and waved it in front of her face. "That's all I've got. I hope you will listen to what He has to say."

That ended the scripted agenda for the evening.

The real fun was just beginning, however. For the next half hour, everyone visited. Music played. Refreshments appeared—brownies, Rice Krispie treats, store-bought and home-made cookies, M&Ms, miniature candy bars. For the calorie-conscious, somebody set out a vegetable tray, with several kinds and colors of veggies circling a container of ranch dressing. Kids ate, told jokes, and even played board games.

Since she knew only a handful of kids, Erin felt a bit like an outsider. Sally introduced her and Jess to some new people from other schools, mostly from Corbin Creek, but as Erin's introversion asserted its dominance, she withdrew, leaned against a wall and watched. That was enjoyable for her and let her reflect on her most unexpected observation of the evening—that all these teenagers seemed to be having a better time together than the kids at all the parties she had ever gone to during her high school years.

"You're Erin, right?"

The question from Rachel Sarks called her back from her daydreaming.

"Yes, hi." She offered her hand, but Rachel leaned forward and gave her a hug instead.

"I'm so glad you came."

"Oh, well, thank you. I came with Jess, Jessica Southard? And Sally Richards."

"I'm so glad. Having a good time?"

Erin shrugged.

"Better than I thought, if you want the truth."

"We're all about truth here." She indicated the whole room, all the group.

Erin said, "Do you remember when we met at ¿Que Pasa? that time?"
Rachel squinted as if trying to recall.

"I'm not sure. Was that when you were with Brad McCauley?"

"Yeah, that was it."

"Then I do remember."

"You gave me a card."

"Yeah, I give out about a million of those a month!"

Erin took a bite of a snickerdoodle that measured about four inches across.

"So, how do you know Sally?" Rachel asked.

"School. I don't know her very well. She talks a lot about how all of her friends here have helped her beat her ..." She stumbled and stopped.

"Her *demon*," Rachel completed the sentence. "Her *eating disorder*. You don't need to sugar-coat it. Sally doesn't. She overcame an eating disorder, and she gives God and God's people credit."

"Yeah, she does. Even more than that, though. She always talks about how you guys have given her life a direction. A purpose."

"Well, that's God's work, not ours. Maybe we've been tools in His hands, though."

Erin took another bite. She was dimly conscious of having said too much.

"What about *you*?" Rachel ventured. "Do you feel like *you* have a direction to your life?"

Not really, Erin wanted to say, but the words stuck in her mind as mere thought.

Different words came from her lips: "What you said about *communication*—that really makes me look at my life this past year."

"Let's sit down."

They removed themselves from the louder bustle in the basement and sat on a couch against a far wall.

"Tell me your story," Rachel urged.

"I'm not sure if I have one. I'm only eighteen."

"Nonsense," Rachel laughed. "Everybody has a story. And they're all fantastic!"

Erin unburdened her soul. She said that she had been slowly coming to realize how many of her troubles came from poor communication.

Family conflicts. Friendship issues. Plus one particular bit of trouble she could never tell anyone about: "If I had only *talked* to my sister instead of *assuming* she meant something that she didn't, then I could have avoided doing the stupidest thing anybody has ever done … And I think, Why can't I talk to people? And sometimes I think it's because I'm too afraid, or too proud. Too proud, and people think I'm humble!"

Rachel patted her knee consolingly.

"We've all done stupid things, bad things. That's what I was sharing about: God has made a way to get past our past."

"That's clever, the way you worded that."

"Thanks! Communication major in college!" She raised her chin in pretended superiority, but her facial gesture collapsed into a giggle.

"While you were speaking." Erin continued, "I was thinking about how terrible some things were that a friend of mine always brags about doing. But then I thought, What if she is lying about all those things? Then I thought, The lying is just as bad, right? And *then* I thought, what about *you*—me, I mean? Here *I* was judging *her*, but my *judging* was maybe worse than anything she had done! I was really confused! I still am!"

Rachel smiled, her lips parted as if forming words that never came. Her eyes studied Erin's face closely. She nodded and her smile grew wider.

"What?" Erin asked. "Why are you looking at me that way?"

"It's just that I'm impressed with you, that's all. Something wonderful is happening in you. You're a senior, right? You said you were eighteen."

"Yeah, a senior."

"What will you be doing next year?"

"Oh! Don't even get me started about that …"

"Okay, okay." Rachel rested her hand on Erin's jeans again.

"And why would you say something wonderful is happening when I just told you how confusing my life is right now?"

Rachel nodded again, then said, "Okay, okay. That message I shared tonight, about the communicating? That came from the book in the Bible called Isaiah. Isaiah was a prophet. There was another prophet, Jeremiah. He was another spokesman to the people of Israel. He spoke for God. And once he said, *The heart is deceitful above all things, and desperately wicked.* So, the reason I said I think something wonderful is going on in your heart is that you sound like you're questioning who you really are. You're questioning your *self*. That's where great things begin."

Eventually students started to leave, hugging, saying good-byes. It occurred to Erin that with so many kids from different schools, some of them probably saw one another only once every two weeks at these "club meetings," as they were called.

Sally and Jess found Erin and asked if she was ready to go.

"I guess so," she said.

Then Rachel interrupted and offered to take Erin home, if she wanted to stay longer. So she said good-bye to Jess and Sally—even giving them hugs.

When only one cluster of students remained, playing doubles ping-pong on a table at one end of the room, Rachel waved for Manny to join them.

"This is Erin Delaney," she said. "We actually met her once before, at ¿Que Pasa?"

"With Brad McCauley," Manny nodded. "And another teacher from your school, right?"

"Yes. Mrs. Hillis. Good memory!"

Once more, Erin explained her connection to Sally Richards, repeating Sally's praise of Young Life for helping her find purpose and meaning for her day-to-day life.

She expected Rachel to press her about her life's direction—especially after Erin had deflected her earlier attempt—but when she looked at Rachel, the woman's face wore that expression of profound interest once again. Rachel seemed to be utterly fascinated by Erin, which filled Erin with uneasiness, fear of vulnerability. Surely nothing about her and her life deserved such attention!

She had to say something, but what?

So she blurted something without thinking: "I guess I don't have any direction or purpose either, if you want to know the truth."

Manny nodded sympathetically.

"Want to hear *my* story?" he asked.

"Okay. I guess." Anything was preferable to having to explain hers ...

For the next ten minutes or so he talked about his college days in California, when he fell for a pretty girl and her lies and "everything went downhill from there." Erin glanced at Rachel, whose eyes were closed. Soon she understood why—Manny had dumped Rachel as his girlfriend to "raise hell" with the new girl. "If there was anything we thought was a sin," he said, "we tried it." He talked about taking part in drinking contests, speeding over a hundred miles an hour on the freeways, lighting firecrackers in the exhaust pipes of school security vehicles, and climbing onto dorm roofs and dropping balloons filled with water or other unnamed liquids onto unsuspecting students below.

Finally Rachel put a stop to his narration.

"I think you've made your point," she said, a hint of sharpness in her tone. "I apologize, Erin, for the graphic details. Sometimes he gets carried away."

"Yeah," Manny agreed. He threw an arm around Rachel. "Sorry. But, my point was, I went about a year without *any* direction. I thought I knew what I was doing and where I was going but ..."

"But ..." Rachel interjected. "*The heart is deceitful above all things.*"

"*And desperately wicked,*" Manny added. "*Who can know it?* Well, I never knew it. I deserved to go early to my grave."

Grave! Graveyard!

"Oh!" Erin cried. "What time is it? I was supposed to meet somebody at nine o'clock!"

They zipped south on Highway 53, although after Manny's California story, Erin imagined it was more of a crawl for him. Passing through Brookstone, Rachel mentioned that Young Life was hoping to find space to rent or buy downtown, a location more central to the region of their ministry than Corbin Creek. They turned west at the traffic light onto Highway 22, picked up speed leaving town, and five minutes later raced across the Junction Bridge. Nearing Green Ridge Cemetery, Erin peered into the darkness and thought she saw a halo of light.

Twenty-five minutes later, forty-five minutes late for her arranged rendezvous with Matt, she pulled into the cemetery and parked beside his van.

She could not believe her eyes.

Matt was shouting her name, calling for her to hurry, waving her toward him with a flashlight. Behind him rose a small heap of dirt, and behind that muttered the engine of a piece of heavy equipment with fork-lift arms, and from those arms—as best as Erin could make out in the sharply focused beam of the machine's headlamps—hung a pair of canvas straps suspending a coffin!

"Where have you been?" Matt asked in a whisper that almost made Erin laugh, considering the racket of the backhoe.

"Sorry," she said. "I lost track of … Matt, what is going on here? What ae you doing?"

"It's Steve!" he said, his eyes scanning the highway east and west. "We dug him up."

"You did *what*? Are you *crazy*? How did you ever …?"

"All it takes is money," he said. "With money you can do anything. I just offered Mitch, the groundskeeper, enough money, and he said okay."

"But isn't it against the law?"

"Probably. I mean, we didn't get permission or anything."

"You're crazy, Matt!"

Yet was this any crazier than her breaking into the offices of her school administrators? Even as she watched the surreal activity, the coffin dangling above the dark hole in the earth, she felt Matt's boldness infecting her, physically. She began to hop up and down with excess energy.

"I heard you talk about this," she said, "but I never expected …"

Matt said, "We waited until half an hour after sunset before we started. The cops usually go past here around eleven o'clock, once each way, so we've gotta get Steve back in the ground by then. It's Chalmers on duty tonight, I think. I don't like him. He's out to get me."

Yet his eager voice told Erin that he regarded his ongoing conflict with the town deputy as a personal competition. He sounded jazzed at the challenge of carrying out this grave robbery under the nose of his nemesis.

Matt jumped toward the backhoe and waved to the operator.

"Hold on a minute!" he shouted. Then he asked Erin, "Do you want to see him?"

"*See him*? Are you kidding? No way!" Just the thought made her nauseous.

"Okay, I'm sorry. I thought maybe ..." He gestured to Mitch to carry on with his work.

The coffin's handles gleamed in the headlamps.

Suddenly a splash of cold reality washed over Erin, who said, "You're sure to get caught."

"Don't be ridiculous. You always say that, and it never happens."

That was true, so far.

"Even if you ... bury the coffin again, they'll catch you. They have ways of figuring everything out, you know. How much did you have to pay this guy?"

"Two thousand now, and two thousand in a month if he keeps his mouth shut."

"You *are* crazy."

"It's only money."

"Right. Like your dad won't find out."

"Quit worrying," he said with frustration. "You're the biggest worrier I know!"

He returned to Mitch to supervise the new burial. On the ground nearby Erin saw a backhoe bucket. She wondered how long it took to dig up a coffin. Weren't they buried six feet down?

She went back to her car and leaned against it, watching the operation while keeping an eye on the sparse traffic going past on Highway 22, praying that Eakin Chalmers was nowhere close. The work at the gravesite went faster than she imagined it would. After the coffin was lowered out of view, Matt jumped into the dug-up area. He was so brave! Evidently he had to undo the straps, which probably meant he had to *lift* the coffin. How scary! Mitch meanwhile swapped the attachments on the backhoe and began scraping the dirt back into the hole. As soon as he could help, Matt took a shovel and rake to the remaining loose soil. They had started by skimming off the layer of grass and setting it aside; to finish their work they manually replaced it and manicured the area as well as they could in the darkness.

In the morning it would be obvious that *something* had happened. Whether you would be able to tell the grave had been dug up, she wasn't sure. Then again, how often did anybody visit Green Ridge Cemetery? There were how many graves? Fifty? Sixty? It was entirely possible that nobody would see the evidence of tampering for weeks.

Maybe Matt *would* get away with it.

He helped Mitch put the forklift into the bucket. Then Mitch moved the backhoe to a storage building at the north end of the cemetery property. He drove away without saying a word.

By 11:15 P.M. everything was finished.

Inside Matt's van, he unfolded the note he had removed from the body's vest pocket—the same note he had hidden there in a panic during the visitation hours for Steve Gutierrez, the note in which Steve supposedly said that he was heading for a meeting with Tolan Myers, the note that represented the last communication from the young man found dangling from a rope the next morning.

"Turn on a light," Erin whispered.

"No way," Matt said. "What if Chalmers drives by and sees it? Come on back here."

She followed him to the back of the van and turned his flashlight on again.

There it was! A note in pencil, written on yellow notebook paper, double-spaced, all capital letters:

MATT—I'M SENDING THIS TO YOU CAUSE I DON'T KNOW WHAT ELSE TO DO. I'M IN DEEP WITH MYERS WHICH I ALREADY TOLD YOU BUT HE'S MAKING ALL KINDS OF THREATS. HE WANTS ME TO MEET HIM TONIGHT AT SCHOOL HE SAYS TO WORK OUT SOME KIND OF ARRANGEMENT HE CALLS IT. I'M SCARED TO GO BUT DON'T KNOW WHAT ELSE I CAN DO YOU KNOW? I'M SORRY BUT I TOLD HIM YOU OWED ME MONEY WHICH WAS WHY I WAS NOT PAYING HIM YET. HE MADE SOME COMMENT ABOUT YOUR LOTTO MONEY WHICH I'M NOT SURE WHAT THAT MEANS BUT JUST SO YOU KNOW. HOPE TO SEE YOU SOON BUT WHO KNOWS…

Tears pooled in the corners of Erin's eyes, but before they could trickle down her cheeks—*rap! rap! rap!* Something banged on the side of the van!

Matt cursed and started sliding toward the driver's seat. Light flashed through the window, which he lowered.

"Mr. Rademacher," came an adult voice, arrogant but authoritative—the voice of Eakin Chalmers.

"Yes, sir," Matt answered.

"What brings you here at this hour?" He directed the light to the back of the van, where it found Erin's face. She squinted and threw up her hands, blinded.

"You have a guest?" Chalmers asked.

"Yes, sir. She's my guest."

"Mr. Rademacher, are you aware that you're on private property?"

"No, sir. I didn't know this was private property. Can't you just come to a cemetery and pay your respects to a friend?"

Erin cringed under her cover of darkness. Matt was maintaining respect and courtesy, but why was he risking escalating the conflict? He needed to shut his mouth.

"Is *that* what you kids are calling it these days?" Chalmers asked sarcastically. His flashlight beam found Erin again.

"No, not her, not Erin," Matt said. "I mean we came to visit Steve Gutierrez. He's buried here."

Shut up, Matt! Erin thought. Was he *trying* to get Chalmers to check out the gravesite?

"And what were you doing in the back of your vehicle? Praying?"

Matt laughed.

"No sir, not praying."

Erin breathed with relief when he said nothing more.

"All right, then. Let's call it a night."

"Yes, sir."

May

10

THE UNEXPECTED AND pleasant visit from her children had an unexpected and pleasant result for Robin Hillis. Peace filled the channels of her heart and overflowed its banks. No longer hiding her secret from anyone in her family, no longer fearing that Anyssa might reveal it to Zeb, she felt like a condemned prisoner must feel at getting a last-minute pardon, how a cancer patient must feel at receiving a diagnosis that the deadly disease has inexplicably, mysteriously, miraculously disappeared, leaving no trace.

She had cheated, she had tried to hide it, and she had been caught.

And now, inexplicably, mysteriously, miraculously, she felt a light and glorious freedom—totally undeserved—from the worry and regret that should have clung to her forever.

Her only apprehension now revolved around her job. The school board was not as forgiving as Zeb—her day of reckoning before them had come. For several days she had talked about her options with Zeb and Anyssa from her family, with Brad and Lydia Knowles at school, and finally with Howard and Jerri Roost across the street.

Everyone agreed that Robin's safest course of action was to tell the truth. They all said she should admit that she had taken matters into her own hands instead of letting the higher authorities deal with the accusations of improper behavior by students or adults at Brookstone

High School, that she should humbly apologize and hope for the best. Since she had been a model employee in every respect before now, she could expect leniency. Everyone agreed.

Except Robin.

Everyone agreed, but everyone was wrong, she believed.

"I can't explain it," she said to Brad the afternoon before the school board meeting. "Maybe I'm all wrong. Maybe I'm overconfident. I'm just feeling *invincible* right now."

"Why would you feel *invincible?*" he asked. The past few days he had reverted to his habit of letting an unlit cigarette hang from his lips, as he had always done in the fall when they had grown close.

"I can't explain that, either," she said. Which was a white lie, the truth being that she didn't want to explain it, not to him, since it involved him. Ever since accepting that Zeb really did forgive her, that a giant shoe was not going to drop from the heavens and squish her like an ugly bug, she had marveled at her suddenly charmed life.

A memory kept coming back to her, the memory of that driver whose wild gestures she had so badly mistaken a few weeks back.

"But I *can* say that life is full of surprises," she went on.

"That's original," Brad joked.

"No, really," she insisted. "You doubt me?"

He smiled around the cigarette in a gently mocking way. So she told him the story about the driver who she was so sure was angry with her and about to scream at her for her lousy driving but all along was really singing and flailing his hands to the rhythm of some happy song on the radio.

Brad nodded politely, still unconvinced.

"I wish I could make you see how much that got to me," Robin finished. "It was just … well, it was more than I could have ever hoped for."

"Why?"

"Because I was in the wrong."

Good things kept happening to her. Anyssa, instead of condemning her for her affair with Brad, had sent her a nice card and followed it up with a phone call, praising her for her change of heart. "Mom," she said at the end of the conversation, "you're still my greatest encouragement!"

Even Bragley had come through for her, finally removing that resistant smudge from her classroom's whiteboard. He took his time, as he always did, but he finally made good on his promise to clean it.

Was it tempting fate to think that maybe, just maybe, she ought to *challenge* the school board rather than knuckling under to their insistence that she cease and desist in her pursuit of the cheaters?

Their grave faces evenly spaced in a semicircle above the level of the floor in the conference room, the five members of the Brookstone School Corporation board, along with their recording secretary, treasurer, and attorney—plus Walter Patingale, the swarthy superintendent—proceeded swiftly through their agenda. The meetings were open to the public, but few people ever attended. Robin decided to wait in the conference room rather than in an adjoining area where she might have waited more comfortably until called for her item on the official docket. She hoped that observing the meeting would ease her nerves.

A few other members of the public were sitting in metal folding chairs on the carpeted floor. Some of them had been invited to give reports or offer their expertise on questions about construction finance, for the corporation was in the early stages of building a new elementary school in the northeast corner of the county. Whenever these people delivered their reports or answered questions, they stood beneath those high serious faces. The arrangement looked deliberately inquisitorial.

Her turn came soon enough, and it started innocently enough.

"Mrs. Hillis, thank you for coming tonight," said Tamara Sax, the current board president. Before Robin could even form the sarcastic thought *as if I had any choice*, Mrs. Sax continued, "You may not know all of us on the board, but I have often bragged about our great English teachers and how much all of you, but especially *you*"—she pointed her pen at Robin—"helped my daughter Serena improve as a writer for college."

The praise momentarily disoriented Robin. For the past twenty minutes she had been steeling herself for what she expected would be hostility.

"Thank you," she said. "Serena was a joy to have in class."

Mrs. Sax nodded to her left and said, "Witt?"

The board members were identified by nameplates, and the face above the plate that said WITTGREN OLANDER sniffled noisily and began, "Mrs. Hillis, we have a report, a complaint I might call it, from Mr. LaGrange and Mr. Myers. Are you familiar with this? Do you understand why we asked you to be here tonight?"

She had anticipated this question and answered with confidence: "I'm not a hundred percent sure I do know. But I suppose it concerns the way I have handled cheating." Then she added, "Cheating by students." That was a fair response. It *was* the student cheating that had been her starting point, the doorway she had kicked open, leading to the discovery that other teachers, administrators, and perhaps higher officials were also involved.

"Yes," Mr. Olander said. He was a farmer, Robin recalled. He had younger kids, middle school and elementary age. "Yes, the complaint is that the principal and assistant principal requested that you leave the, ah, disposition of the cases of cheating to the administration, and that you, ah, disregarded their wishes."

That too was fair enough, she thought. But *disposition of cases*? No farmer talked like that. That was lawyer-speak. Brad McCauley would be gagging about now ... She was conscious of the many faces staring down at her. Had she been asked a question?

"What I have been doing, all along," she said, nervous but bold, "is the same thing I have always done, whatever I think is best for the students."

The face above the nameplate that said REBECCA COLE asked, "But *did* Mr. LaGrange and Mr. Myers ask you to let them handle it?"

"Yes, ma'am. Yes, they did."

"And?" The eyebrows of Mrs. Cole arched upward, creasing her forehead with wrinkles.

"I did not exactly submit to their wishes. Your report, your complaint, is right about that."

Walter Patingale, at one end of the arc of judges, spoke up.

"Why not?"

Robin's paranoia kicked in—she could feel her heartbeat quicken and her skin heating up. She wondered whether any of the school board members were connected to the cheating network—any, or some, or none at all. Patingale, she believed, was dirty.

For an instant, she wanted to cry out, "Because you, Mr. Patingale, are the biggest cheater of all!"—and then lay out the most damning evidence that she and Brad and Erin had gathered. That would dramatically put the truth on the table for everyone to see! But what if the whole board were already compromised? Then her accusations would effectively sign her own death warrant, professionally speaking, and maybe more than just professionally, considering what had nearly happened to Brad on the railroad tracks. She imagined herself being bound and gagged and blindfolded and pushed into a dark van to be driven away and shot in the back of the head and dumped from the Junction Bridge into the Orange River ...

"I guess," she said slowly, measuring each word carefully, "I was so upset about how slowly Mr. LaGrange and Mr. Myers were moving—slowly in *my* view—that I thought it would be best to take matters into my own hands."

Patingale interlocked his fingers in front of his mouth and ran his thumbs up and down his cheeks below his eyes. Everyone else on the board was deferring to him—a reaction that only heightened Robin's suspicion and paranoia.

"We don't need or want *lone rangers,*" the superintendent said severely. "You have a long record of great work at Brookstone High School." He seemed to search for his next words, and his tone turned to soft pleading: "Don't ruin that, ma'am. Stick to teaching our young people to read and write. You do that better than anybody, like Mrs. Sax said earlier. Will you please, please, please let the administrators do *their* jobs, like they let you do *yours?*"

That was crafty, she thought. The words, the logic, all of it was so devious, so seductive and cunning. It made her think once more of that Bible verse about the heart being deceitful above all things, desperately wicked.

How could she say *no* to his entreaty?

She couldn't, and she didn't.

"Robin, I'm so glad you didn't go in there with guns blazing," Brad said.

They were leaning toward each other over the Dairy Queen table, their voices reduced to whispers. Robin at one point, unknown to Brad, had felt under the table for bugs, electronic bugs, but found only the hardened lumps of chewing gum.

"I thought you would be proud of my self-control," she said.

"I am. When I talked to you this afternoon, I wasn't sure what would happen."

"Well, I'm glad that you didn't show up at the meeting. That would have been a disaster."

"Probably," he agreed, crunching on an onion ring. "But I didn't want you to have to go through that without any support. I had to show some self-control too."

"I appreciate that." Zeb was in Dallas for three days. Talking about their self-control meant something entirely different now than it would have meant a few months earlier.

"What now?" she asked. "What's next?"

Since their burglary of the administrative offices, a conspicuous lull had descended over their activity. In fact, they could not determine whether Myers and LaGrange even *knew* that anyone had broken in. Had they known, then their suspicion should have fallen immediately on Robin and Brad, yet neither teacher had heard from the administrators. Possibly Myers and LaGrange seldom got into the filing cabinets in the back closet and would not notice if anything had been rearranged. Or perhaps Myers, failing to crack the combination to Brad's safe, had abandoned it to its hiding place beneath his desk and did not know it was gone. Or maybe Robin and Brad and Erin had done such a professional job of thievery that Myers and LaGrange suspected nothing.

Or, more likely, as Erin had sensibly suggested, their attempt had been so foolish or so brazen as to be inconceivable to Myers and LaGrange.

"What now?" Brad repeated Robin's words. "I'm not sure what else there is for us to do. I get the feeling everything is … I don't know … winding down."

"You and your clocks," Robin joked. Yet she felt the same as he did.

"Look, all we've wanted to do is get the truth out there for everyone to see, right?"

"Right."

"And we agreed that letting the newspaper publish the information was the best way to do that, right?"

"Right."

"Okay, then. I think everything is in Pete Doty's hands now."

Robin stabbed a breaded mushroom with her plastic fork and dunked it into the cup of ketchup. The little act reminded her of her brief vision of violence against her as she stood before the school board, and she asked, "Do you think Pete Doty is in any danger? If Myers came after you, what's to stop him from going after Doty?"

Brad smoothed his mustache, greasy from the rings and mushrooms.

"He wouldn't dare," he said dismissively. "Bullying me was one thing, a part-timer whose contract is up in a few months. But going after a journalist from another city—that would be a whole different level. That's intimidating the press, anti-First-Amendment stuff. Myers would be stupid to even take that chance."

Robin nodded, but said, "He might do it out of desperation, though. If he knew he was about to be exposed."

"Or out of revenge. But it won't make any difference, Robin. Trust me."

He was holding something back.

"Why? What do you know that I don't know? Tell me, Brad!"

He shook his head.

"Please!" she pleaded.

"I don't want to involve you any more than you already are involved, because frankly, I'm more worried about Myers coming after *you* than his coming after me again, or going after Doty."

"It's too late for that! I'm involved up to my eyeballs!"

"I know. I was just hoping." He smiled mischievously. "I was also afraid that Doty would not be safe. So I called him and explained it to him. You know what he did?"

"What?"

"He laughed at me. I'm not kidding you."

"Laughed?"

"Laughed. And you know why? Because we're amateurs, you and me and Erin. That's what he said. Amateurs. And amateurs are always a step behind."

"Brad, what are you talking about?"

He looked around the restaurant and cleared his throat.

When he finally spoke, it was a murmur: "Pete Doty said that somebody contacted the newspaper editors and asked them to not run the story about the cheating—asked, then tried to negotiate, and finally threatened. According to Doty, the newspaper was able to stick to its guns because whenever the story breaks it will break nationwide. Even if the Bridgebury *Courier* backed down from the pressure, there were a dozen other newspapers around the country ready to blow the whistle. Other papers are working on their own local angles, getting all their information, coordinating. At some point somebody in charge will say the word and pull the trigger and all the truth will come out at once. So Myers or LaGrange or whoever was threatening Doty and the *Courier* didn't have a prayer."

Robin sat dazed, another mushroom halfway to her mouth.

"The rest of the way," Brad concluded, "we're just along for the ride."

"That hardly seems fair."

He laughed ironically.

"Maybe it's not fair, but it's better for us. Safer. Unless, as I said, Myers lets hunger for revenge get the better of him."

"I don't think of him as a vengeful person," she said, an image of his puppy-dog eyes floating before her.

"You could be right. You've known him a lot longer. But he's always impressed me as a high-testosterone guy. Always in a competitive mode."

Robin chuckled.

"And what about you, Mr. High Testosterone? You've gone out of your way to challenge him and not back down. You could have walked away from all this trouble many times and gone back to your dissertation."

"I know. I've surprised myself. Why do you think I said we should meet *here* after your meeting?"

"I assumed you were being considerate of me. I assumed you didn't want to put me in an awkward situation by asking to meet at your place or mine."

"You're giving me too much credit."

"Oh." A mild pang of sadness swept over her.

"I just wanted to flaunt everything we're doing in front of Myers, you know? I want him to know we're not afraid of him and we haven't let up despite all his physical and psychological and professional threats. I was hoping he would be here tonight. I was hoping he would see us together and realize we aren't intimidated. I want him to shake in fear because he's going down."

"Wow," she said. "Sounds like *you're* the vengeful one."

Back at home, she kept her promise and crossed the street to let Howard and Jerri Roost know how the school board meeting had gone. Jerri was on the phone, so Howard took Robin into his den, asked her to sit, and got her a cup of hot tea.

She dispensed with her business in a few words.

"I listened to what you said," she explained, "you and Zeb and everyone else I talked to. I took your advice. I told everyone I was sorry and I would let the administrators figure out the best way to stop all the cheating."

Of course, she scrupulously avoided telling him the whole truth. She did not recount the traumatic interior dialogue that had pushed her to the brink of escalating the conflict to the point that the school board would have been left with no other choice than firing her.

"I think that was wise," Howard said. "You've been making a lot of wise choices lately, it seems to me."

She agreed.

However, the unresolved issue of her part in the eventual newspaper exposé stuck out like a speck of dirt or an insect trapped on a newly painted surface. The fallout from that event, if and when it finally occurred, might undercut any of her so-called wisdom …

While Jerri continued to talk in the next room, her voice muted by the walls, Robin said, "Howard, I know Zeb has thanked you over and over for all you've done for us. I just want you to know that I feel the same way."

He nodded humbly.

"The more I think about things you've told us, told *me*, and the further away I get from … from what I did, the more I see how right you were when you were telling us, telling *me*, about how I was deceiving myself. I keep thinking about how true it is. I keep seeing ways that it applies—everywhere I look, in fact."

"Well, it's easier to see how it applies to other people."

"I can't believe how *blind* I was."

"Well, not *you*, not really. That's the tricky part of it all. I've tried to tell you that. It's your *old* heart, the *old* you, that is 'deceitful above all things.' Not the *new* you."

"I know you've said that. It's just hard to accept, I guess."

"Too good to be true?"

"Maybe that's it."

Her eyes studied the Oriental rug in the room. Something in its complicated pattern teased from her thoughts another instance of her colossal capacity to fool herself. For a few weeks in the late fall, when her relationship with Brad was heating up, she had intentionally refrained from giving in to her desire and sleeping with him—convincing herself that she must wait until she and Zeb were divorced. She really thought that hanging onto that single, slender strand of integrity mattered, even while she shredded the rest of her moral fabric beyond recognition.

Howard excused himself to refill their teacups.

Alone, her eyes blurring as they skimmed along the titles on Howard's bookshelves, Robin fell into a spell, entranced by Jerri's muffled voice coming through the wall. Then the door swung open and Howard returned with their tea—but the door stayed open.

Robin heard Jerri say, "That's the way it's always been. He brings out the best in me."

She remembered a time last fall, when despair was pinching out the weakening flame of her marriage hopes and corrupting her friendship with Jerri.

She had knocked on the Roosts' front door. Jerri had answered, the phone to her ear, and waved for her to come in. She was smiling—at

Robin or at the person on the other end of the line—and nodding and fingering the cross on her necklace and saying the same thing: "He brings out the best in me."

Jealousy had surged in Robin's blood. She wanted to jerk the phone from Jerri's hands and wrap the cord around her neck three or four times. It was so unfair that Jerri had such a great husband who was always there and always talking to her and always loving her.

Not until later, after hearing Jerri say the same words in other contexts—"He brings out the best in me"—did she understand that Jerri Roost was not talking about her husband.

11

ONCE AGAIN, ERIN realized, she had been mistaken.

She shivered, partly from the chill, but mostly from the fear and disappointment. Looking down at the waters of the Orange River, the westerly winds of early May flapping her jeans and the meager late afternoon sun lighting but not warming her face, she wondered what she had been thinking when she made up her mind to bungee jump from the Junction Bridge.

Actually, what she had been thinking was simple enough, sensible enough. Taking the long view, she had reasoned that since her earlier experiment in letting Matt Rademacher dangle her from the bridge had turned out safe and even *fun*, she should next try a real jump. Far from frightening her, the dangling over the river had instead left her invigorated, exhilarated, hungry for more—the last thing she expected. Moreover, she saw jumping as another step in steeling her nerves for two imminent conversations that filled her with anxiety: the confrontation with her parents over college, and her get-together with Nathan Dyer later that night, when she wanted to tell him about her hopes for their future.

If she could do *this*, if she could jump off the bridge and trust to Matt's cords and Cody's calculations, then she could stand up to her mother and father and tell them what she wanted to do with her life, what she was going to do, whether they approved or not. And she could risk rejection and disillusionment by sharing her heart and hopes with Nathan.

But now she saw that once again she had misjudged herself.

Today the waters appeared violent and mean, a far cry from their friendly, gentle look from ten weeks before, when thanks to Matt's powerful straining muscles she had effectively *hung* fifty feet up. She remembered feeling that even if he accidentally dropped her, the plunge and splash would be fun and refreshing, more like jumping off a dock into a lake than plummeting from a bridge into the current of a river. But today she could see the reality of the situation. The waters were deep, the river swollen from recent rains and at least a month of spring thaw, its current dangerously swift by Orange River standards.

Another difference between the dangle and this leap was that Matt had pressured her the first time, whereas this time she was jumping— maybe, anyway—of her own free will. In fact, her choice had taken Matt by surprise. He had tried to talk her out of it.

Now he was waiting behind her, quietly observing, having given her all the instructions he could with his thick hands firm on her shoulders. His last words were, "It's up to you now. Whenever you're ready."

She felt the fear, surely enough, yet she also felt a strange serenity floating around and above the fear; or rather, the fear was floating *in* the serenity, which was deeper and broader. The fear was like a little island in the ocean of the serenity. Erin could not shake that image. All that fear—of danger, or of the embarrassment should she back down, or of the disappointment that her sudden reluctance might foreshadow that she would shrink from standing up to Mom and Dad—all that fear was really puny compared to the peace. And she knew where the peace came from, what it represented. It was the sum of all her growth over the past four months. Recognizing this, she imagined the ocean rising and engulfing the little island of fear. She swelled with pride, which tugged the corners of her mouth into a smile.

Some first-time jumpers screamed as they catapulted themselves off the bridge with a running start. Others bent their knees, curled their toes over the edge, and leapt forward, like divers from a platform. Most just leaned forward until their weight carried them out and down.

Erin took a final breath and stepped off.

Oooohhhh! Her insides whooshed away in a sensation she had never known—her legs lost their strength and hung useless, her stomach exploded and filled up her chest, her lungs forgot to breathe, and somehow those feelings all squeezed into some involuntary corner of her brain and she shrieked a long, meaningless syllable.

It was over before her mind could form a coherent idea.

The whoosh softened and the sensations of her limbs and insides snapped back to something like normal as she came to rest for an instant and then rose with a jerk that also softened, and the cycles repeated, the cycles of rise and fall that she had watched from the bridge so many times and now knew first-hand. Those cycles were *oscillations*, she decided, remembering a vocabulary word.

She laughed, and laughed, and laughed.

At Dairy Queen, she and Matt and Cody and Jess further collaborated to eat a super sundae concocted especially for their celebration, a mountain of a dozen scoops of differently flavored hard-serve ice cream with a dozen different toppings and a dozen different sprinkles.

Erin's ebullient, victorious mood spread to the others. Final exams were close but not critical to any of their grades. Graduation was within sight. As friends, they were breathing an early, joint sigh of relief, for the end of thirteen years of mandatory schooling was close enough to taste. And even though that thought entailed a degree of sadness, too, the wistful side of the equation had not yet registered on their collective radar screen. They ate with good will and giggles and great giddiness.

Cody estimated that you could make more than 600 million different combinations of the three sundae components.

"It's too bad, blokes and sheilas," he speculated, "too bad we couldn't have a fourth part, like twelve different kinds of whipped cream." Occasionally he still dropped Australian vernacular into his talk, but mostly that had disappeared.

"Why?"

"Because then we could have a *one-two-three-four* angle on this dessert," he explained, "in honor of Brookstone High School's latest fad, and in honor of the owner of this fine establishment where we have spent so many wonderful times together during our *one-two-three-four* years of high school."

His reference to Mr. Myers was intended to be funny, and Erin giggled, thinking of the silly *1-2-3-4* schemes some teachers were concocting to meet the official demands. She had heard that even custodians were supposed to support the cause.

But Matt grunted and turned morose.

"I'm sorry, Matt," Cody said, genuinely apologetic, realizing too late his rare miscalculation. "That was not very … sensitive of me. Forget I even said it, okay?" He clapped his buddy on the shoulder.

Silence ensued until Jess broke it with a compliment for Erin.

"I can't believe you did it," she said, her used wad of bubble gum lying on a plastic spoon off to the side. Chewing it, while consuming her share of the ice cream, had become too difficult as the gum cooled and hardened in her mouth. "I didn't think you had it in you."

Lately her cousin had been taking a conciliatory attitude. Erin was not exactly sure why, and she didn't bother to try to analyze Jess's motives, which might rebound in the other direction with no warning or apparent reason. Perhaps Erin's break-up with Matt was one factor. Who could say? All through the semester Erin had heard Mrs. Hillis talk about how nobody could fully understand people, that no one could know the human heart except for God. Jess was a case in point.

Altogether that afternoon Erin had bungee jumped five times before Matt and Cody said they were all pushing their luck, that a cop was bound to come along soon—and Matt wanted to avoid a run-in with Eakin Chalmers at all costs. *One more*, Erin insisted, and in the end she prevailed and made a final leap strapped together with Jess in a tandem jump whose hasty calculations by Cody wound up dipping the girls up to their knees in the river. …

As soon as they all reduced the sundae to a swirl of gooey colors, Matt and Cody left, sorry for their quick exit. Everyone understood. Matt did not want to be in the store any longer than necessary. The only person he wanted to avoid more than Deputy Chalmers was Mr. Myers.

Erin's interpersonal antenna quickly picked up that Jess was sidling toward a topic, so she was not surprised when her cousin asked, "So are you excited about winning MOST MYSTERIOUS?" Meaning that Senior Superlative title, of course.

Erin shrugged. She didn't care, one way or the other, about those stupid egotistical honors. They were embarrassing. But her evasive response opened the door for Jess: "I don't know about winning MOST SARCASTIC. At first I was happy to be, you know, recognized for being clever. Then I thought that it might be that everybody was dissing me. What do you think?"

As if Jess really wanted her opinion, rather than her affirmation or admiration.

"I have to admit, you are pretty clever most of the time." To say that much was hardly controversial, since the vote had been unanimous, according to the *Independent Clause*, whose report claimed that the underground paper had a "source on the inside," meaning a Yearbook member.

"Thanks!"

Jess twirled her straw in the melted ice cream.

"What about Matt?" she asked, and Erin detected a tone of worry, of concern. Matt had won that year's joke superlative, MOST LIKELY TO KILL SOMEBODY. His *victory*, if you called it that, filled her with foreboding. His off-and-on depression might not be clinical, yet it was obvious to everyone close to him. So was his occasional temper.

Upon learning that he had won that vote, he had sulked rather than behaving in his usual bombastic manner.

"To be honest," Erin said, "I wish somebody else had won that one."

"Yeah. Me too."

When was the last time they had agreed on anything so thoroughly?

Not wanting their time together to end on such a gloomy note, Erin brought up another topic that was potentially divisive because Erin knew it represented another example of Jess's cheating.

"Did I tell you about my project for history?" she asked.

"I heard McCauley thought it was the greatest project he'd ever gotten from a high school student."

"You did?" Erin was puzzled, for she had not told anyone, even Matt, about her grade—an A-plus—or Mr. McCauley's effusive praise, handwritten for more than a page. "How did you know about it?"

"McCauley told me."

"He did?"

"Yeah. Jeez, Erin, are you deaf, or what? He's been blabbing about it to everybody."

"Oh. I didn't know."

Hearing that was almost as satisfying as reading his comments!

The shared Commons area of Nathan's dorm at Riverside University took Erin's breath away. Its atmosphere—or *ambience*, to use another new vocab word from Mrs. Hillis's class—was so inviting, so comfortable, so mature, so collegiate. She *belonged* here! And that reaction was just one more piece of evidence that she had outgrown high school and was ready for college. More importantly, it was proof positive that she belonged at Riverside University and nowhere else.

Seen from above, the four-story building was laid out in the shape of the letter X. Women occupied the east floors and boys the west, so the vaulted room had a fifty-fifty mix of men and women, mostly freshmen and sophomores. Arranged sporadically through the Commons were twenty or so tables, some round and some square, surrounded by chairs—not hard-backed plastic or metal chairs but thick, cushiony chairs that invited students to lounge or sleep, which many were doing. Except for the low murmur of conversation, everything was quiet. There was no audible music, although many students were using earphones. About half of them were working on laptops or reading.

Bashful about sitting down alone, Erin waited for Nathan along one wall and watched the nearest large-screen TV, its sound muted, which was tuned to a home improvement channel. Young adults wearing masks and gloves were taking sledgehammers to walls, demolishing the old to make way for the new.

"Hi, Miss Mysterious," Nathan's voice floated into her ear.

Great, Erin thought, he's been talking to Jess again.

"Hi. What a cool place!"

"Yeah, I knew you would like it. That's why I said we should come here. Follow me."

He led her past several clusters of students to an empty table along the far wall, beneath a large painting with lots of intersecting lines of different thicknesses.

"Want something to drink?" he asked. "I can get you a soft drink, or tea, or coffee, or bottled water, or ..." He made a gesture indicating that the possibilities were limitless.

"How about lemonade?"

"You got it. Be right back."

Her eyes followed him as he zig-zagged back and forth among the tables and disappeared through the Commons doors. Then her heart began to thud as she rehearsed the things she wanted to say when he returned.

They covered the obligatory topics: final exams for him (this week, mostly finished), for her (in two weeks, no worries); summer work plans (he had a full-time job lined up on campus, she wasn't sure); updates from their mutual friends who had left the area (no real news, except that Lizzie Andrews was going to Japan for the summer); and movies they had seen or wanted to see (both of them couldn't think of any, which threw them into paroxysms of laughter at their boring lives).

She sensed her opportunity, and she seized it.

"I don't mind being boring," she declared.

"I don't either. It's just who I am."

"I know! And we're both okay with that, right?"

"Yeah."

"Okay, so ... do you ever think that maybe ... maybe we should get back together?"

"Oh, Erin," he said, taking her hands—but his tone made her heart plummet—"I *thought* that was why you wanted to talk to me."

Her eyes blurred with tears, but she blinked them away.

He went on: "We've been apart for about a year now, and I still think that what I said when we broke up is true. Remember what I said?"

Erin nodded, her eyes fixed on their clasped hands. She couldn't bring herself to look up, or to repeat his words from a year earlier.

"I said that if we found out that we couldn't live without each other, then we would get back together. And that's still how I feel."

She wanted to pour out her heart, to lay everything on the line in a dramatic make-or-break confession.

But she couldn't.

Whether from her pride or from fear of making herself vulnerable, she couldn't.

And yet—while the throes of that conflict buffeted her heart, the words of Rachel Sarks called to her, echoing down the tunnel of her memory, words bursting with promise and hope.

"Maybe," Rachel had told the room full of Young Life teenagers, "you were *made* for something *special*."

Erin squeezed Nathan's hands, let go of them, and asked, "Do you think you were *made* for something? You know, made to do something in this life? Do you ever think about that?"

A quizzical expression came over his face.

"That's a … drastic change of topic, isn't it?"

Erin laughed.

"I guess so, but maybe not."

She shut her mouth and raised her eyebrows.

"Well," he said, "to answer your question, no. I've never thought about that. I guess I believe I have the freedom to choose what I do with my life. I'm not a robot. Why are you wanting to talk about this? Are you wanting to become a philosopher?"

They shared a laugh.

"No, nothing like that. But I've started to think about it because … well, like you said, I want to have freedom to choose what I do, too. And you know how Mom and Dad, Dad mostly, has these big plans for me to be a doctor and all."

"Yeah."

"And *I* don't know. Maybe I *would* be a good doctor. Maybe I *should* go to medical school. But I don't want to. And so all year I've been worried about that. And Grandpa Dee told me about how Dad sort of let *him* down when he became a doctor instead of being a farmer, and I actually felt sorry for Dad as much as for Grandpa Dee! And then I heard this lady talking about how we all have a purpose in life. She says we are all made for great things, far greater things than we ever imagine. And that got me to thinking, What if I was meant to be something greater than a doctor? What if for me, being in some kind of social work where I help old people is greater than being a doctor? Does any of this make sense? Do you see what I'm saying?"

"I don't know, but I can see you are pretty worked up about it."

"Yeah."

"So, keep going."

She felt the excitement building in her voice: "What if becoming a doctor is not what I was *made* for, and even if I became a doctor and made a lot of money and lived in a nice house and everybody thought I was great, I was really *cheating* myself?"

"Cheating? I don't get it."

Erin sighed. How could she explain it? Nathan did not know the details of the Brookstone cheating scandal, details that any day now might be "shouted from the rooftops," as Mrs. Hillis said. Erin had not told Nathan very much about her exciting collaboration with Mrs. Hillis and Mr. McCauley, even though that alliance was the highlight of the whole second semester.

"I've been thinking about cheating," she said, "because so much of it goes on at school. And then I guess I started to see that there's a lot of different kinds of cheating. Way more kinds than I ever thought of."

She fell silent, thinking of her own December folly, and her suspicion of her father's entanglement with the administrators at school, and Mrs. Hillis's relationship with Mr. McCauley, and Mr. McCauley's cheating on his college work, and that newspaper reporter saying that Brookstone High School was no different from any other school in the country, probably. It was overwhelming, really. Overwhelming and depressing.

And yet, what bothered her more than any of that cheating or possible cheating—and what struck closest to home—was the thought that she might be cheating herself.

Dad's taste in music was okay, Erin had to admit. Now that he had converted the room next to her bedroom into a den, she sometimes heard the strains of Bach or Beethoven or Vivaldi (her favorite) rolling through the walls, or coming through the heating vent in the ceiling, one or the other. Sometimes she wished he would use headphones, but that was asking too much.

That classical sound was okay. It helped her think, actually.

Driving back from Riverside, she had worked up her courage and determined to have it out with him and Mom as soon as she got home. Then, as she slowed down on the road entering Orange Stone, her resolve slipped. Something about her motives was not clear, and she did not want to talk to her parents until everything was settled in her own mind.

She lay in her bed, totally naked under the blanket and comforter, awash in the soft, insistent melody from the den and her own inner dialogue.

About one thing she harbored no doubts—she wanted to go to Riverside University.

But why? Nathan was right on target when he told her that if she came to Riverside, she should do so for her own education and career, not for him or for her hopes about him. That was tough to hear, and it would have brought tears except that he had taken her hands again, and his touch eased the pain of the truth. So did his saying she needed to take the "long view"—that was encouraging because it proved he was really listening to her.

Even more encouraging was that Nathan's words reminded her of Manny Sarks and his story of how he and Rachel had wound up together. After a long time of refusing to believe it, Manny explained, he accepted that being together with Rachel was what he was *made* for. She might not be the prettiest girl in the world, or the richest, but the prettiest or richest girl was not what he had been *made* for—so to go in any other direction would mean settling for something besides the best. Hearing him talk, Erin thought that he might as well have said that to go after any other woman would have meant he was *cheating* himself.

As for exactly how all of this applied to her future with Nathan Dyer, or her college, or her career, or anything else in her life, well, she still had to figure that out.

The music in Dad's den shut off. Moments later the thin, hazy, carpeted line of light seeping under her bedroom door went dark.

An anxious concern for Matt welled up in her heart. It was good that Cody was with him tonight. Matt hadn't said anything about the letter they had retrieved from Steve's grave. Erin wanted to talk to him about it, to learn what he was thinking now. The night in the cemetery, Matt was convinced that the few handwritten words proved that Steve did not commit suicide. Erin did not agree. She saw nothing in the letter to incriminate Mr. Myers. But she didn't want to say so until they could discuss it in a calmer setting.

No such opportunity had come. She was reluctant to broach the subject, and Matt had grown despondently silent about the whole night, not even telling her whether anybody else even knew what he and his grave-robbing accomplice Mitch had done.

Whenever he stopped talking, she worried. She was afraid for Matt.

She remembered something else Rachel Sarks had told the YL kids, something about how to overcome fear. You defeat fear by rising above and beyond it, according to Rachel, and you do that through what she called "perfect love." It was something from the Bible. Erin didn't know exactly what that meant, perfect love, but the image of rising above fear or any kind of trouble made her think of her whirlwind, which made her think of how she had overcome her fear of jumping from the bridge by trusting Matt, trusting that he loved her, maybe not perfectly, but enough that he had proved himself trustworthy when he dangled her over the river, trustworthy enough that she finally believed him when he told her that jumping was safe, and fun, and so she had taken him at his word.

12

J. BRADFORD MCCAULEY dropped his backpack on the weathered boards of the picnic table that sat near a slight bluff overlooking the muddy waters of the Wawachee River. Already this Saturday morning he had found two other venues unsuitable for his work of grading a dozen exams from his Riverside history course. First his apartment and then his grad studies office had failed to cultivate the right frame of mind.

Perhaps this place would work, so far removed from Riverside University and from Brookstone High School. In half an hour Pete Doty was scheduled to meet him on this very spot.

McCauley battled the momentum driving him toward chaos in his thinking. Now, more than ever, he needed to think clearly. The events of the previous weeks had nearly overwhelmed him with their emotional intensity—starting with the brazen break-in at Myers's office, continuing with three unexpected and pleasant surprises that came in the mail, and culminating in the news he had received the night before.

Not just news, but *startling* news.

Gregory Travis was dead.

McCauley kept repeating that fact to himself. Travis was dead. He had passed away peacefully in his sleep, according to the scant information emailed to history graduate students. His cigarette smoking had finally done him in, no matter what the doctors called his official cause of death.

The river slid by, brown and silent. McCauley feared that this setting might be too peaceful to work.

Travis was dead. What exactly did his sudden demise mean for McCauley? For his dissertation? For his academic future?

Especially, what did the professor's death mean in light of the three sudden job offers he had received in one batch of mail?

For weeks he had laid a groundwork for defending himself against official charges of plagiarism, should they arise. Not knowing whether Travis had ever talked to colleagues, McCauley emailed or spoke face-to-face with the other members of his dissertation committee as well as other faculty familiar with his research, asking for their help. He fabricated a believable lie. He claimed that before Travis had been hospitalized, he had told McCauley that he might need to extensively revise one section of his thesis because of "questions of originality." McCauley told the other professors that he had scoured every database and every published bibliography but could find nothing to explain Travis's cryptic phrase. Could they help? Did they know what Travis was referring to? Had Travis made any specific statements to them about McCauley's work?

On the river a pair of long yellow boats passed by, each with four rowers, members of Riverside's Crew Club, their low voices wafting over the waters.

Everyone McCauley had talked to claimed to have no idea what he—or Travis—was talking about. One of them, whose office was next door to Travis's, even suggested that the old professor was probably not in his right mind the past few months: "There were definitely some indications of senility. I wouldn't take anything he said seriously, especially since you were working with him for more than a year before he said anything to you."

Besides Travis, then, no one suspected anything. That revelation should have set his heart at peace, but it did not.

As he had left his office that morning, shuffling along the marble-floored hallway and down two flights of granite stairs and kicking open the exit door, paranoia dogged his steps. Outside, the morning fog had mostly lifted. A few wisps lingered here and there on the broad lawns between buildings. Everywhere on campus the grass was turning green, and buds and leaves were appearing on bushes and trees according to their secret cellular schedules, their internal biological versions of the Universal Clock.

The signs of spring were even sharper here by the river. Redbud trees were blooming, the fragrance of honeysuckle was sweetening the air, and birds were noisily nesting in the trees along the water.

McCauley decided to postpone the grading. His heart was simply not in it. He was excited about the meeting with Pete Doty, but the shock of Travis's death was foremost on his mind.

What he most wanted was least likely. He wanted to talk to Robin Hillis. Since he had told her about Travis's blackmail, he wanted to rejoice with her over the old man's passing. At the same time, however, he felt heavy with ambivalence about seeing her and sharing the news. Why? As much as he tried to avoid the truth, he had to admit it: Robin was turning back to Zeb, turning her back on Brad (at least as a lover), turning her back on her own cheating. Her choice for change, juxtaposed with his ongoing hypocrisy, only underlined the gravity of his own cheating. Travis might be gone, but McCauley's academic future was suddenly pulsing with more promise than it had since Travis's incriminating discovery. McCauley feared that Robin would keep trying to convince him that his best course of action was to acknowledge his error (he *could* always pass it off as incidental, not intentional), modify his thesis, and move forward with no skeleton in his closet. But that course of action would probably mean another year of work (with its related expenses) and postpone his grand entrance onto the stage of scholarly stardom.

And that stardom had never hovered as close as it did now.

Yesterday's mail had included not one, not two, but three offers for employment. All three came from universities west of the Rocky Mountains, and all three had sprung from interviews at the Chicago conference in January. At the time, he had done those interviews only as a matter of formality, not planning to start a serious job search until his Ph.D. was safely in hand. The interviewers had given no indication of special interest in him or his thesis—so the windfall in his mailbox came as a total surprise. He even looked around suspiciously, half-expecting that Kelly Graham, his prank-loving office mate, had put together fake documents to trick him. But two of the three letters had come via certified mail, so McCauley concluded they were genuine. Kelly, as cost-conscious as McCauley, would never have gone to such expensive lengths.

Unfortunately, the offers only complicated his situation. They were all contingent, of course, on the successful completion and defense of his dissertation. To accept one of the jobs would rule out any possibility of revising his thesis to cover up his plagiaristic tracks, which was Robin's solution to his dilemma. "Make a clean start," she kept saying—and her idea certainly had a lot of appeal. But so did taking a position as an assistant professor at a state school in California or Utah or Washington state, far from the personal miasma of his Midwest history. Keeping to his current path, keeping his secret hidden and hoping it stayed that way, was fraught with its own potential peril, no doubt. Should an employer learn later about his academic dishonesty, the revelation would be grounds for his termination and might wreck any chances for other jobs. Still, as McCauley studied the professional landscape, he noticed that more and more cases like his were being swept under the rug of increased academic freedom, an environment that relaxed the standards for the educational use of intellectual property. Even if he were exposed down the road, he might be excused without serious consequences. Who could tell? He might even be held up as a hero for keeping alive a great idea. Stranger things had happened.

The slow-moving river filled his heart with peace. He could sit here for hours, he thought.

He was so close to reaching his goal! The start of it, anyway, the first rung on the ladder. Once he was *on* the ladder, he expected to climb quickly to widespread honor and recognition.

Often he thought of himself as *destined* for that kind of shimmering academic fame. The last time he had met with Erin Delaney before she turned in her fantastic research project, she was bursting with pride at her work. "It's made me think I was *made* to work with old people," she declared. "I never knew that until spending so much time with them, doing this project." For many years, whenever McCauley thought of being *made* for radical historical scholarship, he attributed the plan and purpose to the Universal Clock. That was another way his relationship with Robin was transforming him—the deistic explanation no longer satisfied him. It was too impersonal, as Robin had insisted all along. If there was a power above and beyond this world, he wanted it to have a face and a voice.

Thinking about these things, about Travis and Robin and the thesis and the Universal Clock, unsettled him. He could probably finish his work this spring—at Riverside and at Brookstone—without Robin even learning about Travis's death. Nevertheless, he hated keeping a secret from her because she had been so supportive about Mary Ann Childress and even about Travis. She had never condemned him.

A police cruiser on patrol swung into the parking area nearby. The officer waved to McCauley and drove away. A couple of kids with fishing poles emerged from the trees on the opposite bank of the river.

No, Robin had never condemned him. She had hurt him, though. She had unintentionally belittled him with her criticism of his passivity, even when it shifted to encouragement to fight the Brookstone cheating. When he had changed his mind, he knew he was doing the right thing, yet the fact that it had come at her behest was somewhat emasculating.

On the other hand, once he had jumped back into that fight alongside Robin and Erin, he felt not only justified but also powerful, almost fearless. The night of the break-in, as the three of them hid in the closet and overheard Myers and LaGrange spilling secrets, he knew he was in the right place. He truly believed he would have physically attacked Tolan Myers if he had opened that closet door. Those were heady, intoxicating minutes. The adrenaline rush was thrilling, nearly addicting. For hours afterward he tried to think of similar risks they might take—*he* might take. And earlier that week, when Myers and LaGrange reported to him that they were siding with the six first-semester plagiarists and overturning the failing grades McCauley had given them, he took their rejection in stride. Myers himself, gloating, barely able to contain his glee, informed him of the official decision. Yet McCauley could afford to be patient. He would have the last laugh.

Thinking about *that*—the battle against the cheating and Myers— filled him with energy. One of his grad school classmates owned a gun, and McCauley had even thought about asking to borrow it, for protection. Then he realized he had an even greater weapon in the stolen information. When the time came, that evidence would be worth more than an assault rifle. He had no reason to fear for his safety.

Five minutes later, the sounds of crunching gravel signaled the arrival of a silver Chevy Malibu.

Pete Doty climbed out, dressed like a hiker, wearing boots and a bandana. Without a word he shook hands with McCauley and emptied the contents of his haversack on the picnic table before he dramatically announced: "This is dynamite."

"What do you mean?"

"All this." He indicated the documents, then took a swig from his plastic water bottle.

Doty was medium height and slightly overweight, about forty years old, with short brown hair and pudgy cheeks. The few previous times they had met, McCauley had taken away mixed impressions. Doty laughed a lot and had an easy-going, joyful personality that belied the earnest, serious attitude he took toward his work—toward *this* work, at least. Robin's description of Doty's "presence" was on target if hard to explain. When he spoke, you tended to listen.

He said, "I mentioned that I was moving in this direction once before, but I never followed up with you. I *have* started collaborating with a reporter at the Indy *Star* about this. I've worked with him before on stories that seem … too *big*, I guess I would say, for our local Bridgebury newspaper to try to handle. Are you okay with that?"

Before McCauley could answer, Doty continued, "I'm not really asking, I guess. I'm telling. As I said, this is dynamite. This is a story that needs to be researched and needs to be told. I realize you're right in the middle of it, and what happens when we eventually publish what we have will affect you, so more than anything else I guess I'm just giving you advance notice."

"So …" McCauley began. "So this is all *real?*" He felt foolish as soon as the words left his lips. Still, his question was honest. Until hearing Doty speak so frankly from his more objective perspective, McCauley had nursed a tiny suspicion that everything he and Robin and Erin had been uncovering was all one monstrous mistake—that everything had an explanation that fell far short of criminal corruption.

Doty snickered. "More real than you ever imagined. You need to read the manuscript file you gave me. Myers's book. It spells out everything. As soon as the authorities get hold of it, he's a dead man. Figuratively speaking. Professionally speaking."

After the break-in, McCauley had skimmed the first chapter of the pilfered electronic manuscript, far enough to know he needed to forward it to Doty. Now, based on Doty's words, he was glad he had kept a copy.

Doty stared out over the river, pensively.

"You going hiking?" McCauley asked.

"When we finish here. Lemme show you what all we have."

They sat across from each other at the table, and one by one Doty went through the documents. McCauley was stunned. The files they had copied from Myers's computer, according to Doty, included lists of students, parents, faculty, civic leaders, business figures, even school board members who played some role in propping up the system, whose roots went back for at least ten years. There was proof that Myers accepted bribes directly from parents, who were more than happy to "invest" in their children now to save possibly tens of thousands of dollars of college costs later. There were organizational charts and files that "read like start-up materials Myers could send to other officials or school systems." There were tips on how to dig up dirt on opponents, and what dirt was best for keeping participants—teachers, students, and parents—quiet. There were audio files, taped telephone conversations between Myers (and sometimes LaGrange) and various interested parties from elsewhere in Indiana and from other states.

Doty swept the separate piles of material into a single stack and stuffed it back into a file folder.

"Now," he said, "let me try to give you a handle on the ..."—he dramatically spread his arms—"the *scope* of all this. And by *this*, I mean all the work that you and Robin Hillis and your student Erin have done." He pointed at the manila folder.

Then he chuckled in a simpering, almost condescending manner.

"Have you looked at the documents I sent you? The transcripts and all?"

"Not as thoroughly as I want to," McCauley replied, truthfully but defensively. "I've just been too busy." He rested his hand on his own folder of ungraded papers. "I was hoping to get to them today, if I ever got through these tests. But no, ever since your stuff arrived in the mail, it's been sitting on a table at my apartment. Even Robin has looked at them more than I have."

"Well, then, let me give you a summary."

Doty shared what he and his Indianapolis colleague had discovered about similar cheating scandals or rumors in other parts of the country. Editors and publishers were beginning to coordinate their efforts with the intent of going public together on a particular date—as yet undetermined but likely before the end of the month.

"The financial evidence is the most interesting," Doty said. "There's the usual stuff, like records of payments, bank account information, and so on. And there's a bunch of files on paying off government officials most likely, because instead of names we're finding codes like CC1, SB2, and so on. The guy from the *Star* says he's seen those items before, and they probably stand for School Board, County Commissioners, things like that. There are also records of payments received from transfer students—some kids or their families are paying $25,000 to get into Brookstone. Everybody wants to come to your school because they think it guarantees they can get into pretty much any college in America. Myers and LaGrange are raking in a ton of money."

"How much?"

"It's hard to say. There would be a big margin of error, but I would estimate in the hundreds of thousands of dollars per year."

"Are you kidding me?"

Doty shook his head and gazed expansively over the river.

"So you see, what we're doing—what you and your friends started—is major. It's a good thing you're on your way out of the area, because once this hits, your life might get pretty uncomfortable. You can't ruffle the kinds of feathers we're talking about, with this much money involved, and not expect a lot of blowback."

McCauley's thoughts rushed to Robin. What would her future be like?

"Do you feel safe?" Doty asked.

"What does *that* mean?"

"I'm serious. You've already been attacked and had your apartment broken into, right? What makes you think it's over?"

For all of McCauley's recent muddled thinking, and for all his slowness to see the truth, he now accepted that he held the upper hand over Myers. Over the past few days he had envisioned confronting Myers in a dramatic way, asking for payment to withhold the evidence—what a turnabout that would be!—or forcing Myers to resign or retire from his job. McCauley's leverage was indisputable, even if Myers didn't know about it. But would those financial records and other documents be admissible in a legal courtroom, since they had been obtained illegally? McCauley didn't want to think about getting lawyers involved.

"It's probably not over, is all I'm saying," Doty went on.

"So ... what do we do next?" McCauley asked.

"Wait, there's one more thing. You really need to read that manuscript file. It's the most damning evidence, assuming it's Myers's real story. He actually says in there that he wants to set the record straight and come clean."

"I don't get it."

"Can't you see? He's probably going to ride this cheating train as long as he can. Then when it runs out of track, he's already got a back-up plan to keep making money, by writing a book and probably becoming a star consultant or witness on the other side."

McCauley shook his head in reluctant wonder. Every time he thought he was giving Myers his due, the old cheater showed him a new level of cleverness.

"I should just send copies of the file to everyone who might be able to do something about it," McCauley suggested. "Anonymously."

"Except as you've told me, you don't know which people are trustworthy and which ones aren't. Half your recipients might be part of the system."

"Right."

"I really do have leverage against Myers now," McCauley said, aware of his pleading tone. He wanted Doty to agree with him. "He has to know I've been in his office and gotten my safe back. He may not know we stole computer files, but if he comes against me in any way now, all I have to do is drop a hint or two about what I know."

Doty eyed him, calculating.

"You could do that," he nodded. "But remember this. If he gets wind of what we're doing, he's liable to disappear before he is brought to justice. He has the means. He probably has enough money in hidden accounts to be someplace like Brazil tomorrow. So unless you absolutely have to, don't let him know what you know."

"All right." He exulted in the fact of his power—he was in a position utterly upside-down from what he was used to.

"You're doing a great thing," Doty said. "You have a lot to be proud of."

McCauley beamed. Hearing this from Doty somehow made him want to carry the campaign even further, even if that was no longer necessary. He could relax now if he wanted, kick back and wait for the newspaper's bombshell report. But he burned to go the offensive, to keep taking the fight to Myers.

He thought of something else: "Did you find anything to explain those numbers, *1-2-3-4*, that kept showing up on the files?"

"Oh, yes," Doty answered. "Those numbers mean a lot of things, it looks like. As Myers and LaGrange refined their scheme, they referred to it as the *1-2-3-4* system. Some of the audio files called it "twelve-thirty-four." Whatever, Myers was really proud of that, in his manuscript. They used the numbers a lot of ways. On one level, they talked about success at Brookstone being as simple as *1-2-3-4*. Each number stands for a link in the chain, so to speak. One is attitude, two is high expectations, three is tradition, and four is something else abstract like that. The manuscript says the school would talk about *1-2-3-4* all the time, put it on signs, posters, you name it."

"Yeah, that's been going on all year," McCauley agreed.

"But then there was another meaning," continued Doty. "He actually spells this out in the book! One stood for students, two for parents, three for teachers, and four for community leaders—and all four were different constituencies or groups served by the system, and all four were part of the overall revenue stream. He tries to go *literary* at one point and sets up a table metaphor, with the *1-2-3-4* as the four legs. He goes into terrific detail. You've gotta read the manuscript."

Doty returned his folder to his haversack.

"That's all I have for now," he said. "I'll keep you in the loop, and you do the same."

"Great," McCauley said. He regretted not having met Doty until this late hour of his time in the Bridgebury area. Everything about the man impressed him.

"You know, there was rather famous suicide here a few years ago," Doty said, nodding toward the river. "Upstream maybe fifty or sixty yards, as I recall. One of your Riverside grad students."

"I've not heard about that."

"Some guy drowned himself. Just dropped into the river and gave up. It made a splash—no pun intended—because a lot of people said there was no way you could actually drown yourself, so it must have been homicide. Then it came out later that he had a lot of bizarre ideas about life, mental problems I suppose."

"Weird," said McCauley.

"And another time, some kid drove his car into the river right off this landing, then waded out of the river and walked all the way back to Bridgebury. That *was* part of a homicide. Lots of weird things happened here."

"What's your point?"

"I don't know. Just don't do anything stupid, all right?"

"Don't worry."

"Take care," Doty returned to his car, left the haversack, and began striding through an open area next to the restored French fur-trading fort that was the centerpiece of this small tract of state park land. Soon he disappeared over a hill toward the river.

McCauley unzipped a side pocket on his backpack and withdrew a folded paper, which he carefully opened. After talking to Doty, he was thankful that he had listened to Robin's advice and made a copy of what he now held in his shaking hands—the so-called suicide note from Steve Gutierrez to Joe Floyd. For the fiftieth time at least, McCauley read the short message. For the first time, he began to comprehend its structure:

Dear Joe—

Here's the money I owed you. Sorry it took me so long to pay it. I also want to tell you a few things I found out recently.

ATTITUDE DON'T REALLY COUNT FOR NOTHING IN OUR SCHOOL. MONEY IS WHAT TALKS.

HIGH EXPECTATIONS…RIGHT! THE ONLY THING THEY EXPECT IS ME TO KEEP MY MOUTH SHUT. TOO BAD FOR THEM.

TRADITION. DON'T EVEN GET ME STARTED ON THAT. ITS THE BIGGEST CROCK OF YOU KNOW WHAT I EVER SMELLED. I NEVER KNEW UNTIL MYERS JUST TOLD ME ALL ABOUT IT.

HARD WORK, WELL, ALL I GOT TO SAY ABOUT THAT IS THE HARDEST WORKING PEOPLE ARE THE ONES TAKING ALL THE MONEY AND FOR WHAT? JUST TO KEEP THE LIE GOING ABOUT MIGHTY BROOKSTONE HIGH. IT ALL MAKES ME WANT TO PUKE.

THAT'S IT I GUESS. THANKS TO MYERS NOW YOU CAN SEE WHAT I THINK ABOUT SUCCESS IS AS EASY AS *1-2-3-4*. IT MEANS SOMETHING NOBODY KNOWS ABOUT OR NOBODY IS BRAVE ENOUGH TO SAY IT OUT LOUD. WHAT A LOAD OF BS!!!!!

McCauley breathed through his nose. Since first seeing the note in ¿Que Pasa?, neither he nor Robin had come up with any theories about the *1-2-3-4* pattern or imagery in the note. Plainly it had something to do with the Brookstone slogan on one level, but what more was Steve Gutierrez getting at through his broken, enraged language?

Myers must have showed Steve what was really going on behind the scenes, McCauley surmised, *just like he showed me. He is so arrogant. He thinks nobody can touch him. But he can't get away from me now.*

He shouldered his backpack and went down the sloping, furrowed concrete landing to the river. Its muddy waters lapped against the banks.

13

FOR A CHANGE, Erin Delaney felt free of pressure.

Three colleges had accepted her for admission (one of which she had actually applied to) and it was only a matter of time until she had the inevitable confrontation with her parents. However, her father had just spent four days at a convention for cardiologists in Dallas, which gave her a breather from his nagging about her paralysis over a college decision. And since he had come home, the backlog of work at his office in Bridgebury was occupying his every minute and diverting his attention.

As for Matt, she had successfully ended her relationship with him. In fact, breaking up at the baseball game had been so easy that she feared something had gone terribly wrong—or maybe something now would go terribly wrong as the universal scales returned to equilibrium. Matt talked to her every day, often reminding her that she had agreed to help him with an "assignment" whose deadline, he claimed, was fast approaching. Being "just friends" with Matt was turning out to be far more gratifying than she ever would have imagined, so she did not mind the one remaining commitment to him. Except for his unwillingness to talk about Steve Gutierrez and the grave-digging adventure, he was treating her as well as ever. At least he hadn't frozen her out of his life altogether, as some guys did with their ex-girlfriends.

But best of all, earlier that day she had done her required "oral interview" with Mr. McCauley to review her research project. A week before, she had received back the written part, with not only an A-plus grade but also a full page of handwritten praise for her persistence, originality, and passion. So she knew she had passed the assignment with flying colors. Still, the ten-minute, face-to-face meeting was the highlight of her day.

Mr. McCauley started by reminding her of the reason for the interview.

"In college, and beyond college, you won't have many paper-and-pencil tests with mostly multiple choice and fill-in-the-blank answers," he explained. "You'll have to talk to people and think on your feet. So consider this little meeting as a way to get some practice."

"Right," she said. He had repeated the same spiel in class every time he reviewed the parts of the overall project assignment.

Erin was a little nervous that he might ask her something she would struggle to answer, but no—all he wanted was for her to explain how the project had helped her (a) grow in her understanding of her subject matter, and (b) grow as a thinker or as a person. That was all! She easily talked for ten minutes, covering every angle she could think of about the experience of doing her own oral interviews with the Lake Haven residents, school work that led her to volunteer to come back in her spare time and serve the elderly folks by reading newspapers, magazines, letters from loved ones, recipes, chapters from her textbooks, and especially, sadly, obituaries. Erin could have told stories for hours. She never even got to part (b) of Mr. McCauley's question. As her answer expanded, shooting off onto various tangents as she thought of them, his smile kept widening beneath his bushy mustache. Finally he laughed and cut her off, saying he had to get to the next student.

"But one more thing," she said, bursting with emotion. "I just have to thank you for helping me so much and letting me change my project and showing me *how* to change it." She shook her head and looked away, fighting back tears. "Really," she finished, "it was more than any teacher has ever done for me, more than I ever imagined. More than I deserved."

A stretch of silence followed, which made her glance up. Mr. McCauley was staring at her with an odd expression on his face, but he never stopped smiling.

"Your project was—is—fabulous," he said. "I was honored to help you with it. If I were going to keep teaching here, I would ask your permission to use it in the future as a model for everyone else. You really are good at research!"

After school, swelling with pride, she hurried to Lake Haven to share the great news with Grandpa Dee.

She set a bowl of freshly popped corn on the table and salted it liberally, the way Grandpa liked it. He had excused himself to use the bathroom. Next to the popcorn she placed her research paper and a DVD—he would probably not even know what the shiny disc was—to spark conversation. Outside, through the sliding glass door to his patio, she could see across the way that the fountain had been turned on in the pond, and an arc of water was shooting from the mouth of the concrete statue of the child, a sparkling parabola. Funny, she had never noticed the irony before, the contrast of the child in the middle of an old folk's home.

Final exams were next week. Later that night she was planning to join Jess and Matt and a few other history classmates at Jess's house to start reviewing for their exam. Mr. McCauley had given them a long list of terms to know and promised extra credit if they created note cards. Those definitions would be only a small part of the exam, of course, but any excuse to be away from her house was welcome.

Far and away, the most interesting part of her life right now was her ongoing furtive alliance with Mrs. Hillis and Mr. McCauley. A few weeks earlier they had sneaked into Mr. Myers's office and copied the files on his computer and recovered Mr. McCauley's safe—what could possibly top that excitement! Maybe that was how Matt and his buddies felt, living on the edge with their incessant wagering and bungee jumping. But the *secrecy*, that was what made her adventure so fun and special. Hour by hour she sat next to friends and acquaintances who had no clue what she—their humdrum, boring, antisocial, nondescript, plain-Jane classmate—was up to behind the routine scenes of school life. They were busy with sports and prom preparation and college plans. She was about to turn the school upside down.

According to both Mrs. Hillis and Mr. McCauley, so far there had been no repercussions from their burglary. That meant one of two things, they figured. One, there was no knowledge or suspicion of their activity. Two, Mr. Myers and Mr. LaGrange were quietly planning a counter-attack of some kind. The teachers thought that Mr. Myers had to know the safe had disappeared from his office, meaning they were biding their time, waiting to respond—and then Mr. McCauley would spring into action, revealing the devastating information that would defeat the crooked administrators and topple the corrupt system. However, Erin thought it was equally likely that Mr. Myers did *not* know the safe was gone because he had taken it only to send a message to Mr. McCauley, not to steal it contents, and that once he had stolen it he forgot about having it in his possession. After all, they had discovered it stuck under a table, out of the way, basically invisible in the office.

Erin heard a thud and a whimper from the bathroom.

She hurried to the closed door and called, "Grandpa? Is everything all right?"

"No," she heard him cry. "I fell!"

She opened the door and found him sprawled on the linoleum floor, grimacing and trying to pull himself up to a sitting position. Then he screamed and grabbed at his thigh—and one leg looked a few inches shorter than the other. Erin panicked. Thoughts bounced around inside her skull, intersecting in dizzying angles. She knew that older people often fell and had brittle bones, and that nobody was sure whether a broken bone resulted from falling or caused the falling. She fought to ignore that trivia and focus on Grandpa Dee.

The next hour passed in a painful blur. Somehow she must have called her mom, or called 9-1-1, or called the Lake Haven office. Somehow she must have called somebody, because help arrived in waves, first the Lake Haven staff, nurses and doctors, then paramedics in an ambulance. Erin watched in a daze, blankly munching popcorn. Her mom arrived as the paramedics struggled in the confined space of the bathroom to move Grandpa and lift him, screaming in agony, onto the stretcher. Then, as he was being wheeled out to the ambulance, her dad arrived and immediately took the lead in directing the paramedics to his choice of a hospital—in Bridgebury, not Orange Stone—and in assuring Grandpa that everything would be all right. Erin was impressed with her dad's authority, composure, and compassion. She had seldom seen him in his professional element. Once the paramedics understood he was a doctor, he was permitted to ride in the ambulance.

Erin rode with her mother to the hospital. On the way, Mom said that Matt had called her three times after school and sounded anxious over the phone.

"I don't care about him right now," Erin insisted, honestly.

At the emergency room they waited in a comfortable area with a TV playing *Wheel of Fortune*. Erin made a mental note of the total prize amount—$48,000—to tell Grandpa Dee. Meanwhile, her mom made phone calls to Patti and Sarah, leaving messages for each. Then she paced nervously and kept getting drinks of water in cheap conical cups from the bubbling dispenser in one corner. Uncle Jerry arrived, followed soon after by Uncle Chuck, and they conferred with Erin's mom in low voices.

Thirty minutes later Dad came out and ushered them all back to see Grandpa, who was lying down, his lower half covered by a white linen, an IV drip already hanging from an aluminum pole next to his bed. Dad said it was a pain-killer. Grandpa's eyes were open but distant, studying the ceiling.

"He's a bit out of it right now," Dad said. "But we can talk to him. He's scheduled for surgery in an hour."

"So fast!" Chuck blurted.

"There's no reason to wait," Dad explained softly, efficiently. "It's a clean break, the kind elderly people get all the time. They'll screw a brace or plate onto the bone to give it more strength, and they'll actually have him up on his feet in a day or so."

"Will he be able to walk again?" asked Erin.

"Yes. But he may need a walker or a cane. We'll just have to see, as he goes through therapy. The nice thing about Lake Haven is that he can go through the rehab right there."

Erin wondered why they wouldn't just bring him home to their house, at least for a while.

She hovered over Grandpa until his eyes focused on her. His mouth formed words but Erin couldn't hear him. Finally she just said, "We're here with you, Grandpa! You'll be well soon!" And she kissed his smooth forehead.

At Dad's suggestion, they went for Arby's sandwiches then returned to the hospital. Erin decided to stay through the operation. Fortunately she had brought her history homework with her. Chuck and Jerry left, intending to keep in touch and come back if necessary. Dad came and went from the emergency area. The surgery was supposed to take only an hour—amazing, in Erin's opinion. Within the span of less than six hours Grandpa Dee would fall, break his hip, be taken to a hospital, have the break set, have a metal piece attached to the bone, get stitched back together, and be up taking a few steps. Her Dad kept telling everyone that nothing in that painful sequence was out of the ordinary.

She felt so comforted by Dad's expertise and command of the situation—but her spirits took a nosedive when he sat down next to her and said, "Let's talk about college."

She shut her book nervously.

"Let me get a drink first," she said. On her way back, she lingered at a wall decorated with nature photos, trees and clouds and wide-open spaces. She didn't want to argue with her dad right now. She would rather be wading in the Orange River at the Junction or dangling her legs from its bridge. Why would Dad bring up such a sensitive topic at such a terrible time? Shouldn't they be worrying about Grandpa?

She steeled herself as much as she thought possible.

"I keep opening your mail from Princeton," her dad began, "because you just seem to ignore it. This latest piece is asking you to confirm your acceptance. Why haven't you done that?"

She wanted to just shrug and plead her busy-ness and lack of time. Instead, she told the truth: "Dad, I have been trying to tell you this for months, every time you bring it up. I don't want to go to Princeton." Then, before he could respond, she added, "I want to go to Riverside. I want to go to Riverside and study forestry." She elected to keep her mouth shut about her more recent interest in elderly care.

Dad nodded and looked at the floor.

After a spell of silence he said, "I thought we had agreed—"

She cut him off, anger surging in her soul.

"*I never agreed to anything!* You and Mom agreed, but you never gave me any say!"

"But don't you want to—"

"No, Dad! I don't!" The she felt suddenly embarrassed, for she had no idea how he was going to finish his sentence.

Her emotion, however, apparently convinced him that she did know. He said, "Okay. I see ..." She wondered what he saw.

She explained in clear words and a calm tone that on her own, she had already applied to Riverside, paid the small fees out of her own money, and been accepted. Dad continued nodding, grasping for words.

His reaction startled her. Never in her life had she seen him speechless, and after watching him take such confident control of the situation of Grandpa Dee's accident, she wondered what had suddenly paralyzed him. Surely not her standing up for herself!

She actually felt embarrassed, sorry for him, so she looked toward the ceiling, where a fan was rotating rapidly, silently. Her thoughts shot to the Junction Bridge, to the whirlwind, whose memory kept swirling new insights into her introspection. Gradually through the school year she had sensed that something or someone was trying to help her, reaching into her life—not as obviously and violently as the whirlwind, perhaps, but with equal effect. For a while she imagined it was Mrs. Hillis; then she thought or hoped it was Nathan. Neither choice seemed right. Now, watching the spinning blades above her, she entertained the idea that it might be *herself.* It was hard to believe.

Her father said, falteringly, "I also thought we ... Don't you want to go to the best school we can find? Even if your grades aren't perfect, there are ways around that, too."

He did not see her roll her eyes. *Ways around that* ... right.

"I could just see you as a doctor of some kind. I've always had that dream, that maybe we could even be in practice together."

"Dad!"

"Don't you see that we're just doing what's best for you?"

She could stand it no longer.

"No, Dad! I'm glad you have a career you like, but *the Good Lord didn't make everyone to be a doctor!*"

As she rose in agitation, he slumped backward in his seat. Erin could see that her words had hit home—Dad looked as though she had just announced that she was pregnant or ashamed to be his daughter, or that he was a quack with a medical license from a fly-by-night internet college. Like Grandpa Dee two hours earlier, his lips appeared to be forming words that carried no sound.

Finally he mumbled, "Okay. We'll talk about it more later."

Erin sought the best way to renew and amplify her objection. She sensed she had gained momentum in the debate. She had an advantage and wanted to press it, just as she had learned to do in the game of Risk. However, she was spared the trouble because at that moment the surgeon pushed into the room, smiling, reaching to shake her dad's hand.

"Everything was smooth, Sam. No complications of any kind. He'll be fine."

Her dad's emotions rallied. He thanked the surgeon, whose name badge read LANCE, four or five times.

Then Erin received a jolt of surprise—Matt Rademacher walked into the waiting room.

Plainly he felt out of place, and plainly he felt the only way to justify his presence was to give her a hug, which he did, clumsily.

"I heard from Jess," he said. "Is he okay?"

"The doctor said the operation went fine," she said. Then, with no time to weigh the possible consequences, she tugged on his jacket and pulled him toward the water cooler, saying, "I'm so glad you're here." Just in case Dad wanted to renew his college-application assault, she might be able to use Matt as a human shield.

Content that her father was out of earshot, she gave Matt a blow-by-blow of their confrontation. She searched the lines of Matt's face for sympathy, but found none. He was here for another reason, she remembered now.

"What is it?" she asked. "Mom said you were trying to get me."

Now it was Matt's turn to look troubled by the presence of other people nearby. He set his heavy hand on her shoulder, whispered, "Outside," and guided her into the lobby area.

"Matt, you're scaring me," she said.

"Come on."

She followed him out the door and along the sidewalk, where, finally satisfied with their privacy, he turned toward her, his face white with the illumination from the nearest parking lot light, and said, "Myers wants me to kill McCauley."

14

SPOTTING CHEATERS WAS easy, now that she knew their signs and secrets.

Robin Hillis circulated among the tables where nearly a hundred students were taking their final exams in English. A few years earlier, Brookstone had adopted a schedule for finals structured around courses rather than class periods. Everyone took his or her math final on the same day at the same time, for example. The same for social studies courses, for science courses, and so on. For English, that meant every student in the school was simultaneously taking an exam in either the Media Center, the cafeteria, or the gymnasium. Robin and one other English teacher, Butch Young, were supervising the Media Center testing.

And dozens of students were cheating.

Everything she and Brad McCauley and Erin Delaney had learned during their investigation had turned her into an expert. She noticed some students giving undue attention to their water bottles, and others coughing repeatedly into their hands or carefully folded handkerchiefs. Still other students kept carefully adjusting and readjusting clothing, shirts or dresses or scarves, or slipping their feet into and out of shoes. She wondered why so many students were removing eyeglasses and cleaning them—but she assumed that was some new tactic or technology, some new attempt by cheaters to keep one step ahead of whoever might try to stop them—if anyone would.

Yes, if anyone would even try. Did anybody really care? She was happy that the other English teacher in the room was not Mitch Adams, whose name had come up in many of their stolen files and documents as a teacher clearly in league with Myers and LaGrange. She wasn't sure about Butch Young, either, but she had no evidence that his hands were dirty.

Moving stealthily among the tables, she began jotting down her observations. Names. Objects. Clothing, accessories. Postures. Gestures. Patterns of behavior.

Even if she turned in her suspicions and evidence to the administration, nothing would come of it. Even if she caught a cheater red-handed, nothing would come of it. Still, she felt her enthusiasm for justice swelling.

What could it hurt to blow the whistle? Not long ago she had feared that her role in the secret crusade might culminate in her firing, but not now, for the momentum had shifted when they hacked into Myers's computer. Without having any solid reason for her confidence, she imagined that Myers and LaGrange were back on their heels, "fighting defensively" as Erin had called it, using a bit of military terminology she had picked up from the game of Risk. And with an outside party in the form of Pete Doty now waist-deep in information and involvement, the war against cheating really would be finished, soon enough. The moment the story broke in the media, Myers and LaGrange and countless others would be exposed for the frauds they were.

She dared not become overconfident, though. They might still suffer casualties from a defiant, desperate enemy. Brad claimed that history was full of examples. And even though the school board had let her off with what amounted to a slap on the wrist, she knew they could change their minds any time—especially since the superintendent, Walter Patingale, appeared to be as dirty as Myers or LaGrange.

Robin breathed in deeply and let out a prolonged, profound sigh.

What an emotional roller coaster she was riding! The last month had hurtled her through sorrow and release, grace, anger, pride …

Her momentum was taking her in the right direction, though. For the first time in many months she could honestly say that.

Here she was, disgusted and outraged by the school's cheating culture. Yet only a few weeks before, she had finally told her husband about her cheating, her affair with Brad McCauley. For far too long she had postponed that confession, even as their love rekindled—the last thing she ever believed could happen, a miracle, really. Yes, she had actually rejected Brad and reconciled with Zeb. The night when she tearfully blurted the humiliating truth, Zeb simply said, "Well, that was *my* fault, *too*." Oh! She deserved to be spat on and abandoned—really abandoned, forever—but instead Zeb had taken part of the blame! There had been a time when his little word *too* would have filled her with fury, for she wanted to lay the blame *entirely* in his lap. Then for a time she conceded that they shared in the guilt equally. More recently she had admitted that everything was her fault. And finally he had absolved her! She did not deserve such mercy.

She had been saved by grace, as she was always being saved by grace. This time it had come through her dear neighbors, Howard and Jerri, but more so through Zeb. And behind it all, of course, too big and too obvious and too unchanging to think about, behind it all stood the grace of heaven. After months of pleading with God to vindicate her before her wayward husband and to condemn Zeb, God had done something marvelously greater.

Life was bursting with irony, though. Tragic irony? Maybe. The next time she talked to Brad after telling Zeb about him, she was curious to see what Brad would say. He knew that sooner or later she was going to tell Zeb, and the time when he might have hoped to win her back had passed.

Yet he tried.

"You need to think for yourself," he said. "You can do whatever you choose."

That statement was ironic, considering their many arguments about his clockwork philosophy, which denied the reality of free will, of people making real choices.

"You are your own person, Robin," he said.

"Not really," she replied. "I'm not really my own. I've been bought and paid for."

"By Zeb?" He laughed cynically. "That's a funny way to describe marriage."

"No," she started to say, "I mean—"

What was the use? Brad could not understand. For all his intelligence, he could not understand. No matter how long and how hard she tried to explain, he could not understand. That was the biggest irony, the tremendous chasm between them.

She was bought and paid for. The great truth whispered along the infinite corridor of eternity and nestled in her heart.

She counted her blessings while she walked home after school, but her anger about the school cheating did not subside in the least.

Across the street Lena and Philip were playing baseball catch. Robin waved and Lena called, "You're almost done!" probably referring to finals week, not knowing that the kind statement could cover so much more.

Inside, she called Zeb and confirmed that he had a meeting in Bridgebury and planned to eat in town. He said he would be home by nine o'clock. How nice it was to be able to trust him again, to know that he really would be home and snuggling with her before a TV movie or sitting nearby while she graded final exams.

What a joke! In truth, final exams were the last thing on her mind. Did they really mean anything?

She made some coffee and sat down at her computer, drafting an e-mail message in her mind. Her plan proceeded in fits and starts. Within an hour she had decided to send the accusatory e-mail and attach all the documentation she had assembled during the English exam. Among the electronic evidence that she and Erin and Brad had filched from Myers was a mailing list. Pete Doty had combed through its contents and believed it to contain the names of everyone remotely associated with the *1-2-3-4* system—students, parents, teachers, administrators, school board officials, even local business leaders. Using a junk account that Zeb had set up with a bogus user name, Robin sent the e-mail to everyone on the list and copied the governor of Indiana at his general government address listed on the state web site. He was scheduled to be at Brookstone on Friday.

She also copied Doty. Only after she hit the send button did it occur to her that maybe, just maybe, Doty too was part of the scandal.

Next she put together flyers. Under a bold heading CHEATERS she spelled out her accusations and names of her suspects, both students and teachers. She found some colored copy paper and printed about a hundred flyers in various colors. Inspecting them, she found that the printer's ink cartridge had run out near the end of the job.

That did not matter.

For dinner she microwaved leftover chicken and rice. Then she called Brad, whom she had not seen at school that afternoon, and told him what she had witnessed proctoring the exam.

"I'm going back there tonight," she said. "Tomorrow morning everyone in the school will know what happened!"

"What are you talking about?"

She outlined her plan.

"Be careful, Robin," he said. "If Myers even suspects his empire is about to crumble around him, there's no telling what he might do."

"I know, but I can't sit and do nothing anymore. Any word from Pete Doty?"

"No. Last I heard, he's still thinking the story may run any day now. He said for maximum effect they would want to run it to coincide with the governor's visit. He also said the paper would never blindside a local school, so an editor or the publisher will give LaGrange or the school superintendent a heads-up."

"You mean ... what? They might *not* run their story?"

"No, I don't think that's what he meant. But they would give the school officials a chance to respond to the allegations or the evidence. Doty said that some of the problems are legal, so the newspaper is forwarding evidence to law enforcement people, too."

"It keeps getting bigger and bigger. What about you? Are you still planning to confront Myers? To rub his face in it?"

"I don't know. I'd like to. I really think I could end everything at once by just showing him what we have and demanding that he resign."

Around 7:15 Robin walked back to school, flyers in hand. She worked in her classroom for forty-five minutes then made a tour of the building and found it empty.

Her heart started to thump. She wished Brad were with her, to encourage her and protect her. Despite her anger, despite her belief in their cause, she feared coming face-to-face with Myers—and possibly staring down the barrel of his gun.

She began by taping flyers to the columns in the Atrium, creating a vivid juxtaposition between the airy studiousness of the Greek philosophers and her charges of academic corruption. She put flyers on random lockers then thought of a better idea—she looked up the locker numbers of students she knew had cheated that day and targeted their lockers. She papered over the photos of the school's academic superstars with flyers; she stuck flyers on the milk shake dispensers in the cafeteria and the soda pop machines in the athletic area; she slid flyers under locked doors of classrooms and administrative offices.

All the while, she kept thinking that she would never be running this race to the finish line unless she had returned to Zeb. She really wished he were here, even more than Brad McCauley.

Myers never appeared, but more than once she caught herself humming the senior song "I'll Take My Chances."

She ducked into restrooms and placed flyers in the stall doors, on the mirrors, on the paper towel dispensers. Then, as she was leaving the girls restroom closest to her classroom, she heard footsteps go past. They sounded too light and hurried to belong to Myers, so she felt brave enough to peek out—and she saw Erin's tall, slender form receding down the hallway and into her classroom.

Robin followed her. When she entered the door, Erin was sitting on a table, tears streaming down her face.

"Erin, what's wrong? Is it your grandpa?"

Erin collapsed in her arms, shaking her head, shuddering and sobbing.

"It's all my fault," she gasped, repeatedly.

"What's your fault?"

Robin was seized by a sudden certainty—the certainty of an English teacher who knew intuitively the way stories unfold—that something crucial was impending, rushing toward her at fantastic speed.

"Matt," she gasped. "He's going to kill Mr. McCauley. Tonight! And I helped him!"

15

HER VISION BLURRED by tears, Erin was barely aware of Mrs. Hillis nudging her into the hallway, shutting off the classroom lights, locking the door, and guiding her along with a motherly arm around her waist. They reached the Atrium, where they sat, surrounded by flyers proclaiming the day's travesty. Erin was just taking notice of their damning accusations when Mrs. Hillis said, "Shhh!" and led her to a spot in the shadows of a larger-than-life cardboard cutout of the governor set up that day as part of the festivities to come.

Erin felt adrenaline coursing through her, stimulating her, dispelling her emotional lethargy. Her eyes cleared and even her hearing grew acutely sensitive. From one direction footsteps approached, fast footsteps. Mr. Myers came into view, hurrying toward his office. He stopped at the door, fiddling with his keys beneath the security light above him on the wall. Then he paused, snatching the flyer from his door and flinging it aside with a string of profanity that reverberated ominously through the hollow Atrium. He disappeared into his office, leaving the outside door wide open.

Mrs. Hillis whispered, "Don't move."

Then Erin heard the creak of the door to the inside office. After some echoes of banging, the inside door slammed. A moment later Mr. Myers hesitated at the outside doorway again, a glint of light reflecting off his bald head and another from the metal object in his hand—his revolver. Erin gasped. She lurched backward, but Mrs. Hillis's steady hands gripped her shoulders.

Mr. Myers hurried away, his cell phone ringing.

Mrs. Hillis tugged at Erin's sleeve and they headed in the opposite direction. Soon they burst outdoors through a little-used exit into a dark parking lot.

"What is going on?" Erin asked.

"I should ask *you!*" Mrs. Hillis replied, an edge in her voice. "What is this you're saying about Matt killing Brad? And where is my—? Oh, I walked!"

For the first time ever, Erin heard Mrs. Hillis utter a swear word. Just as quickly she apologized and said, "Come on. Talk to me!"

They hurried along Dogwood Avenue.

Erin tried to talk, truly she did, but her thoughts were so muddled and fragmented that Mrs. Hillis became frustrated trying to assemble the scraps together into an intelligible account. Finally she started asking simple, pointed questions for Erin to answer, and by the time they made it to the Hillis's front porch swing, a coherent story was spilling from Erin's lips.

Matt, she said, held fast to the belief that Mr. Myers was responsible for the death of Steve Gutierrez, either directly by murdering him or indirectly by pressuring him into taking his own life. Throughout the current school year, Mr. Myers had pressured Matt to pay Steve's debt, and then Matt had incurred a debt of his own when Mr. Myers falsified some transcripts that went to several colleges where Matt was applying.

"That was his big mistake," Erin said. "He keeps saying he wishes he never asked Mr. Myers to do that. His life has been miserable ever since. It was already miserable because of Steve, but it got worse. And then he won the lottery."

"What did *that* have to do with anything?"

"Mr. Myers started asking for more money."

"I can't *believe* this. Why didn't you tell me this before, when we were doing all our detective work?"

Erin looked away. She had never heard Mrs. Hillis so angry.

"Matt didn't want anybody else to know."

"Okay, okay," Mrs. Hillis said, distracted. "But what about Brad? Why are you saying Matt wants to—"

"*Because he told me!*"

"But *why? Why* would he want to do that?"

Erin tried to explain but kept veering off on one tangent after another. Once again Mrs. Hillis refocused her with questions, listened to Erin's answers, and said at last:

"So, what I'm hearing is this: Once Brad started making waves, by not knuckling under to Myers and not overlooking the cheating that he caught, Myers went after him big time. And he had Matt doing his dirty work, right? Like beating up Brad and tying him to the railroad tracks, and stealing the safe from his apartment?"

Erin sniffled and nodded.

"We were pretty sure it was Matt involved both times," Mrs. Hillis said, "but we didn't want to tell you."

"Why not?" But Erin already knew why—Mr. McCauley and Mrs. Hillis suspected that *she* was a *spy*, really in league with Matt and Mr. Myers. Then why did they keep working with her? She recalled something Mr. McCauley had said once, in class, about the military strategy of keeping your friends close but your enemies even closer. She grew desperate now, trying to figure out the implications for her …

Then Mrs. Hillis answered, "Because we weren't sure, and we didn't want you to get hurt, or Matt for that matter. We knew whatever was going on, Myers was in back of it."

"Oh." She was stunned. "But … how did you know Matt was involved?"

"Your perfume. Brad smelled it at the railroad tracks, and … well, I never told you this either, but I was in Brad's apartment when Matt and somebody else broke in. I smelled that same fragrance there. So we figured it was Matt. He must have been with you before he came to the railroad tracks, or the apartment."

Erin felt the blood rising to her cheeks; she was thankful they were sitting in shadows.

"Actually, it's maybe not that I was with him," she said. "He likes that perfume so much he sometimes sprays it on his clothing. A good luck charm kind of thing, I think."

Mrs. Hillis chuckled.

"Anyway," she said, "this explains a lot of what's happened ever since we broke into Myers's office. We've been pretty certain that Myers knows we got the safe back, but we don't know what he knows about what we know. Does that make any sense?"

It did, perfect sense.

"The conflict has gone to a new level. And the danger. We made the last move, and now it's Myers's turn, and we're just waiting, wondering what he will do next."

Erin felt squeezed again. She stood up and settled on the porch rail, facing Mrs. Hillis. Something was bothering her, something she was trying to put together about Matt's behavior over many weeks. When they broke up at the baseball game, he had mentioned vaguely that he might need her help later for a final "assignment."

Now she knew what that was.

She blurted out, "Matt said Myers wanted him to get rid of McCauley. He never said to *kill* him, but Matt knew that's what he meant. He said McCauley had to be 'eliminated' or 'erased' or 'made to disappear.' Those were the exact words he said!"

Erin shook with rage, with an acute awareness of her impotence at being caught up in something too big to understand or fight. She turned to look at the road while she struggled to regain her composure. Dimly she felt her conscience complaining that she needed to use *Mister* in front of the teachers' names! How silly! Like a tidal wave, her anger smashed her scruples.

She faced Mrs. Hillis again and continued: "And Myers said that if Matt took care of that, then he wouldn't owe him anything. His debt would be paid in full. But I still don't know why Matt would have asked me to help him *so long ago*. He only got this 'final assignment' a few days ago, when I was with my grandpa at the hospital. Matt showed up there, he was so upset. But it was like a month ago that he first said anything about me helping him. I don't get it."

"I do," Mrs. Hillis said. "It's perfectly obvious, isn't it?"

Once again Erin felt glad for the darkness.

"Look," Mrs. Hillis said, "Matt was at the railroad tracks, and at Brad's apartment. So he knew that Myers was after Brad. So naturally he must have thought anything else Myers would have him do would involve Brad."

Erin sighed. Mrs. Hillis and Mr. McCauley were such clear thinkers!

"But Erin," Mrs. Hillis began. She rose, reached over with both hands and set them on Erin's shoulders. "Why do you think this is *your* fault?"

"Because when Matt called me earlier, he asked me to contact Mr. McCauley and have him meet me at the Junction. I was supposed to tell Mr. McCauley that you and I would meet him there to talk more about the cheating investigation. He wanted me to make up some lie about our finding new evidence, whatever it took to get Mr. McCauley to show up."

"And you did it?

"Well, sort of."

"*Sort of?* What does that mean?"

"First I argued with Matt. I told him he couldn't do something like Myers was asking. And then Matt said not to worry, that he was going to set things right, *set everything right*, he said."

"Meaning what?"

"I don't know. He wouldn't tell me. He just kept saying not to worry. So … I called Mr. McCauley, and told him to go the Junction. But then I told him why. The *real* reason, I told him the *real* reason."

"You warned him, then." Mrs. Hillis paced the porch.

"Why would Matt want to meet him at the Junction? Why not Dairy Queen?"

"Because nobody else would be there. It's away from everybody, and dark, and Matt has spent so much time on that bridge that he knows it backward and forward. He even found a place on the bridge to store bungee cords so he doesn't have to carry them around in his van all the time, and, and …" She slumped under a burden of guilt. "This is why it's my fault: Matt used me to get at Mr. McCauley. He knew Mr. McCauley would believe it if I said it had to do with our cheating investigation."

"Erin, do you really think Matt is going to try to kill Brad?" That sharp edge had crept back into Mrs. Hillis's voice.

Erin stared at the dark porch and mumbled, "He *could* do it. I think he would do *anything* to get clear of Myers."

"Okay then," Mrs. Hillis announced with finality. "We have to try to stop him. When are they meeting at the Junction? What time did you tell Mr. McCauley?"

"Matt told me to make it eleven o'clock."

"Where? Down by the river, or—"

"No. Matt insisted they meet *on the bridge*. On top, on the side. Where they bungee jump from."

"Come on."

They went inside for Mrs. Hillis's car keys. The message indicator light on her phone was flashing, so she pushed the PLAY button, and Mr. McCauley's nervous voice poured from the speaker. After starting to give a detailed message, he cut it off and said that Robin needed to call him at once, that this was an emergency. Mrs. Hillis punched the DELETE button, remarking that it must be urgent if he had risked leaving a message that her husband might hear. She swept her keys off a counter, along with her cell phone, and they rushed to the garage.

"Dial Brad's number," she told Erin as they backed out and headed up the street. She rattled off the ten digits. "Then hand me the phone."

Erin wished Mrs. Hillis would put the conversation on speaker. Mr. McCauley did nearly all the talking. Mrs. Hillis just held the phone to her ear and nodded, said "yes" several times, and asked a couple of questions such as, "He actually said that?" and "And then what did he say?" At last she said, "Be careful!" Then she handed the phone back to Erin.

"What did he say?" Erin asked excitedly. "Did he talk to Matt?"

"No."

Erin waited, wondering.

"He talked to Myers," Mrs. Hillis finished.

"Myers? Why? I don't get it."

"Neither do I."

They sped east on Highway 22. In the passenger-side mirror, Erin watched the twinkling lights of Brookstone recede behind them. The dashboard clock read 9:42. As soon as that early time registered in her thinking, she asked, "Where are we going?"

"To the Junction—before Matt and Brad."

"Why?" She leaned forward with anticipation, longing to hear Mrs. Hillis's plan.

"I don't know. I'm making this up as I go."

"Shouldn't we call the police?"

"Maybe. Probably. I don't know." Mrs. Hillis slapped the steering wheel, agitated. "Brad specifically said to *not* call the police. He said he had a plan."

She gripped the steering wheel tightly and swore again.

"*Brad* has a plan," she whined. "*Matt* has a plan. *Myers* has a plan. Everybody has a plan but *me*."

"I don't have a plan," Erin offered.

"Maybe it's just as well …"

A quiet minute passed, the rumble of the road almost soothing beneath them.

"I have been so afraid for Matt," Erin began.

"I know you have. You've told me all about it."

"I know, but …"

"But *what?*"

"I haven't told you everything." Erin did what Mrs. Hillis was always telling her and other teenagers to do: She got specific. She rattled off the scary statistics from the pamphlets she had picked up from the school's Guidance Office about teen suicide: 50,000 suicide attempts by young people aged 15-24 in Indiana during the previous year; a dozen youth suicides daily in the United States; and for every "completed" suicide, as many as 200 "incomplete" attempts. Then she regurgitated material from her sister's college psychology textbook about warning signs such as depression and withdrawal, anger and threats of revenge (like Matt sometimes breathed against Myers), and risky behavior (like the bungee jumping).

Mrs. Hillis listened respectfully but said nothing, her eyes glued to the road.

Everything Erin had learned, she summed up, convinced her that Steve Gutierrez's death was truly suicide. But it did more. It also got her thinking about Matt, because all the warning signs fit him and his mood swings and recklessness. A final discovery—that gamblers had higher attempted suicide rates than anybody—added an exclamation point to her research.

"But then I saw I was wrong, all wrong, even about *that*," she said. "I thought Matt was thinking about ending his *own* life, but it wasn't himself he was thinking of killing. It was Mr. McCauley, because he had a job to do for Myers."

"No, Erin, no," Mrs. Hillis said forcefully, shaking her head. "That can't be it. Listen, your heart is in the right place, but you're just not thinking straight. You just don't have enough … experience to know how to figure all this out. I'm not even sure *I* do."

Then Mrs. Hillis launched into a mini-lecture on Type A and Type B personalities, claiming that Erin's home life fostered Type A when her natural inclination was toward Type B and that the clash between the two was responsible for the pressure she always felt.

"It's not *only* your home life," she clarified. "I'm not blaming your parents. But you are being made to grow up too fast by the whole school culture. You, Matt, everyone."

Mrs. Hillis parked about a quarter-mile west of the Junction at a small turn-off where every autumn beneath a grove of shade trees farmers sold sweet corn from heaping trailers. They hiked east toward the Junction, retreating into the tangle of bushes and trees whenever a car passed. As the terrain rose, Mrs. Hillis said, "We need to find a place where we can't be seen but we can see what happens."

Erin immediately thought of the instrument room beneath the bridge and described it, but then she admitted, "You can't *see* what happens on top; you can only *hear* it."

"That might be the best we can hope for. Let's check it out."

As they climbed up to the bridge, Erin's adrenaline surged again. What was this thrill? She had never thought it exciting to break rules or put her life in danger before. Everyone always said high school and college were times of transition, but she never expected the changes to be so intoxicating. Truly, she was risking a lot right now.

She led Mrs. Hillis down the ladder and along the lower parapet. Far below, the Orange River gurgled lazily.

"Are you afraid of heights?" Mrs. Hillis asked, clutching the railing.

"I thought I was, until I ..." She admitted that she had used the bungee cords, for jumping but even just for hanging, and found the experience surprisingly delightful.

"How do you even know about this place, this room? We're probably breaking the law right now, aren't we?"

Erin stifled her reply. Yes, it was no doubt illegal, but she didn't care because it was so exciting and important. She slid her hand along the ledge above the frame of the metal door to the room that Cody called the bridge's "research data center." Her fingers closed on the key.

"Where *are* we?" Mrs. Hillis continued, her fear evident to Erin as she felt for the keyhole and shoved the door open, its metal scraping against the concrete floor. Erin groped for the light switch in the dark and flipped it on. Then she replaced the key and shut and locked the door.

"Cody says this is the room the engineers use to set up their experiments. All the measurements and data come here and get transmitted to the labs at Riverside. Something like that. Cody knows a lot of the engineering students."

"Can anybody outside see that we're in here?"

"No. There aren't any windows."

"Good." Mrs. Hillis took a deep breath. "So, Erin. You don't have a plan, but can you *think* of one?"

She shrugged: "No, but we can wait here. It's more than an hour before Matt and Mr. McCauley get here."

"No. Not that long."

Once again, Mrs. Hillis seemed nervous about something. The small room's fluorescent lights threw harsh shadows on her face. Shivering, Erin plugged in the space heater beneath the counter that ran the length of the room and contained three computer monitors, all turned off.

"Okay, Erin. I'm going to tell you what Brad told me, about his conversation with Myers."

Sensing the gravity of the moment, Erin sat in one of the cold aluminum chairs. Mrs. Hillis followed her lead.

"Brad said he decided that things had gone far enough. He was tired of always looking over his shoulder for Myers, and he was tired of waiting for the story to come out in the newspaper. Personally, I think he just wants to rub Myers's face in it, get revenge for the trouble Myers has caused him. He has to get the victory, in his mind.

"But whatever it is, once you called him earlier tonight, he decided he had to make his move. He called Myers and told him that it was over, the whole cheating system, the payoffs, the falsified records, all of it. He said he had all kinds of evidence that would bury Myers and wanted to meet him. He said he told Myers that maybe they could come to some arrangement that would save Myers from embarrassment, and Myers took the bait—probably he figured Brad meant he wanted some money. But that's not what Brad meant. He said he was going to demand that Myers resign or else he will turn over the information to the authorities."

Erin followed along until this point.

"Huh? What does that mean?"

"He's bluffing, Erin. That story is going to come out in the media no matter what. But Myers, when he sees what evidence Brad has, might resign, thinking he will escape any further trouble. Like I said, Brad just wants to rub Myers's nose in it.

"When I talked to him, he said Myers wanted to meet tonight in his office, but Brad demanded they meet at the Junction. For some reason I can't figure, Myers agreed to that. Brad said he could tell Myers was calculating, and then Myers said something about a graduation gift for Brad. I have no idea what that means."

Erin said, "But I don't understand. If Mr. McCauley is already coming here to meet *Matt* ..." She floundered, trying to fit together the puzzle pieces.

"That's the thing," Mrs. Hillis said. "Brad and Myers are supposed to meet at 10:30, before Matt ever shows up. Brad is planning to get Myers to give up before anything else happens. At least that's what I *think* he's planning."

Erin checked the time on her phone: 9:47.

"We can't just wait here," she said. "We won't know what's happening. We should wait outside this door, on the ledge. That way we can see down below, when anybody drives up. And we can at least hear whatever happens up top, on the bridge."

Mrs. Hillis threw up her hands.

"I guess that's what we'll have to do, then."

They slipped out of the room and pulled the door shut behind them. No sooner than they had settled themselves on the edge with a clear view of the landing below, an automobile turned off the highway and screeched to a halt. The dim illumination from a single yellow floodlight high on a telephone pole was enough for Erin to see that the car was the Volvo belonging to Myers. He left his headlights on and switched to his high beams.

"Don't worry," Erin said with assurance. "He can't see us." The teenagers had determined all those details over the years of Junction parties.

Mrs. Hillis wondered aloud, "Why would he be here so early?"

Myers stood beside his car and rotated, looking in all directions.

"He's scouting, surveying," Mrs. Hillis said. "He's planning something. Keep your phone handy. We might have to call the police whether Brad wants us to or not."

Myers slid back inside his car and backed it up until it was obscured by several pyramids of gravel. His car door slammed shut. Soon his form reappeared under the halo of lamplight and headed for the bridge. He vanished in the darkness. A few minutes passed until Erin heard his footsteps above them.

"What's he doing?" Mrs. Hillis whispered. "Is there any place up there that he can hide?"

Yes, there were several places, spots next to concrete and steel posts. Although Erin was not a Junction regular, she had heard others talk about avoiding traffic headlights on the deck of the bridge by ducking into the shadows. As a noisy truck rumbled over the bridge, Erin told Mrs. Hillis what she knew.

They heard Myers's footsteps scrabbling back and forth. Then they ceased, and except for an occasional car or truck passing overhead, they heard nothing.

Presently another vehicle arrived below, wheeling through the long cone of the overhead light before coming to a stop. It was Matt's van. Erin and Mrs. Hillis could make out the shape of Matt leaving the parking area and moving toward the bridge. Erin checked her phone: The time was only 10:03.

She tensed and quit swinging her legs off the parapet, as though her stillness would enhance her hearing. Matt's heavy footfall came to a stop nearly directly above their heads. Erin could envision him taking his usual position with his legs dangling over the edge and his arms hanging over the rail. If she leaned out and looked up, she could probably see his feet. He would be watching for Mr. McCauley's motorcycle.

At such a short distance, he might hear her and Mrs. Hillis whispering, so by the light of her phone she pressed a finger to her lips. Mrs. Hillis nodded.

Time slowed to a crawl. Every thirty seconds or so, a vehicle crossed the bridge. Erin supposed Matt was still seated over them and Myers was hiding nearby. A terrible possibility occurred to her—what if Matt and Myers were working together to get rid of Mr. McCauley?

From far off Erin heard the increasing volume of a motorcycle. Then came a succession of downshifts, after which the headlight of Mr. McCauley's bike swept across the river and under the bridge before he shut off the engine and the light. A moment later a flashlight began weaving its way across the parking area and jerking up the incline to the bridge.

Erin's heart plunged with new fear. In the next few minutes, she would know whether she was right to have trusted Matt when he promised to make everything right, or whether she and Mrs. Hillis should have gone to the police. She could still shout up to Matt, but the instant the idea occurred to her she heard voices above.

"Well, here we are." That was Mr. McCauley.

An unintelligible and then unexpected sound dripped over the edge of the bridge—crying. Then came Matt's cracking voice: "I'm so sorry, Mr. McCauley! I'm so sorry! I slashed your tires and I broke into your house and took your safe and I—" Then a vehicle passed and his words were drowned out, but Erin knew he was simply finishing his admission of guilt for the railroad incident.

The next words she heard were more of Matt's: "You need to quit your job at Brookstone, resign or retire or whatever. That bastard Myers is out to get you. If you don't disappear then he's going to do something worse than so far …"

Mrs. Hillis's arm wrapped around Erin's shoulder and they leaned together, listening.

Mr. McCauley's voice spoke calmly, reassuringly: "Matt, you don't have to worry about any of this anymore. Myers's days are numbered. You never should have had to face any of this anyway—"

Then the mocking voice of Myers broke in: "How very touching. How very, very touching. No, don't come any closer! Keep your distance!"

Erin could hear Matt scraping on the concrete, rising from his position. Another car passed, and a horn blared.

"Yes, this is a gun," came Myers's voice. "McCauley, as I promised, I've brought you a little parting gift. How very convenient for me to find you both here. Matt, I'm disappointed. I give you a golden opportunity to make up for everything you owe me and you turn sissy on me. I set it up so McCauley comes right to you and you still can't come through. You and Gutierrez—what a pair."

"Tolan, give it up," Mr. McCauley said evenly. "Everything I said on the phone is true. But what I didn't tell you is that I'm not the only one with the information. We've handed it over to the press."

"Oh, I believe you, Brad. Because less than five minutes after you called me my phone rang again and it was an editor at the Bridgebury *Courier* telling me they will be printing their exclusive story tomorrow and asking for my reaction."

"And?"

"And what?"

The conversation now was between the two adults only. Erin wondered where Matt was, what he was doing. Probably just watching and listening, frightened, sorry, amazed.

"And what *is* your reaction?"

"We knew this day would come, sooner or later. And we're prepared. We have contingency plans."

Mr. McCauley said: "If the reporter from the newspaper is right, you'll head for South America."

"I'd not thought of that. But where I'm going, nobody will be able to touch me."

"Okay. So what's your end game?"

"That's simple enough. Since Matt here was unable to carry out his final assignment, I have to come in and clean up." The next ten

seconds were impossible to hear as another vehicle rumbled past. "…
shoot both of you and let the river take your bodies downstream. Hell,
by the morning you might be as far south as Attica or Terre Haute. Or
I'll put weights on you so you sink. I haven't quite decided that yet. I
like to keep my options open. It doesn't matter. Nobody will find you
and nobody will care. And McCauley, if you disappear, that will cast
a lot of doubt on your so-called evidence. LaGrange and I, we figured
you from your profile—you're a bit of a sissy too, but you like to make
big splash whenever you have a chance. You were hoping to go out with
a bang, disgrace Brookstone with the governor on hand. Well, I've got
news for you: You *are* going to go out with a bang and you *will* make
a big splash, literally!"

Erin screamed, but the noise was virtually swallowed up by the loud,
long blast of another car horn and the screech of braking tires. She heard
grunting and panting and the three voices shouting and swearing—and
somewhere in the middle of the noise came the pop of a gunshot. Mrs.
Hillis began yelling "Brad!" so Erin shouted Matt's name, and as two
heavy vehicles passed overhead, perhaps semis, one from each direction,
their headlights reflected off the girders—and glinted off an object that
dropped out of view and into the river with a quiet *plunk*.

The next thing Erin knew, a much larger mass, a dark blot against the
night sky, plunged past her and then came bouncing back in a manner
that was ominous and obscene. Matt's breathing came in great huffs.
Mr. McCauley shouted, "Where did he—what happened?"

Erin gasped, and Mrs. Hillis's arm tightened around her.

McCauley's flashlight beam fell on the body of Tolan Myers, bobbing
from the end of a bungee cord wound around his neck.

For Erin, the next two hours passed in fuzzy, disconnected impressions. There were sirens, lots of sirens—so many sirens that she thought
that every available cop in the county must have descended on the
Junction. Except for the crackle of police radios, the bridge itself grew
eerily silent as traffic was blocked off from both east and west. When
students started to arrive, summoned through an untraceable network
whose original node was a phone call from Matt to Cody Summers, they
had to come on foot in converging migrations from either direction.

She remembered her parents arriving, her mom flustered and her dad stoic, and holding her for so long that she wondered whether they were impostors. She heard Matt answering questions with a couple of refrains: "for Steve" and "that bastard." When the police were finished questioning them, she went to Matt and hugged him for a long time, but she had to ask if he killed Myers, and he said he wrapped a cord around his neck during the struggle for the gun, and Robin pointed out that the cord had gone around Myers's neck *many* times, and Matt said, "That's right, four times. *1-2-3-4.* The bastard!" She remembered the police separating her from Mrs. Hillis, and from Matt, so that each "witness" could give a statement independently. The reporter from the newspaper was there, Pete Doty, joined by other reporters and photographers, and the Bridgebury TV-18 station also had camera crews and reporters on hand. She remembered hearing Mrs. Hillis tell Mr. McCauley that now the morning paper would have a hard news story to go with the first install-ment of their expose of the cheating. She heard a TV correspondent, her face lit up during a live report, announce that in light of the school tragedy, the much-anticipated visit by the governor the next day had already been cancelled. Later she heard Darly Jones, whose mom was a school board member, say that school would be suspended until further notice. As Erin mingled in her dazed condition with other students, she heard somebody blaring the senior song, "I'll take My Chances," from a car stereo until others with wiser heads prevailed on him to be more sensitive—just another volley, she realized, in the eternal tug-of-war of transition between adolescence and adulthood. She heard police discussing the necessary search for a weapon allegedly thrown into the river. At one point, feeling a gust of wind, she drifted apart from Mom and Dad, stepped cautiously to the bridge railing, and looked down to the spot so precious in her memory, where she had watched awestruck while the whirlwind created the waterspout that had swept across the bridge where she now stood, and she wished with all her might that another whirlwind would rise up and sweep away everything bad that was happening. And perhaps most memorable of all, a searchlight was turned on from the ground below to assist the emergency personnel in retrieving the body of Tolan Myers, and when its brilliant cylinder of light found the dangling corpse, even Tyler Batta, Brookstone High School's recently crowned SENIOR BIG MOUTH, fell utterly silent.

16

AS A CONSUMER, J. Bradford McCauley thrived on garage sales.

Years of low-paying work and graduate school had hardened his "cheapskate" approach—that's what Robin Hillis called it, correctly—and attuned his eyesight to spot every orange-and-white sign advertising sales along rural roads, city streets, and highways like State Road 53, where he had stopped to browse on this sunny Friday morning.

His eyes ran along a line of tennis shoes laid out on a section of faded, threadbare blue tarp. They looked too large, he thought, but he couldn't afford not to check, so he held one shoe sole-to-sole against his own before dropping it back on the tarp. Unconvinced, he tested every shoe the same way, with the same results.

He had plenty of time on his hands.

Getting fired from a job had that effect.

The axe had fallen a week earlier, the morning after the death of Tolan Myers at the Junction Bridge, the death at which McCauley and Matt Rademacher had been the primary witnesses, the death that was technically still under investigation by state police but would surely be ruled accidental (or a matter of self-defense, if blamed on Matt) for lack of evidence to the contrary. As soon as news about Myers spread, school was cancelled the next day, of course, the last day of final exams pushed back to Monday, and the governor's scheduled visit postponed indefinitely, probably forever. All those decisions were made and announced in the wee hours of the morning after.

Shortly after dawn, McCauley received a phone call from the Brookstone School Corporation office—not from Walter Patingale, who was conveniently out of town—requesting his attendance at an emergency meeting at 9 A.M.

Curious, he complied.

Basically, they fired him on the spot. The justification they gave was airtight: He had "misrepresented" his employment history on his original job application four semesters back by not disclosing that his previous high school teaching contract had been terminated because of the trouble with Mary Ann Childress. Lawyers for the corporation presented evidence in the form of newspaper articles, legal documents, and minutes of board meetings from the Ohio school where McCauley had once taught. He did not dispute the facts. There was no need for any kind of formal hearing at which he might utilize legal representation or try to fight his dismissal. He sat through the proceedings with an air of indifference, answering respectfully when addressed, waiting and wondering if anyone would ask about the tragedy that had taken place less than twelve hours before.

Had he chosen, he might have asked why the board had not taken action on the Childress information earlier, since they had possessed it all along. This he knew from having come across the documents in the trove of information spirited away from Myers's office the night of the daring break-in. He might have asked, except he already knew—the board, or Myers more likely, had sat on the information, hoping to leverage it to influence McCauley, and, failing that, holding it until it was needed. When he was asked whether he wished to make any statement in his defense, he declined, except to say that he had committed vandalism at the school the previous evening, defacing property by putting up hundreds of flyers with detailed charges of cheating. As long as he was going down, he might as well shield Robin from any fallout.

He could afford to be magnanimous. He expected to be getting a real job in the not-too-distant future.

At the yard sale, a folded copy of the Bridgebury *Courier* sat next to the cash box on a card table just inside the garage. Catching sight of it,

McCauley could not help but think about the events of a week ago or the newspaper's six-day series of articles that concluded this morning.

His presence at the sale was not at all coincidental. He had contacted Robin, and, learning that her husband was on a business trip, told her he would be at the sale for the first thirty minutes or so if she wanted to talk. She *might* come, she said, but he knew she *would* come. She had to be just as curious to compare notes as he was.

Mixed in with a pile of worthless electronics, McCauley found a pair of cheap wall clocks, a buck each. As much as he wanted to take one, he knew he should not purchase anything now unless it was essential. Soon, hopefully, he would be making a major move. He ought to be reducing, not adding to, his store of possessions. He didn't even want to have to rent a trailer from U-Haul. He envisioned shipping everything to his destination and taking his motorcycle on the cross-country trip.

Over the next five minutes, several women about his age appeared at the sale, most with toddlers or baby strollers. They sifted through the clothing items for sale, all organized efficiently by size and type. Shirts occupied one table, pants another, and behind those was a sagging rack of hanging coats and jackets. The women were near enough that McCauley could overhear their small talk. All of it centered on the Brookstone scandal.

"You'd have to be crazy to think that our little high school could really be graduating so many kids to go to Harvard and Stanford," said one mom, holding up small dresses, examining them closely, suspiciously, looking for stains or other defects. "I can't say any of this really surprises me."

Another woman, the top half of her face hidden behind large sunglasses, agreed.

"This kind of stuff always starts at the top," she added. "I never did like that Walter Patingale, even before he got hired by the board."

They speculated about the whereabouts of the superintendent. One article by Pete Doty in the *Courier* series had implied that Patingale improperly allowed his business interests to become entangled with his public education position. However, he was reported to be somewhere in Washington or Oregon, possibly in negotiations for the sale of his business. He remained unavailable for comment, according to his lawyers.

"I'll *bet* he's unavailable," a third mom muttered. "Unavailable and never coming back, you can be sure."

McCauley found a few motorcycle accessories for sale, but he didn't need anything in that department, either. He kept reminding himself that as soon as he landed somewhere, he would start scouring garage sales for necessities. Better yet, he would start pulling down a decent salary, which would set him free from his long slavery to flea markets, yard sales, and thrift stores.

One woman kept going inside the house and coming back out, lugging cardboard boxes held together by packing tape, boxes that yielded up more trinkets and treasures for sale. McCauley took her to be the homeowner. As she set out new items on an empty table near the customers discussing the scandal, she joined their gabfest. McCauley listened with greater interest. Her contributions made it plain that she had children in high school, but the name on the mailbox, CHAMBERS, was unfamiliar to him.

"I don't know what to think," she confessed, peeling pre-printed price labels from a sheet and pressing them onto small toys. "When we ask Jeremy and Keely about it, they say they don't know anything, or they say it's blown all out of proportion. But I don't know, reading all those stories this week, I wonder what all goes on that our kids don't know about. Or maybe they *do* know but don't tell *us* anything. I just don't know."

To continue eavesdropping on the gossiping moms, McCauley loitered at a table with boxes full of books whose spines and titles, he noticed, faced outward and ran the same direction. He appreciated such attention to detail by the owner of the sale. For several minutes he combed through a paperback medical dictionary, looking up his different ailments. The truth was, he felt physically better now than he had all year, maybe because his mind had been distracted from his body by all the things going on his life. He listened to the women and their ongoing commentary on what one of them called "the biggest story in these parts since Abraham Lincoln's funeral train came through." That reference drew a chuckle from McCauley, for he knew the historical allusion was accurate.

All week, beginning the previous Sunday, the *Courier* had parceled out its damning exposé of the Brookstone High School cheating scandal in a scathing six-part series titled Mask of Excellence, with the letter *s* in Mask replacing a letter *R* that had been crossed out. The sheer volume of information was enormous, and on the third day, the newspaper announced that in response to popular demand, it planned to print a special section as an insert the following Sunday that would contain all of the thirty-three articles published during the week as well as hundreds of letters to the editor, most of which had never been published before.

In his Riverside University graduate office, McCauley had saved each daily issue. Information that he, Robin, and Erin Delaney had played a part in bringing to light appeared in more than half the stories, by his count.

The articles covered the whole gamut of angles to the scandal.

The first day's package included a historical overview with a colorful, detailed timeline credited to a graphic artist from *USA Today*. Surely, McCauley thought, the fact that the *Courier*'s parent corporation had lent its expertise to the local story testified to its importance. According to Pete Doty's research, the seeds for the scandal were sown in the middle 1980s and probably fell from the hand of Morland Harte, a Riverside business professor better known as the architect of the CUPP program. That cooperative effort between Riverside and Brookstone led to student cheating, faculty bribery, and parental pressure, according to the article. Evidently it began when Harte, whose grandson was a Brookstone student, paid Myers to alter transcripts to help a student get into the University of Chicago. McCauley remembered Doty saying that Myers's manuscript referred to such a bribe as "the spark that lit my fire"—which Doty derided as a "dead metaphor." Harte himself was long gone, having taken a government job in Washington, D.C., after retiring from Riverside. He had died three years earlier.

One set of articles dealt with the demographics of the scandal. Student cheaters fell into several categories, defined and described in a "Who's Who" sidebar. At the top of the food chain were CUPP participants who needed good grades to enter the best colleges, whose class rank was vital and forced them into cut-throat competition with classmates. Often they faced unrelenting pressure from immature, competitive parents. McCauley figured Cody Summers and Lance Tracer fell into this category. Next came CUPP students not quite so intensely focused on excelling in the classroom who nevertheless had to at least *pass* the program to qualify for college. They just wanted to survive the rigorous studies with decent grades to get into good second-tier schools. Jessica Southard and Matt Rademacher were examples, McCauley thought—and probably also Steve Gutierrez. Another group comprised non-CUPPers who simply needed to graduate from high school to get jobs. To that end, they pressured CUPPers for assignment and test answers and paid them to do homework, write papers, or even take final exams in their places. Even though these students were not in direct competition with the CUPPers, they were still competing with other non-CUPPers, especially in courses graded on a curve. McCauley knew two students identified in this group, Molly Traxton and Tory Johnson, who both were quoted in the article. The "Who's Who" also considered non-cheaters at both the CUPP and non-CUPP levels. Those in CUPP recognized the slanted playing field, but their protests always went first to their parents, whose attempts to bring the problem to the attention of school officials always ran into a brick wall with Myers. When honest students approached teachers but found them deaf to their pleas, the students suspected some teachers were dirty, too. The whole analysis suggested that over time, cheating had spread by a trickle-down effect from the strongest students to the weakest.

As for Myers, McCauley was delighted to see a story about the dead man's egotistical manuscript, unfinished, which according to Doty's report came from "anonymous sources close to the author." The article quoted extensively from the electronic file that McCauley, Robin, and Erin had copied from Myers's office computer. Its quotations alone painted Myers as crooked administrator looking out for Number One, not for the hundreds of students under his charge.

McCauley kept his ears open as he browsed at the yard sale. In a dog-eared volume called *Encyclopedia of Popular Music: 1960-79*, he thumbed through the pages to find the Bruce Springsteen entry. Its material was superficial and dry, the old photographs comic.

The women shoppers, having picked over the kids clothing, were now debating the *extent* of the high school corruption. One of them was striving to interpret an article in that day's paper that attempted to quantify the problem with the aid of an expert from Riverside, an expert not in statistics but in psychology.

"He said," the woman explained, "that you could take the estimates from school officials and then make adjustments because of the way everyone exaggerates from human nature. There was a lot more psychological mumbo-jumbo, but this guy said it was safe to say that the percentage of students who cheated regularly was probably about fifty percent, and he said that everybody, those who did cheat and those who did not, everybody *believed* the ratio was way higher. That was from human nature, too. The cheaters overstated the problem to justify themselves. The psychology guy called that 'safety in numbers.' But the non-cheaters felt outnumbered and overwhelmed by cheaters, so they overestimated the amount of cheating too."

McCauley realized that Erin Delaney belonged in the latter group. Because she was so socially reserved, she did not realize there were a lot of honest students—she happened to be influenced more by the cheaters like Jessica and Matt.

"Find any bargains?" came a familiar female voice.

He turned and smiled at the friendly face of Robin Hillis.

¿Que Pasa? was relatively empty. Day by day, Riverside's Maymester students were clearing out from campus, and summer classes didn't start until the following Monday. McCauley and Robin chose the most private booth available and sat across from each other.

McCauley sensed Robin's nervousness but felt powerless to dispel it.

He decided to try humor.

"Know anybody who needs a history teacher?" he asked. "Twice-terminated, no less?"

Her eyes reflected a sorrow he did not mean to elicit.

"I wish I knew what to say," she replied. "First of all, I need to thank you. I didn't hear until yesterday that you … took the fall for me at that school board meeting."

He waved it off, saying, "It was nothing. It was the least I could do."

"But …"

"No, really. They were going to fire me regardless, so I thought, Why should you crash and burn with me? Why should you be a victim of collateral damage?" He chuckled at his own violent imagery. "You know what I wish, though?"

"What?"

"I wish I had thought of *resigning* first, before they ever fired me. I would have quit just to spite them. And it might help me in the long run, professionally."

"Was Patingale there?"

He shook his head and smirked.

"No way. Pete Doty says Patingale is hiding out somewhere in Washington. For business reasons, supposedly. "

"Right!" Robin hissed, her ire rising. "He just doesn't want to come back and face the music."

"Doty says Patingale for years has been siphoning off profits from the cheating network to pay business debts."

They ordered an appetizer, quesadillas, along with soft drinks.

Robin wanted to talk about the week-long deluge of negative publicity for the school. The *Courier* articles had implicated far more teachers than she ever thought could be involved, she admitted sadly, as well as corruption on the school board that went far beyond Patingale.

"I just want to try to get my mind around it," she said. "That's why I came to see you at the sale. I thought that together, we might make some sense of it."

"Okay."

"Okay. We already knew Myers was the … what, brainchild? Or at least the local point man, if it turns out that the problem is really nationwide."

Again, McCauley felt an odd detachment. His future was tugging him away from Brookstone, Indiana. Yet he understood that the whole mess would remain painfully present for Robin.

"Right," he said. He would let her process out loud, if that helped her.

"And it looks like he was running a tight-lipped network of teachers and counselors. Everything was free of documentation, except for the electronic files we took."

"Right," he repeated, "but look at the real source of the problem. It's money. It's always money."

Doty's investigative reporting concluded as much. Profit was the key for Myers. He accepted bribes from parents to change student grades even over teacher recommendations, and some of that money he reinvested by paying the teachers in his network for their cooperation and silence. He also ran the Dairy Queen, which gave him financial leverage with students. The kids who worked there were paid well to keep quiet about his ring. If they wouldn't work for him, or if they caused trouble, he had the power to change their grades at the wink of an eye. One of Doty's articles described the DQ store as the geographical nucleus of the corruption.

"Is it, really?" Robin asked. McCauley looked her squarely in the eye, expecting her to explain what else it might be. But her question hung in the air.

She abruptly changed the subject.

"The whole atmosphere at school has changed," she said. "Everyone is suspicious of everyone else. And I don't mean only the teachers who were named in the articles. Everybody wonders about the teachers who *weren't* named. Now all of us are going our separate ways for the summer. I'm afraid to see what the school will look like next fall!"

He nodded and leaned back from the table as the appetizer arrived.

"Do you see what I'm saying?" Robin pleaded. "People that I've worked with for years are probably wondering about *me!* Some of them probably think I'm part of the problem."

"Maybe so," he said, "but as soon as everyone knows what you've been up to this year, with me and Erin, then you'll be a hero."

"I don't *want* to be a hero!" she emphasized, shifting in her seat. "I wish none of this had ever happened! I wish I had nothing to do with it! I wish I could take one of your clocks and just turn back time, go back to before any of this started!"

"But it started before *you* ever got to Brookstone, from what I'm reading," he pointed out.

"I know. It's so depressing."

He tried to put himself in her shoes. Doty had uncovered corruption way worse, way more widespread even among the faculty, than Robin had ever believed possible. Many teachers were passive accomplices who encouraged cheating by looking the other way whenever they caught offenders. Others were more active participants who bent rules in various ways, by leaving copies of tests to be stolen, by intentionally making scoring or recording errors in favor of students, by changing grades already entered into the gradebook under pressure from Myers or in response to bribes from students or parents, or by offering students creative ways to "work out" their inflated grades.

"What about LaGrange?" McCauley asked. "I can't decide how to judge him in all this."

"I think he's going to get off scot-free. I mean, he will lose his job, but I don't think you can prove he's broken any laws. If he's not ready to retire, then he'll pop up as a principal somewhere else, based on how he oversaw one school's turnaround, how he engineered the tremendous rise in one school's academic success. If our students are superstars, then he's the principal of the superstars!"

"Do you think that's right? Is it fair?"

She shook her head, the gesture oozing uncertainty.

Honestly, all the evidence was inconclusive regarding LaGrange's role. Pete Doty and the other newspaper reporters and editors covering the story—just like McCauley and Robin and Erin—could find no unambiguous link between LaGrange and the cheating, or even between LaGrange and Myers. The name of the principal simply did not show up in any of the documents. As soon as the *Courier* stories first appeared, the school board suspended LaGrange indefinitely, with pay. LaGrange himself did not try to hide from the media spotlight. He was quite visible, expressing sorrow at the death of his friend as well as dismay at the allegations against his long-time assistant. He seemed confident that he would emerge unscathed.

"I'm not sure myself," Robin said. "He's awfully slick, awfully clever."

McCauley said, "I think in some ways maybe all he is guilty of is weak leadership. He never investigated any allegation because Myers was always assuring him he would take care of it. Maybe the bottom line is he's just a weak principal."

"Right," Robin said sarcastically. "Well, how can we prove it's anything more than that? What we heard LaGrange saying on the phone, when we were in the closet—we cannot prove even that! Erin turned on her recorder, but after that only Myers did any talking. There isn't any proof that LaGrange was even there! It's our word against his, if it ever comes to that. How can we prove it?"

"*We?*" McCauley asked sharply. "*We* are finished. *I* am, anyway."

"I know. But the state is going to do an official investigation, and I'm afraid he'll get off scot-free, like I said."

"At least it's not the *school board* doing the investigation," McCauley said. "They're as dirty as anybody."

"I suppose." She sounded unconvinced about that, too. "Maybe it's just proud parents and alumni on the board who don't want to see the school exposed as a fraud. Maybe they admit there is a small problem, as with any high school, but they have no idea how bad things have gotten."

McCauley's own convictions about the board rose to the surface.

"I don't think so," he said firmly. "If Patingale is corrupt, then some of the board must be corrupt, too."

"The truth will come out," Robin replied. "That much I'm sure of."

"But how long will it take?"

She shrugged.

"Not long, I hope. Things have happened pretty fast this past week."

Robin reviewed how the fallout had come, fast and furious, starting last Sunday. Resignations, firings, transfers, threats, lawsuits. College admissions had been rescinded, scholarships revoked. Overnight, it seemed, scores of parents, implicated or afraid, put their houses up for sale, went into hiding or took early summer vacations. McCauley had not heard any of these details.

Their quesadilla plate lay largely untouched, leading their server, on her next pass, to ask, "Is everything all right?"

McCauley and Robin locked eyes and laughed together.

"The food is fine," he said. "We're just … preoccupied."

The day was lovely. Sunshine poured down from a high blue sky. They walked to the Engineering Mall on campus and watched the fountain, its jets of water rising and falling in programmed, colorful rhythm.

"So what have you been up to since last I saw you?" Robin asked.

He chuckled.

"Since that night on the bridge, you mean."

"Yes."

"Well, it's been hell. Interesting, but hell."

Twice detectives questioned him about the night of May 23 and the events leading up to it. He had no qualms about telling them everything—every word out of his mouth was easily corroborated by Robin, Erin, and even Doty—and doing so felt like a great psychological purge. As Robin kept saying, this seemed to be a season for secrets to be told, for hidden truths to come to light. For McCauley, the shock of seeing and remembering Myers's body bouncing obscenely on the end of the bungee cord made him want to put as much distance as possible between himself and Brookstone High School. Already fired, he nevertheless finished scoring his one class's final exams, mechanically, superficially.

The request for the second interview by the detectives worried him until he realized they were only trying to make sense of the forensic evidence. Matt Rademacher alone had seen what happened between McCauley and Myers. For a few seconds, as Matt wrestled with Myers and McCauley had twisted the gun from his fingers and flung it over the side of the bridge, he had lost sight of them in their close groaning scuffle. Exactly how Matt had wound the cord around Myers's neck so quickly, McCauley did not see. But he harbored no doubts that Matt, with his athletic agility, linebacker's quickness, and powerful arms—all boosted by the adrenaline frenzy of the moment—could physically overwhelm the smaller assistant principal. Under interrogation that seemed pointlessly repetitive, McCauley finally blurted out: "Why don't you work on getting at the *root* of the problem?" And the lead detective, taken aback, asked, "All right, then. What *is* the root of the problem?"

The detectives asked him to try to remember any further details. They gently suggested that he might be forgetting details he didn't *want* to remember because they were too painful. He was not fooled, though. He saw through their ploy. They were insinuating that Matt did not *need* to kill Myers, that he could easily have disarmed and disabled the older man.

And they were insinuating that McCauley knew this.

When McCauley tried to give this point a fair hearing, though, all he could think about was that if ever there were a crime of passion, this would qualify. If ever there were a case of legitimate self-defense, this was it. The false accusations made against him by Mary Ann Childress seven years earlier still stung, and their memory made him want to ensure that Matt Rademacher got every benefit of doubt.

He told all this to Robin as the sun warmed their faces.

"Brad," she asked, "I want to ask you two questions. Do you mind?"

Her reticence seemed out of character. He tried to read her face.

"Sure," he answered.

"Okay. Please don't take this wrong—I just need to know."

"Sure. Okay."

"What really happened on the bridge that night?"

Involuntarily, his gaze drifted back to the fountain and rested there.

How could he tell her, when the memory of those harrowing moments had grown blurry from their never-ending playback in his mind?

For a moment, alone with Matt on the bridge, he felt sure he was getting through to the troubled teenager, and hoping to calm Matt's agitation he opened his mouth tell him about the imminent media revelation that would end the assistant principal's reign of terror—then Myers himself had interfered, bristling with his arrogance and brandishing the gun they had seen in his desk drawer—at which point Matt, moving with startling quickness, shot upward from where he knelt sobbing on the bridge deck and tackled Myers, grappling with him, their interlocked bodies illuminated by the headlamps of a passing vehicle whose screeching tires and blaring horn were cut off by the gunshot, which ricocheted off a girder, evidently, and then McCauley, acting on instinct, he guessed afterward, seized the weapon from Myers and flung it over the edge, and his eyes followed it, relief flooding his whole being, but when he turned back around, he saw Matt push Myers off the bridge, but there was no cry, not a sound from Myers although Matt, grasping the girders, screamed a long angry curse, and McCauley rushed forward to grab Matt, afraid he was about to leap to his death, when from somewhere below he heard female voices calling, familiar voices, and he aimed his flashlight down toward them, but it lit up Myers's hanging body, his face swollen from the cords about his neck, and McCauley groaned inwardly and thought: "What have we *done?* What have *I* done?"

He poured out all he remembered to Robin in an incoherent stream, even as his vision never moved from the fountain, transfixed by its tranquil, colorful pulses. Gradually he felt pressure on his hands, warm and gentle pressure from Robin's fingers.

"I'm so sorry, Brad," she said.

Time passed, how much he could only guess.

"What was your other question?" he asked at last.

She had not let go of his hands.

"What are you going to do about your dissertation?"

He returned a squeeze and withdrew his hands.

"I still have to decide," he said. "And soon."

June

17

"SO, IT'S VIRGINIA Tech, I hear," said Aunt Jennifer. "Best forestry degree program in America, your dad says."

Erin let her shoulders sag. The main reason she had come to Jess's graduation party was to find a safe harbor from the stormy weather she faced at home from her father, who, once he understood Erin wanted to study forestry or conservation or something in the realm of natural resources, set his sights on tracking down the best college for his last daughter—best for *him*, really, best for his ego. That's the way Erin understood his recent *monomania*, to use a vocab word that had stumped her on her final exam in English. Dad was obsessed with her college choice. One evening he had even tapped on her bedroom door, entered with a clipboard as if she were his patient in a hospital room, and stood at the foot of her bed reading the statistics he had collected in his search for the perfect school, for *her* perfect school, he said. She refrained from pointing out that Riverside was rated tenth nationally in forestry (and would cost only half as much). Dad would have scolded her for her willingness to settle for a second-rate school.

Thankfully, her college plans interested nobody else at the graduation parties. The exploding high school cheating scandal crowded out other usual teenage topics of conversations, of course, just as it had dominated phone and party chatter all week. That was fine with Erin, sort of. She was happy to roam free from her dad's meddling. However, the scandal was an unwelcome subject, too, because most of her classmates now knew that she had played a role in uncovering it.

"Maybe," Erin replied to Jen. "I'm still holding out for another possibility." Meaning Riverside. Erin was curious to see how Jen would respond to her less-than-hearty judgment of Dad's endorsement of a college Erin had never heard of before the middle of May. Jen nodded and changed the subject, raving about the fruit salad filling one section of her plate. Instinctively, Erin knew that Jen knew about her preference. Dad must have told her that, too.

Today was Sunday. On the calendar, Commencement lay five days away, Friday night. The graduation ceremony was about the only part of the year-end schedule not thrown into a tizzy by the recent events, by the death of Mr. Myers, by the firings of several teachers and resignations of a few more, by the suspicious absence or disappearance of Mr. Patingale, by the announcement of an official investigation by the Indiana Department of Education *and* the Attorney General, and by the daily barrage of ever-worsening newspaper stories that made the whole school look rotten to the core. Even the annual year-end Senior Picnic had been postponed from this afternoon until next Sunday.

Erin looked across the patio, past her cousin Jeremy shooting baskets, and her eye fell on a picnic table where Matt was holding court with a circle of friends. Ever since the night Mr. Myers was killed, Matt had risen in the esteem of many Brookstone students. Tyler Batta had conducted, edited, and published online an "investigative interview" with Matt sitting in darkened silhouette and speaking in an ominous, mechanically altered voice, describing what happened on the night of May 23 and in the months leading up to the tragedy. Needless to say, the publicity made Matt (and Tyler too) instant celebrities. On the flipside, it frustrated the police in the early days of their work to get at the facts behind the death and any illegal activity going on at the school.

She really wanted to talk to Matt. He had told the police and Tyler that he had acted in self-defense when he struggled with Mr. Myers and his gun and shoved him over the railing and off the bridge. For the time being, no charges were being contemplated against him. Still, Erin wanted to talk to him. She doubted she would get the chance—he was riding a wave of sudden popularity that might not subside for weeks.

"Erin, where *is* Virginia Tech?" came a boy's voice. "Blacksburg?"

Her shoulders dipped even further. Aunt Jen must be spreading the "news" to every student at the party. Or, more likely, Jen had told Jess, and Jess had broadcast it to everyone else in Party Land.

"I think so," she said, turning to look at Cody Summers directly. To be honest, she wasn't sure where the four-year prison was located.

"You *think* so?" He left the logical second part of his question unasked.

"Cody," she said imploringly, pulling him by the wrist to a more private place in the yard. "Listen, we've had a great year, right?"

"Sure. Pringles?"

He pointed the open can toward her as if aiming a toy cannon in her direction. At his party, earlier in the day, a number of senior friends had pitched in to buy him a set of eight cans of his favorite snack chip, each in some exotic flavor. This one was Jalapeno Pepper.

"No thanks." She gestured toward Matt and his fans across the way. "How's Matt doing? What do you think? I haven't been able to get close to him since ... you know."

"Yeah, I know." He fell silent, carefully weighing his next words. "Matt sure is enjoying his fifteen minutes of fame."

Allusion, Erin recalled, a vocab word she had remembered on the English exam.

Cody went on, "I'm happy for him—about *that*, anyway. It sure is good to see him feeling like there is no pressure on him anymore."

"Has he said anything to you about what happened that night?" She searched his face. "I feel like ... I don't know. I'm just afraid, I guess. Afraid he's not told the whole truth, and afraid that when he does he may be in more trouble than ever."

Cody took a deep breath and let it out in a slow hiss through pursed lips.

"Nobody can know what was going through his head while he was wrestling with Myers," he said. "Nobody will ever know. I'm not sure *he* knows. There was so much pressure, so much trouble he was trying to get away from. He told me that Myers wanted him to get rid of McCauley, but he decided at the end that he couldn't do that. But what he finally *did* do, that's something we can never know. Only McCauley might know. Other than McCauley, what Matt did is between him and ..."

Erin nodded. She tried to fit together Cody's understanding with her own, and found them compatible. These days, she didn't know whom to trust, but throughout the school year her respect for Cody had blossomed into admiration, especially when she heard that even before the past week's revelations, he had quit hiring himself out to write papers for other students.

"Okay," she said. "Thanks, Cody."

Erin shot baskets with Jeremy, partly for the amusement of getting caught up on his budding romantic life—he admitted sheepishly that he had given up on the girl of his dreams from the sleepover, when he doggedly pursued Erin about her perfume, and was now "interested in somebody new"—but partly for the comfort of being *with* somebody. Wherever she went among the groups of guests at the party, she felt out of place. Everyone was talking about the cheating. Students that she suspected had not cracked a book all year had obviously devoured each and every word of the week's press coverage, not only the stories in the Bridgebury *Courier* and Indianapolis *Star* but also in the Pritchard *Herald-Journal*, a weekly that had joined the media circus. Unfortunately, in Erin's opinion, the tone of the talk from her classmates was excited rather than ashamed. About every other conversation dealt with new ways to cheat that the newspaper series had revealed. Most of these methods depended on emerging technologies and materials that had not yet made it to small-town or rural high schools. She heard Cara Eberle rave about software that allowed you to scan a nutrition label on bottled water and digitally alter it, inserting test answers or formulas that would be formatted to look the same as the original information. Not to be outdone, Bill Frost described wireless earbuds that college students employed during exams, enabling them to somehow use their cell phones to contact friends on the outside for answers. Erin found herself enthusiastically invited into some discussions by classmates who apparently figured that since she had helped pull the rug from under the Brookstone system, she must be privy to all sorts of secrets that they wanted to explore—in order to enhance their own stature in the culture of dishonesty. They were all graduating in five days. Then what? Plainly, Erin could see, they all intended to transfer their "skills" to college. They asked her about Facebook and other tools for cheating that one article in the *Courier* had detailed in yesterday's package. She herself knew little about those kinds of internet fads, but throughout the week she had talked to Jess and learned that "everyone" wished they had known about the social media "tools" before now. They were all voracious for short cuts, addicted to laziness, passionate to play the game even in the wake of the scandal. The reporting had implicated the adults only and at worst characterized the teenagers as victims. That had been the only problem with the media coverage, Erin believed: Not a *scintilla* (another vocab word from the final exam) of blame had fallen on the students. That was why so many classmates were eager to hear her "view from the inside," as one of them called it. Not everyone was so welcoming, however. A fair number of students at the party hushed their voices when she came near, uncertain or leery about whether she was trustworthy, whether she was for them or against them.

She pried Sally Richards away from Cody. They had finished the year as boyfriend and girlfriend, even though Erin recalled Cody telling her that they were drifting apart—way back on the day of the Super Bowl, the day Erin had embarrassed Matt in the winner-take-all Risk game, a day three months earlier that now seemed like a lifetime ago....

"I'm about partied out," Erin confessed. "I'm glad my mom and dad didn't insist on throwing a party for me."

"Yeah, they get to where they all seem the same," Sally agreed. "The cake with the picture on it, the scrapbooks or slide shows running on a big TV screen, the punch, the book you're supposed to sign. Still, I like seeing everybody. Who knows? After next Sunday, we might not see each other ever again, some of us."

"That's true," Erin acknowledged. But she didn't add that there were a bunch of classmates she wouldn't mind never seeing again.

"Have you been at school any this week?" Sally asked.

"No. Not since my last final. On Tuesday."

"I have, just for baseball." The state tournament was in progress. Brookstone's team had played during the week, and lost, ending its season. Sally had served as a team manager.

"The day after we got beat, I was there helping collect all the uniforms and equipment and stuff. It was funny, because I didn't feel very sad about the season being over; but when the custodians mowed the field and were cleaning it up, getting it ready for the picnic, that's when I felt really sad."

Erin remembered driving past the school and seeing that work in progress. Whatever team had defeated Brookstone had shot a ton of confetti into the air from the pitcher's mound as part of the post-game celebration, forcing the grounds workers to bring out the machines with the giant vacuum hoses usually reserved for sucking up leaves in the fall. As Erin watched, the image of the whirlwind at the Junction rose in her mind for the millionth time, swirling like a stubborn ghost. If only a whirlwind would drop out of the sky and whoosh away all the ugliness from the school! When she saw that Bragley the janitor was operating the leaf vacuum, she remembered that once he said he could clean anything, given enough time.

"Erin!" came Aunt Jen's voice, breathless. "You have a phone call." Her tone was ominous. "It's your mom. She's at the hospital. Something's happened to your grandfather."

Her heart fluttering, she paced the waiting area at the end of the hallway from Grandpa Dee's room.

Strokes, the doctors said. Or ministrokes. Erin wasn't clear on the difference, or whether there really *was* any difference. Dad would explain everything when he came to them.

"Don't *worry*," Mom kept repeating, which only made Erin worry more.

Finally Mom said, "Ministrokes are not that serious, most of the time. They are common in old folks."

If that were true, then Erin would feel better about the emergency. However, she feared that her mother was just trying to say something comforting, regardless of its truthfulness. Maybe Mom was trying to convince herself.

She went on, "When *my* dad was near the end, he had ministrokes too. They didn't affect his speech or his motor skills, like *strokes* usually do. Not at all."

Near the end. Erin didn't like the sound of those words.

Down the hall she saw her dad appear, walking toward them. She wanted to run and meet him halfway, but that would only confirm to Mom how worried she was. So she waited.

"Well?" she asked when Dad was close enough that her question could be asked without shouting. "How is he? What happened?"

Dad sat down, took a deep breath in, and exhaled slowly. He lifted both hands, palms toward them, a gesture that Erin took as a plea for everyone to be calm.

Then he spoke: "Okay. Okay. It looks pretty certain that Grandpa has had a series of TIAs, transient ischemic attacks."

"Oh, no!" Erin shrieked. Energy drained from her body, and she collapsed onto a couch. "Transient … *what?*" Whatever they were, they sounded scarier than a heart attack.

Dad went on in an even tone: "They are usually called ministrokes. They are probably not serious, but it sometimes takes a few days to figure out how serious they are, how much damage they might have caused. They are not serious in themselves. The downside is, they are often a warning sign for a full-fledged stroke. And that would be more serious."

He went on to explain that TIAs took place when blood circulation in the brain was temporarily obstructed from blood clots or constricted blood vessels. He gave a lot of statistics and talked about "lesions" and "white matter disease." The numbers and medical jargon annoyed Erin. Then he said that when TIA victims later had regular strokes, they occurred as early as forty-eight hours afterward—so the doctors would be monitoring Grandpa closely for several days.

The others in the room remained silent. Her uncles nodded gravely.

"Can they do anything?" Erin asked.

"Well, yes and no," Dad replied. "Most of the things done to treat people who have TIAs, we're already doing for Grandpa. There are dietary changes, aspirin therapy, things like that."

She waited for somebody else to talk.

"When will he be able to go back to Lake Haven?" she asked.

Dad sighed heavily.

"I don't know," he said bluntly. "I don't know if he *will* be able to go back."

"Why not?" She felt panicky.

"Depending on any damage the TIAs might have caused, or if he actually has a stroke, it's possible that Lake Haven will not be able to take care of him. It may not be the best place for him anymore. Plus, we still have to see how well he comes back from the broken hip. He'll still be in rehab for some time, and the TIAs will probably push back his recovery from that. So, let's just wait and see—"

Erin interrupted, "But can't he come home and live with *us?*" She looked around at the uncles. "With *any* of us?"

They all looked so grim!

"Well?" she insisted.

"Let's just wait and see,' Dad repeated, but his tone of voice was no different from when he said they would "wait and see" after Erin began to speak up about her college hopes.

After a moment of silence, Mom said, "I've called Patti and Sarah but had to leave messages."

About ten minutes later, Dad returned from another visit to Grandpa's room and escorted them all back to see him.

He looked okay—far better than Erin envisioned. She feared he might have a droopy face or glassy eyes or drool dripping from his lips, but no, thankfully, none of those frightening things had come to pass. He recognized all of them and smiled and apologized for all the "fuss" he was causing. Her father and both her uncles cried, "Oh, no, Dad!" almost simultaneously, and Erin rushed forward and took one of his hands, which felt bony but warm and squeezed hers with clear reassuring firmness.

They talked to him until Dad said, "Okay, we probably ought to let him rest now."

Erin asked if she could stay the night in his room, but Mom shook her head and Dad said, "Not tonight, Erin. He needs to just rest. Maybe later. Let's wait and see."

"Okay." She squeezed Grandpa's hand and let go of it gently. She left the room quickly, before the others, and when she made it back to the waiting area, she was surprised to find, sitting in a chair, leafing through a magazine, humming contentedly and twirling her hair, Rachel Sarks.

Erin recoiled at the thought of her family finding her with Rachel, although she could not explain why. She stammered out a flustered hello and asked, "Why are *you* here?"

"For you," Rachel said. "Sally called me and said you might need a friend. Something happened to your grandfather?"

"That's right."

"Is he …?"

"He had a stroke, or a ministroke, or something." She glanced anxiously back down the hall. "Do you mind coming with me?"

"Sure, whatever you need."

She took Rachel down another hallway.

"It's just that I'm having a hard time with my parents right now."

Rachel's arms flew around Erin in the same kind of friendly hug that Mrs. Hillis had given her to sustain her through the tortuous times of the school year.

"*You* need to come with *me*," Rachel said.

Erin submitted quietly. They retraced their steps, passed the waiting room where the others had returned and were loitering, and entered the nearest elevator. Rachel certainly knew her way around the hospital. She pressed the button for the third floor of the seven-story building, and when they exited, she pointed down the hallway and took Erin through a door with a sign that said CHAPEL into a compact room about fifteen feet square with thickly padded pews of dark polished wood, tall yellow-tipped candles, and stained glass windows lit from behind for effect.

It was a cozy, intimate place. They were alone.

Erin braced herself for the inevitable, for Rachel to start talking about God, and Jesus, and her purpose in life, and how Jesus was there for comfort in times of trouble, everything she was accustomed to hearing from this woman at the two club meetings she had attended and from their other chance meetings. Most of those times she had felt safely distant, insulated by layers of other people who comprised the "intended audience," as Mrs. Hillis would probably call it. Not now.

Instead, Rachel asked, "So what's the trouble with your parents?"

Such a simple question!

Yet something about it seemed all wrong.

On one level, Erin welcomed the chance to spill her guts to someone like Rachel, who was close enough to care but not too close to be nosy, but also far enough away to be safe yet not so far away as to be irrelevant. Erin would love to just vent her frustration to relieve the ever-present pressure from her Dad!

On another level though—maybe it was the "longer view"—she sensed through an unfamiliar but insistent and powerful instinct that simply baring her soul, as good as that might feel, was not the answer to her problem. She was growing up. Everything that had happened to her during this topsy-turvy school year was part of her growing up, getting ready to leave the past behind, strike out on her own, and live her own life. Her opposing the cheating scandal, and dating Matt, and working on the research project with the old folks at Lake Haven, and refusing to just knuckle under to Dad's wishes for her future, and even stumbling into this strange friendship with Rachel Sarks—all these separate strands of her senior year were part of a pattern, she was sure, even if she couldn't quite make sense of the pattern yet.

"It's not really my parents," she said with conviction if not clarity. "It's more than that."

"It always is."

"What does *that* mean?" She gently pushed herself away from Rachel on the pew, sliding a few inches on the cushion and turning to face her. "What do you mean?"

Erin feared, temporarily, that Rachel might be offended by her tone of voice and her gesture. However, as she searched Rachel's face, what she saw was a contradictory mixture of excitement and restraint, as if Rachel was about to burst from anticipation, as if she was longing desperately to say something but wasn't sure if the time was right. Rachel was studying *her*, Erin realized. Rachel's gray eyes were brimming with a joy that they could not hide and were straining mightily to contain.

She *knew* what it was, or at least what Rachel would *say* it was. She had heard Rachel and others, even other Brookstone students, talk about it at the club meetings. For years she had gone along with the popular mockery against the One-Tracks, not exactly comfortable with laying a sarcastic label on them but sharing the belief that something was not quite right about them.

Now she was not so sure.

"I'm so glad you came," Erin said.

Twenty minutes later, she peeked back into the waiting room, found it empty, and walked back down the hall to Grandpa's room. Everyone was gone except for Dad, who was talking to a nurse.

"We wondered where you had disappeared to," he said. "Mom already went home. You're stuck with me."

Which was exactly what she wanted.

Once they were in the car, Dad behind the wheel and focused on the road, she said, "I'm sorry about making a big case about where Grandpa lives. I know it's not my decision. It's not my place to say where he should live."

"No," he chuckled in agreement. "But a few years from now, you and your sisters will be making the same decisions about Mom and me, probably. Did you ever think of that?"

"No." There were a thousand things she had never thought of. Every new day seemed to add a few more.

He reached over and patted her knee.

"When that time comes, I know you'll do the right thing. You make good choices."

"I *do?*"

"Sure you do."

"But ..." she struggled for the best words, for words that would not sound accusatory. "It seems like you're always telling me the opposite."

"Hmm," he mumbled. "Maybe it does seem like that. Maybe that's because the only time I ever say anything is when I disagree. But most of the time you make good decisions, so I don't say anything. You should take my silence as ... approval."

That was something else she had never thought of.

Dad said, "You make a lot of good choices."

"What about college?"

"Hmm."

He fell silent, but Erin knew it did not signal approval this time.

She waited as long as she could bear before blurting out, "Dad, I'm going to Riverside. I won't go anywhere else."

"Hmm."

"That's all you can say? *Hmm?* Say something! Say some words!" Her audacity, welling up from something hot and thick and strong in her blood, startled her.

"You want to study forestry, natural resources, something along those lines?"

"Yes, but not at Virginia Tech. It's not important for me to go to whatever the number one school in America is. Can't you understand that?" Her tone teetered on the edge of disrespect, so she softened it: "Please tell me you understand that."

"Well," he grumbled, "I don't *understand* it, Erin."

Great, she thought, her heart sinking into despair. *Just great*. So many times during the school year she had taken chances and things had gone in her favor. She was probably due for something to go against her. Or, as Matt and his gambling buddies would say, the long arm of the law of averages was balancing things in her life.

Then Dad said, "I don't understand it, but I *am* willing to *accept* it."

"You are?"

"Yes, if you want to try it." He reached across and ran his hand through her hair. Whenever he did that—which was not often—she wondered whether he wished at least one of his children had been a boy.

Nevertheless, his simple affirmation opened the locks to a flood of other worries that she felt compelled to share with him. She said she was afraid that subconsciously she might be going to Riverside simply because Nathan Dyer was there, but Dad assured her that "those things have a way of working out." Similarly, she feared her interest in forestry might have come from Nathan switching his major to the same field, but Dad pointed out that nearly half of college students changed majors anyway, and she could do the same without much trouble as long as she didn't wait too long.

"I think maybe I should just start out in general studies," she suggested. "Then I could wait a year to figure out for sure what I should major in."

"See?" he said again. "That would be another good decision."

She could tell he was struggling to keep calm—and succeeding.

They passed the cemetery on Highway 22 where Steve Gutierrez was buried, where she and Matt had spent some memorable moments, and where Matt had actually dug up the coffin in another amazing chapter of the incredible story she had helped write.

Dad saw her looking toward the graveyard and said, "Hey."

"Yes?"

"What do you hear from your friends? From Matt? I'm just curious. What did he have to do with what happened to Tolan Myers?"

"I still don't know about that," she said. "I wish I did."

She was being totally honest. It felt good to be totally honest with her father.

"Okay, okay. Then, what about you and Matt?"

"Well, we're finished. We were finished months ago."

"And Nathan?"

She laughed. Her romantic life was not something she was ready to talk to him about. From her experience with Matt, though, she had learned that it would be foolish to try to force anything with Nathan, or to expect that they could start all over again. If that were to happen, it would have to emerge naturally.

She answered, "I don't know about that either, Dad."

The weather was warm enough that he parked in the driveway when they got home. Erin said she would stay on the porch for a while. Her father tousled her hair again, pulled her head toward him in a gentle hug, and went inside.

She took off her shoes and socks and crossed the cool lawn to the tire swing hung from the ancient hackberry tree. For the next half hour she swayed back and forth and twirled lazily in the darkness, breathing in through her nose the sweet aroma of honeysuckle and lilac. The breeze was just right, she thought, not too strong to make her cool, but strong enough to clear the air and make the stars brilliant and sharp. Any more, whenever she felt wind she thought about it being either violent and destructive or comforting and cleansing. Even her whirlwind, for all its tornadic fury, had refreshed her soul and cleaned up everything in its path.

Dad's unexpected consent to her college hopes began to sink in. Her sense of relief, of having had a great burden lifted, was palpable. She was actually going to Riverside University! She wanted to call Nathan and tell him, but probably she should wait. If she waited too long, though, Jess would tell him first.

Then she smiled: Jess did not even know, not yet.

Life was so unpredictable! She had hoped her senior year would be a time of clarification, of coalescing direction and focus and planning. Instead, all it had become a cauldron of seething uncertainty. Even with the Riverside issue resolved, she felt no more certain about her life. Honestly, she did not know whether forestry was really a suitable major or career, and she was more up in the air about Nathan than ever. Her father's blessing on her choice should have relieved her; instead, she seemed more anxious than ever. She knew why, too. She knew that if she failed now, if her dream did not come true, she would have no one to blame but herself. That was a whole new kind of pressure to deal with.

Another scary thought clouded her outlook. What if Dad changed his mind? What if his approval turned out to be only temporary—a unilateral ceasefire while he dealt with the more important problem of Grandpa Dee's health?

Somehow, though, all this new turmoil was all right. She could live with the uncertainty, the lack of clarity.

She kept looking at the stars.

Then a new idea occurred to her, a magnificent idea that made her feel even smaller than she did from swaying alone beneath the glorious expanse of the skies. She considered that her earlier thought about setting her college decision in the "longer view" of her whole life was itself too narrow, because her life was just one of many—and what was going on in *every* life and how they were all interconnected was the real "long view." What, if anything, she asked herself, could possibly unite all people in all times and places?

As quickly as she raised the question, she knew the answer. At least she knew what the One-Tracks would say was the answer. It was surprising, if not downright frightening, how much the One-Tracks were on her mind right now. Her original opinion about them—that they were brainwashed by a lot of harmless nonsense—lay shredded at her feet.

Whatever they believed and talked about was definitely *not* nonsense, and now she wasn't even sure it was harmless. The biggest surprise of all, however, was that everything about them was turning out to be so *practical*. She never imagined that could be true. Yet tonight, when she needed somebody to listen to her, to encourage her, to tell her she was okay, to just *be* with her, where was Matt? Where was Jess? Where was Nathan, or Cody? Where were her parents or her sisters or her uncles or even Mrs. Hillis? Nowhere in sight. No, only Rachel, a One-Track woman she had not even known a few months ago, had come to help her.

The stars twinkled merrily. A couple of years earlier in an earth science class she had learned about the stupendous distances of the stars and galaxies, millions and billions of light-years, too far to fathom. Yet really they were so close. A whiff of wind rustled the new leaves in the tree and wafted the smell of honeysuckle through the yard. Erin felt the cool rough grass between her toes, and she listened for the song of crickets, aware that the weather was still not warm enough for them to thrive. She loved nature—she worshipped nature. If passion were the only factor, then she was *made* for forestry.

But—

Another One-Track idea intruded on her reverie. Manny Sarks had told the club that each one of them had greater glory than anything else in creation. They were more glorious than anything in the heavens or on earth, more glorious than any waterfall or canyon or mountain or any animal or bird or butterfly or flower or tree or leaf.

More glorious than the stars. More glorious than her whirlwind.

That was hard to believe, but wonderful to imagine.

18

J. BRADFORD MCCAULEY needed to get on with his life. The death of Gregory Travis, whom he had never replaced on his Ph.D. committee, had nevertheless led to a postponement of his first meeting for his dissertation defense until Friday, two days away.

And now, stewing in the delay, McCauley was anxious in an entirely new way. He had no doubt that his dissertation was polished to perfection, a scholarly gem of deep substance and high style. He had no doubt that he could defend it against any question or objection from his two remaining committee members in the traditional tussle that was really a mere formality. For all intents and purposes, he had finished his work; he awaited only the routine stamp of approval from the powers that be.

Yet ... he was apprehensive.

Not because he feared being exposed for his academic fraud, either. On that count he felt safe. His careful checking had satisfied him that nobody besides Travis knew about James West's original thesis from the middle of the nineteenth century.

All the same, as he approached the Riverside Engineering Fountain and dropped his backpack on one of the arc-shaped sections of concrete bench that together circled the landmark, he heard an imaginary clock ticking. Time was rapidly running out. He must decide going into the meeting on Friday whether or not he would tell the truth about his plagiarized doctoral work or plunge forward into his career knowing that in his own way he was as big a cheater as Tolan Myers, Walter Patingale, and countless Brookstone High School students.

He heard a clock ticking, and it was not the Universal Clock. Never had he recognized with such lucidity that a moment of decision lay at hand—that he himself must make a choice, that he could not figuratively sit back and let some vague fate decide his destiny. All the philosophy he had believed in for years and discussed with Robin Hillis for months was just irrelevant theory compared to this real-life issue.

McCauley squinted upward at the clock tower. Whatever ticking he imagined he heard did not come from the tower, whose machinery had been out of order most of the spring semester.

The Engineering Mall was nearly empty, most students having left for the summer. A jogger appeared beneath the elevated walkway joining the Materials Engineering and Electrical Engineering buildings, and McCauley followed his slow but regular route along the front of the Mechanical Engineering building, his white shirt shimmering in sunshine, contrasting with the green ivy crawling up the walls behind him. His eyes left the jogger and settled on the ivy.

Yesterday, even lunch at ¿Que Pasa? had failed to settle his thoughts. He had gone there half hoping to see Manny Sarks, because whenever they met by chance—the only way they ever did meet—McCauley always left refreshed and upbeat. Sarks was about the only person from Indiana he would miss, other than Robin Hillis, when he finally packed his bags and headed wherever he headed next. But today the mystery man, who came and went like a leaf on the wind, was blowing somewhere else.

After lunch McCauley hopped on his motorcycle and rode for nearly two hours through random towns north of Bridgebury, avoiding Brookstone and the Junction Bridge, obsessing over his Friday defense.

Crazy ideas came and went. He could announce to his dissertation committee that his whole four-year course of study had been an exercise designed to show how easy it was to fool the experts, that his thesis was really recycled. How would they react? They might not be amused. It was not worth the risk. He could claim that because of the tragic events at Brookstone and his personal investment with the people involved, he was not psychologically fit to continue with his program. That might buy him time to think through his options more thoroughly. His craziest idea was to go to Robin's neighbor, the man who helped her and Zeb navigate the treacherous waters of their failing marriage, and ask for his help. That was ridiculous, of course. The man would figure out who McCauley was after the first few words of conversation.

He also knew that all his worked-up worry about the dissertation masked the simpler truth that he really wanted to see Robin once more, to say good-bye, to reach some sort of personal closure with her. The night of Myers's death they had talked after the police were through with him, mostly comparing notes, trying to fill in each other's missing information. A few days later they had met at the garage sale and spent two hours together. Even then, however, their time was spent analyzing the aftermath of the scandal's revelation by the media. Since then, silence had ensued.

Night fell. McCauley went back to his office and called the Hillis home to determine if anyone was there. When Robin answered, he hung up immediately. Okay, she was home. What about Zeb? As he pondered what to do next, he was aware of his own boldness but also the futility and simple *wrongness* of using it in this way. Yet he instinctively felt that the decision he must make about his professional future involved her. Why? Because she was the only living person who knew about his academic crime?

He rode north to Brookstone, past the landmarks of his last twelve months—the Dairy Queen, the farm fields, the Amoco terminal's huge tanks, the railroads, the town's street signs. He circled the school. At the front entrance he paused, his jaw dropping at the vandalism: Kids had knocked the façade off the pillars and spray painted CHEATERS and more vulgar words across the marble and limestone pavement. McCauley wheeled into the rear parking lot and stopped in the corner near the baseball field. Its lights were on and a man on a roaring John Deere tractor was mowing the outfield grass while sprinklers watered the infield in preparation for the Senior Picnic on Sunday, two days after a commencement ceremony that in the light of the untimely end of the school year could hardly be more ironic.

McCauley set his helmet on the back of his motorcycle seat and dropped his gloves into the storage box. He ran his fingers through his hair and walked toward Dogwood Street.

What exactly were his intentions? Who could tell? If he had learned anything in the past nine months, he had learned that it was fruitless to try to dissect his own motivations. Pride, lust, fear, sorrow—they all mixed together in a stew of unfathomable thickness that gave birth to his thoughts and words and actions. One thing was sure. His old ideas about the Universal Clock, once so unshakeable, no longer brought him any comfort or peace. They were ideas, maybe even reasonable ideas, but the crucible of the past year had tested them and found them insufficient. He was making decisions now, not merely watching and waiting to react to circumstances that were really the results of decisions made by others, not by the inscrutable force of fate.

However, the Founding Fathers had believed in such a force, and even personalized it. The philosophy may have failed him, but his dissertation's central points were valid and professionally valuable.

If he decided to move forward with them.

Far down Dogwood Street he saw a couple coming toward him on the sidewalk, illuminated briefly when they passed under a street lamp. The short slender form of Robin was unmistakable; at her side, he concluded, must be Zeb. McCauley's heartbeat quickened as it had when Robin had first called him *dear*, as it had when they had spied on Myers and LaGrange from their secret-infested closet, as it had when Tolan Myers pulled the gleaming revolver from his jacket on the Junction Bridge.

He hid between two houses, behind a flowering shrub in the darkness. Robin and Zeb passed, holding hands. McCauley heard the sound of humming but no words.

When they turned the corner at the end of the block, he emerged and followed. They angled into the street, timing their crossing to allow a single slow-moving car to pass. Their general direction took them toward the school. Then McCauley noticed people going into the old church with the impressive stained glass windows lit up from within the sanctuary. Once, Robin had mentioned that this was not their church but they often attended its mid-week services.

McCauley crossed back over to the school at the intersection but kept his eyes on Robin and Zeb, who chatted with another couple beneath the canopy over the church's main entrance. At last they went inside.

McCauley's eyes climbed the church steeple, then fell to the ground. He sighed. He was no nearer to deciding how to handle his dissertation dilemma. His aimless wandering had occupied half the day but brought him no closer to conclusion.

Above him the First Fidelity Bank sign dominated the Brookstone skyline, brighter by far than its small-town competition, like the moon among stars.

McCauley sighed again, deeply frustrated. The night was just beginning. If he wanted, he could ride for hours more, to Indianapolis or Chicago. But what was the use?

A particularly vivid line from one of Bruce Springsteen's songs rose in his memory, a line about everybody running but finding nowhere to hide.

He looked back at the tall steeple. ...

Now, eighteen hours later, he was no closer to deciding what to do.

Three times since losing his job at Brookstone, he had cleared his schedule and his mind and cleared out from the familiar environments of his graduate office and his apartment in order to seriously weigh his job offers. Each time he had reached the same verdict about which university made the best fit for him. Unfortunately, that verdict, for all its merit, was not the real decision facing him.

He had known that for some time now.

He had hoped that the troubling specter of his conscience, awakened through his discussions with Robin about the Universal Clock and what she regarded as its moral impotence, would withdraw or weaken after his relationship with her cooled. That did not happen. Whatever had been brought to life during his close hours with her had assumed a life *apart* from her, forcing him to question whether it had ever been dependent on her to start with. Afterward, analyzing it with as much detachment as he could manage, he marveled at his own blindness. How could he have missed something so obvious? How could he have missed the truth that nothing besides a profound sense of moral outrage—something his

Universal Clock could never generate, even hypothetically—could have sustained him and Robin for all those months they had spent rooting out the cheating?

And now that same sense or instinct was focused like a laser beam not on the Brookstone scandal but on his own academic crime.

His interpretation of the Founding Fathers was changing, too. He saw that he was wrong in thinking of them as heroes, wrong in the realm of his deistic framework, which insisted they did not really make any choices. They did what they did in leading a rebellion against the most powerful empire on the planet and establishing a whole new nation because they had no freedom to do otherwise. How could they be heroes if they couldn't help but do the things they did? That question, once he asked it, was impeccably sensible. It came to him as a shock.

When all these dots connected in his thinking, he faced a crisis on two fronts, one professional and one personal.

First, he wondered what would happen to the integrity of his basic argument about the Founders and their faith and the Constitution. Would his thesis crumble from the tension of the newly unmasked inconsistency? No, thankfully. That inconsistency would not necessarily destroy his scholarship—you didn't have to buy into everything you studied. Lots of intellectuals made respectable careers as experts on people and ways of thinking they didn't personally believe. Everything he had researched was still valid. The religion of Jefferson, Paine, Franklin, et al. had plainly shaped the founding documents of the nation, regardless of whether their philosophy was correct.

Second, McCauley began to reexamine his own beliefs. His faith in the faith of the Founders was ebbing. The blame—or the credit—for that went to Robin. At first her questions had seemed nagging and nitpicky, but they had lodged like seeds in the soil of his mind, eventually sprouting, opening his eyes to the weakness in his point view about life and love and history and everything else. And now, ultimately, they were if not flourishing at least strongly rooted and healthy, sending out intrusive, irrepressible new growth into every area of his thinking.

And as his final months in Indiana came and went, there was one place where much of that nagging, nitpicky, irrepressible growth was intruding more and more—his dissertation—and one place on campus where he was acutely aware of it—the ivy-covered engineering buildings that he passed going to and from his graduate office. The university, a land-grant institution established at the time of President Lincoln, had by original statute and later tradition decreed that all its academic buildings have red brick exteriors. Ivy respected neither the law nor convention, however. It had overgrown the particular buildings along McCauley's daily route, and even though it had not yet assumed the deep green color that would prevail until October, its lighter spring green had banished its dead winter brown.

Day by day McCauley watched the changing color. He began to think about what effect years of ivy growth would have on the brick and mortar beneath. Over time, the network of tiny roots must weaken and disintegrate the stone. At what point he noticed the analogy between the ivy and his changing ideas about the Universal Clock he could not positively say; nevertheless, the parallel between the two was fixed in his mind now, so much so that whenever he saw anything similar, like sections of sidewalk left jagged by the action of unseen tree roots, he wondered how his own philosophy was being undermined.

He gazed at the buildings for a long time, dazed, barely aware of the rush and hiss of the fountain nearby.

For all his work to expose the cheating at Brookstone and for all his agitation and rumination about his own academic malfeasance, he made no decision about how he should proceed until Lawton Overholzer called him late that Wednesday afternoon.

"Seems like you've been avoiding me," he observed wryly. "Everything okay?"

McCauley did not know whether Overholzer knew about his trouble at Brookstone High School. Perhaps the old college prof didn't know and didn't care. Even his college colleagues had no excuse to not know after today's news, though—the ongoing coverage in the Bridgebury *Courier* had led off with a page one story reporting that police would reopen the case of the death of Steve Gutierrez. Maybe Matt Rademacher was right. Maybe Myers was to blame.

"I've been busy," McCauley replied lamely. He was less busy right now than he had been for years.

"You haven't returned my phone calls or replied to my emails," Overholzer pressed on. "Mine or Renee's. We just want to confirm that we are still on schedule for Friday."

"Yes," he said. Overholzer, his graduate thesis adviser, and Renee Dolch, another professor in the History Department, were the remaining two thirds of his committee now that Gregory Travis had passed on.

"Yes," McCauley repeated. "Yes, I know you wanted me to confirm. Sorry I haven't gotten back to you."

Overholzer caught the incompleteness in the statement, the hint of uncertainty in McCauley's voice.

The professor asked, "But ... what?"

"Right," McCauley answered. Dread rose in his chest, tightness. He took a deep breath, and then, without understanding exactly why, without knowing how the months of subconscious erosion by the invisible ivy in his mind had changed him, he went on: "I'm not going to defend on Friday. I'm not ready."

"*Not ready?*"

"I have to make some changes."

"What?" Overholzer was flabbergasted.

"Look," McCauley explained, "in the last year or so, Gregory Travis convinced me that with a little editing I can get my dissertation published. That idea really appeals to me. But I'm not going to go for that until I make some changes. If this is going to be *my* book, with *my* name on it as an author, then it has to be perfect. It has to be saying exactly what *I* want it to say. I have to make some changes. They're not major, but they won't be ready for Friday."

"What, then? Next week?"

"No. More like next fall. Next Christmas."

"Brad, you can't be serious! You already have job offers—good ones! Why would you want to stay around here another semester? I'm not even sure you could get any more fellowship money. How will you afford it?"

McCauley had already thought of that obstacle. Without his part-time job at Brookstone High School, his money issues would only get worse. All the same, he was willing to teach a couple of Riverside classes in the fall while he tweaked his dissertation. Riverside wouldn't cut him off.

Overholzer made one more attempt to get through to his bullheaded student.

"Are you sure about this?" he asked. "You're sure to sail through on Friday. Then you could make any changes you want before you publish."

"I'm sure," McCauley answered firmly. "I'm absolutely sure."

"All right, then," the professor said, his voice rising in resignation.

He walked away, never asking about the specific changes McCauley wanted to make. That was just as good—McCauley did not want to lie to Overholzer's face. This way McCauley himself could save face, essentially, by revising his dissertation to incorporate James West, to give him the credit he ought to get, even if he had been dead and buried for more than a century. As for McCauley, his role would shift from being the pioneer and developer of a new theory to being the discoverer and champion of an unknown pioneer of intellectual thought.

In the wake of his decision, a growing restlessness compelled him to leave his office and pace the hallway. Finally he left the building. Thinking about the repercussions of what he had done brought a kind of vertigo. Yet he was sure he was doing the best thing, the right thing. He walked past the greening ivy of the Mechanical Engineering building into the wide open vista of the Engineering Mall, whose fountain seemed to beckon him. Its colored, hissing jets relaxed him. Above and beyond the line of engineering buildings, high in the sky, he followed the flight of a vast flock of birds, hundreds if not thousands, circling in carefree synchrony.

He inhaled deeply, freely. The resolution to his problem was not everything he had hoped for—not originally, at least. But it was all he could hope for now, if he wanted to ensure his professional survival and satisfy his conscience. The crucial idea about the Founders and the Constitution would get the hearing it deserved in the academic forum, the man who had first proposed it would get the recognition he deserved, and McCauley would launch his career on the wings of a decision he would never have to hide.

19

STRAINS OF MUSIC reverberated down the hallway. They struck
Robin Hillis at first as simply mysterious, then as faintly memorable,
and finally as uncomfortably familiar. The song was "Down to the
River," and the voice unmistakably belonged to Bruce Springsteen.
What Robin could not figure out was who would be in the building at
this time on a Sunday, and why that person would be playing music by
that particular artist.

She shuddered.

The last person she wanted to see face-to-face was Brad McCauley.

She could reverse direction and take another route to the Main
Office. Curiosity got the best of her, however, and compelled her to
continue, to see if it really was Brad. The music was definitely coming
from Bill St. Clair's social studies room, which Brad had used last period
every day during the school year. Its door was propped open by a book,
as though whoever was inside didn't care if the sounds were heard but
was more cautious about letting anybody look inside.

A number of questions occurred to Robin, assuming it *was* Brad
in the room. One, why was he here at all, since he had been fired two
weeks ago and presumably told to get his possessions off the premises
ASAP? Two, how did he manage to get into the building? Three, why
was he calling attention to his presence with the signature music?

Breathing a prayer of thanks that she was wearing soft canvas shoes, she paused just outside the door. A flood of impressions overcame her, mingled thoughts and feelings about the past year but more vividly about the past week. So much was happening, day by day, that she wanted to discuss with Brad! Since the last articles had run in the newspapers, more chaos had broken loose. The community air turned dark with accusations and allegations, recriminations and retaliations. Chatter over bins of produce at the Dan's IGA grocery store or drinks at the Corner Bar. Letters to the editor of newspapers. Facebook postings. Graffiti on the school building, on abandoned barns, on train cars. Legal action, including lawsuits against the school corporation and individuals, parents and even students. The tiny town of Brookstone, once so secure in its reputation, found itself the center of a swirling storm of bitter controversy. Robin had never seen anything like it.

The angle of vision afforded by the door's small opening let her see only the back of the classroom. She could hear somebody in the front.

Gently, she swung open the door.

Brad was sitting at the desk, one drawer pulled out, a paper box open on the floor. The music issuing from speakers on a counter along the side wall was loud enough that he did not hear her come in. When she was close enough, he noticed her movement and looked up.

His startled look made it obvious that he was not expecting to see her.

He hustled to the music player and turned down the volume.

"Hi," he said. "Fancy meeting you here."

She wished now that she had avoided the room altogether.

"Hi," she answered. "I'm just … cleaning up my room for the summer. And picking up mail."

He nodded.

Neither one spoke. She wished the music were louder, now.

"Well?" she asked.

"Look," he said. He sat down on the polished wooden surface of the teacher desk. "I'm not sure why this is so awkward, but it is."

She laughed and felt the pressure relax.

"Brad," she asked, "why are you here? Aren't you supposed to be long gone? I thought you had your Ph.D. defense last Friday? I thought you would be as far away as you could be by now."

He nodded again, reflectively, and let a slow sigh blow from his round cheeks.

"Yeah," he said. "A lot has happened even since I last saw you."

So, he had stories to share. She was not sure she wanted to hear them.

"Why are you even *here?*" she asked again, hoping to rivet his attention on the immediate and spare them any temptation to relive the past.

"Well, because I actually have a few personal belongings I left in this room. Not many, but important to me. I'm surprised they're still here, to be honest. Bill St. Clair was kind enough to leave them untouched, but I really expected that LaGrange or the school board would have come in and … I don't know, tried to erase any signs that I had ever been here."

Just hearing the principal's name on Brad's lips made her want to continue the discussion they had begun the day they had met at the garage sale, shared a snack at ¿Que Pasa?, and said good-bye at the Riverside Engineering Fountain. After that, she really believed she would never see Brad McCauley again. But here he was—the one person she most wanted to process with, and the one person she most needed to distance herself from.

He said, "Robin, I'm sorry. I came on a Sunday intentionally to avoid running into you. I figured that after all we've been through and all you're wanting to do with your life, I'm the last person you would want to run into."

She laughed and asked, "Then why do you have Bruce Springsteen singing at the top of his lungs and bouncing off the lockers up and down the hallway?"

He laughed too. Seeing the smile beneath his bushy mustache filled her with happiness.

"I guess my penchant for rebellion won out over my discretion," he offered.

"I guess so."

"The picnic is this afternoon," he remarked.

"Yes. I don't suppose you're going?"

"Officially I'm not supposed to be on school property. I had to sneak in here as it was; it reminded me of our snooping adventures this spring."

The answer to one of her questions dawned on her.

"Let me guess," she asked. "To get in the building, you used that key that Matt Rademacher showed us."

"Yeah. I was shocked that it was still there in its hiding place."

A new song started—"Born to Run," the one that Brad said had launched the young Springsteen onto the national scene way back when. Lately she had reconsidered that song's passionate lyrics in the more permanent light of her running a race marked out for her. The song always bothered her because its speaker was running *from* real life.

Robin remembered something else.

"Oh, in my purse, in my room, I have a tape to return to you."

"Don't bother," Brad said. "Keep it for old times' sake. Or throw it out. Whatever. I won't be offended."

"It's really great music, great poetry," she said with a level of passion that she instantly regretted—but some impulse was surging inside her, some urge to tell the truth. "I was going to toss it, but I couldn't. Too many of the songs just … resonated. They described *me* over the last year or so. I feel like such a hypocrite for the way I made fun of you and criticized you for your music tastes last fall when you gave me the tape. A lot of the last year for me has been deception and fantasy—that's my fault, not yours, and I'm not blaming you for any of it—and so many of the songs talk about how easily we let our fantasies take over our lives …"

She paused, recognizing that she was rambling, saying far more than she should, possibly hurting this man she had no right or desire to hurt.

"You're no hypocrite, Robin."

"Oh, but I *am!* You don't know what I was thinking all along with you! I kept thinking you were running from the truth, running from who you really are, and putting this stupid 'Born to Run' philosophy up on a pedestal and worshiping it. When really it was *me!* I was the one running from everything I believed in! I was running from my husband, from my promises, from my family, my friends, my history, my … Oh!"

"Well, you came to your senses, I guess."

"Yes!" She nearly shouted the word, exuberant with gratitude that she could. "But *you* are not to blame! It was …" She stopped again, afraid that whatever she said to finish the sentence would be dangerous.

She thought of one song on his tape, "Jungleland," whose lyrics haunted her with their eerily incisive, convicting power and whose blend of guitar and piano was so intoxicating that she wondered how anybody could *avoid* being trapped in a net of flesh and fantasy, as the song put it. How seductive!—both the imagery of the song and the truth it described! One line said something about two lovers taking a "stab" at love, but in the aftermath Robin saw that she had been stabbed by her own carelessness and stupidity and selfishness. Her inner English teacher surfaced long enough to wonder whether Springsteen the songwriter, like all the great poets, chose that word *stab* for all of its possible interpretations ... or was it just a lucky stab of a word choice? Could he have possibly known what that word might mean to the vast unnumbered listeners who would populate his bright future? How old would he have been when he wrote that song? Probably not even as old as Brad ... Now her mind was awash in other remembered songs from the tape. There was one called "Glory Days" about the snare of nostalgia, which sent a pang of ambivalence rippling along her soul, for she must forever turn her back on all the precious times with Brad, she must not even think about reliving them. Sin was delightful for a season, as the biblical proverb said, but that season had passed for her and this man, that season that she could see now was a deadly dance swaying between the worlds of real and unreal from "Jungleland." Oh, she wished she could recall the exact words!—but probably it was best that she couldn't, that she was forgetting them, that the season of selfish sin was slipping away.

"Say no more," Brad said graciously.

She looked at the box on the floor and chuckled, struggling for a graceful way to exit the conversation and the room.

"To be honest," she said, "I waited this long to come in and start my spring cleaning because I didn't want to risk meeting you."

He smiled.

"So both our plans backfired," he said. "I guess we were *fated* to meet."

"Maybe." She shrugged her shoulders.

"I'm joking," he said.

They both laughed. It felt good. The way they were finishing felt good.

The music in the room had looped, she realized. "Down to the River" was playing again. Its words about the curse of memories could not be more ironic. She would never forget J. Bradford McCauley.

"When you publish your book," she blurted out, "promise me you'll send me an autographed copy."

"Okay," he said slowly. "I'm not sure where *that* came from."

"The song," she explained vainly. "The song made me think of ... never mind."

"All right."

"What about your defense?"

"Postponed."

"Again?"

"Yep."

Obviously he did not want to talk about it.

"What's next for you, then?"

"I have three job offers."

"Congratulations! I never had any doubts!" She wondered how that reconciled with his still unfinished dissertation; however, she quelled her curiosity. "Where are they? The schools?"

"All three out west."

"I'm so happy for you, Brad!" She congratulated herself for not saying she was *proud*, as a mom might say.

"It's everything I've been working for, I guess."

Another spell of awkward silence fell.

"Well, I need to go check my mail," she said.

A tap at the door drew their attention. The familiar form of Bragley filled the doorway with an unfamiliar addition to the ring of keys at his side—a holstered handgun.

"Everything all right?" he asked. "Anything I can do to help you?"

"Everything's fine, Bragley," Robin replied. "What about you? Is everything okay?" She gestured toward the gun.

"I started carrying this little baby for protection when no one else is in the building," he said. "You know, after everything I read in the papers. One of those stories said that burglars got in at night and stole a bunch of records and that's how everything got out. That's a little bit too exciting for me, if you know what I mean. And that Rademacher kid, me and him was friends, and when I heard he maybe had something to do with what happened to Tolan Myers ... I decided it's better to be safe than sorry, if you know what I mean."

He regarded McCauley suspiciously.

"He's with me," Robin interjected. "I let him into the building."

"Right," Bragley said, apparently unconvinced. "Well, don't work too hard."

They listened to his steps retreating down the hollow hallway, echoing off the metal lockers.

Brad closed the desk drawer and settled a lid on the paper box.

"My work here is finished," he announced, "if you know what I mean."

Robin smiled.

"I do know," she said. "And it was very good work."

Three hours later, she was shading her eyes from the bright sunshine on the thick grass of the baseball field.

"When you read as many stories as I do," she said, "when you do that for a living, then you start to think of everything in terms of stories." Next to her, Erin Delaney clapped her sandals together to knock off bits of mud. Her bare feet were almost invisible in the grass, newly cut but cut high. "People, events, everything. You develop a sense for the rhythms of stories occurring in life. You get a feel for beginnings and endings. And right now, everything feels like an *ending*."

Erin listened respectfully and then said, "But commencement was Friday night, and it means *beginning*."

"I know, but ..."

They were having a playful argument, the kind that Erin thought should typify the ideal relationship between young adults and grown-ups, the kind she had wished for with her parents and other significant adults all through her high school years—and the kind that Robin too welcomed. Erin had taken issue with Robin's opinion that the whole day smacked of *endings*. And because Robin was able to sympathize with Erin's point of view, she was only half-heartedly trying to prove her point, which was equally valid—but did it really matter? On a lovely day like this, and after all they had been through together, did it really matter?

Before Robin could flesh out her thoughts, a football bounded off the ground nearby, followed soon after by the lumbering form of Matt Rademacher, shirtless, smiling and sweating, who retrieved the ball and with a pronounced grunt heaved it back to his buddies. Trotting away, he managed a brief "Hi, ladies!"

From Erin's happy perspective, this day suggested nothing resembling an ending. If anything, the annual Senior Picnic was exploding with the sensations of summer, the season it informally inaugurated every year. Erin had been to these celebrations before, with her older sisters, so she knew what to look for. The hundred or so new graduates and their families scattered around the baseball field and its grandstands could not have scripted any prettier weather for their celebration. The yellow sunshine poured down warmly from a cloudless sky, the temperatures hovered in the low 70s, and the pennants around the outfield fence fluttered in light puffs of wind. The fragrance of lilac and early heliotrope, with a hint of geraniums, hung in the air from neighborhoods around the school. From the loudspeakers positioned on the corners of the press box blared loud pop music interrupted by occasional announcements from Coach Batta. On the thick outfield grass, students tossed footballs and Frisbees, played corn hole and washers, and gathered in groups large and small to pose for pictures and sign yearbooks. Six grills, set up in the infield, sent up billows of smoke, and parents and other school boosters wearing aprons and chef hats mingled around them, chatting and laughing and cooking hamburgers and hot dogs. Nearby, an array of side dishes, desserts, and chips were laid out on tables. Cans of soft drinks bobbed in a pair of tubs filled with ice water, while four tall coolers dispensed lemonade and water. Despite the year-end turmoil that had led to postponement of the annual event, nobody was complaining today.

"It's just a feeling I have," Robin went on, despairing of making Erin understand. "You go right ahead and enjoy it for yourself."

Robin was well aware of all the joy and life around her, and she appreciated it. Yet she saw deeper into the truth. She knew: Many seasons *were* ending. Ironically, thankfully, what might have been the most expected but disappointing ending had been averted by Brad McCauley's sacrificial gesture before the school board. Robin debated whether or not to tell Erin about that. Now that their friendship had been forged in the fires of their teamwork with Brad, Erin certainly had proved herself trustworthy. She deserved to know. Then again, the cheating scandal and its aftermath had left its mark on her. No teenager should have to face what Erin had gone through.

"I'll talk to you later, then," Erin said, and she headed toward the nearest cluster of classmates.

Robin smiled, looking forward and backward at the same time. Try as she might, she could not resist the mental exercise of piecing together the timeline of what had happened and when, of who knew what and when.

She remembered vividly Brad's phone call on the rescheduled last day of final exams. He had already given his exam, the day before his firing, and for some reason finished scoring the tests and even calculated the semester grades for his students. Now he wanted Robin to turn in his final grades. When she took care of his request the next morning, she discovered that he had obviously been in the building at some point and left a card in her faculty mailbox. It was a simple thank-you card that also addressed one of her fears by stating (with no explanation) that she would never be penalized in any way for her night-time flyer binge that embarrassed and angered so many teachers and students when they came back to school three days after the death of Myers. Over the weekend, police had declared the school part of the crime scene, sealed the doors with yellow tape, and refused admittance to everyone, even Principal LaGrange; the flyers, therefore, greeted everyone the following Tuesday morning. Later that day she learned how Brad at his school board termination meeting had claimed that he was responsible for those flyers. Robin suspected that the board, kept informed by Patingale and LaGrange, probably knew this was a bald-faced lie. In their administrative calculus, however, they wisely decided it was better to fire Brad, who would be leaving anyway, than to fan the flames of the scandal by launching an internal investigation whose end point would simply underscore the school's titanic hypocrisy.

Yes, Robin's temper tantrum warranted her dismissal. She had made unprovable accusations and named names. Even if she could produce evidence to support her allegations beyond her own say-so, she had intentionally circumvented the prescribed protocol for professional grievances, which was part of the master teaching contract. At the time, of course, she had not thought of any of this—but Brad had thought of it. He had thought of *her*.

There was enough hypocrisy to go around. Her own and her school's, to be sure. Watching the families spread around the baseball field, though, Robin was even more upset by the hypocrisy or crime that might never be known. So many parents were guilty. She had no way of knowing which ones were involved and which ones were innocent. All the same, she knew that many of the moms and dads celebrating their children's graduation today had encouraged their kids to do *whatever* it took to succeed, and that word *whatever* was a net cast wide enough to catch lots of behavior that was unimaginable but real. Too many parents did not care enough—did not love their sons and daughters enough—to insist on integrity. Many of the parents themselves, lacking any true morals, were nonetheless more spineless than wicked. Some were possibly oblivious. Others had no excuse. They were more actively and malevolently engaged in the competition for success and honor, offering bribes or gifts or favors to teachers in return for good grades for their kids. One of the newspaper articles reported that parents threatened teachers and even pressured the academic rivals of their own children. And the kids? Most of them knew which teachers were honest and which were not. In the end, certain students who were exposed as cheaters still got their good grades this year. A couple were even co-valedictorians.

All of it was shameful, Robin said to herself, absolutely shameful. Yet everything that she and Brad and Erin had done might make no difference. Even the nationwide media exposure might prove to be just an insignificant drop in the ocean of cheating.

Between the first base line and the dugout, Bragley was putting new plastic liners in the trash bins. His gun was gone. Robin smiled with appreciation. Bragley transcended the ebb and flow of politics in the school just as low-level government workers survived post-election purges.

She rejoined her husband near one of the grills, where he was gabbing with Howard and Jerri Roost. Brookstone's graduates and their families were extended perpetual invitations to the Senior Picnic; however, few took advantage of the gift. The Roosts were an exception.

"You'll never guess what Howard and Jerri just told me," Zeb said. He and Robin were still riding the wave of their rejuvenated marriage, but Robin believed the real reason Zeb had come to the picnic was in hopes of seeing Brad McCauley, should he make an appearance. Zeb was just curious, she thought, not vengeful.

"These days," she replied, "I would believe anything." Her reconciliation with Zeb was nothing short of a miracle.

Jerri said in a low voice, "We heard about the cheating long before it was in the media. After you were asking Lena and Jack about it, they told us. And ever since that day, we have been praying for the school, and for you and all the others who were trying to get to the bottom of it."

"Thank you," Robin replied. What else could she say?

Howard added, "What's happened—the way it has all blown up, with the newspaper coverage and all—has been amazing. I know it looks bad for the school, but in the long run, this is the best thing that could have happened. We couldn't have asked for anything more."

Robin nodded politely. She was not entirely sure she agreed. However, it was good to be done hiding secrets—of all kinds.

Zeb was nodding and smiling at her as though he had some wonderful secret to share.

Their good news came in waves. A week earlier, Zeb's up-in-the-air job situation had finally been settled. As part of its restructuring, Key-Comm had not exactly eliminated Zeb's job but instead was hoping to create a new position that would fit his needs and abilities more closely. Best of all, the new job's travel requirements would be only half those of his current job.

Robin felt so unworthy! She did not deserve such a forgiving husband. She did not deserve to keep her job. From somewhere beyond the outfield fence she heard a car horn and remembered the driver she thought was angry with her but was really joyful.

Overhead a plane buzzed, trailing a banner: CONGRATS GRADUATES! Erin Delaney squinted into the sky to read its message, then dodged a parade of seniors led by Cody Summers and Gordie St. James circling the field hoisting the aluminum foil trophy they had earned for their washers championship. Meanwhile, Matt was soliciting offers for payment if he climbed one of the telephone poles to the very top. Nearby, Tyler Batta was testing his new video equipment—a graduation gift—by capturing different scenes and providing running commentary. In the stands, the more popular girls were signing each other's yearbooks in combinations of bright felt-tipped marker colors, never relenting in their complaints about the exorbitant cost of the publication. Not far away, Jeremy Southard was watching the girls. Erin giggled.

She felt the happiest she had been the whole school year. That morning she had visited Grandpa Dee at the hospital. His ministrokes, scary as they were, had not affected him in any noticeable way. He was resuming his daily exercise to recover from his hip surgery, already walking with a walker and handling his physical therapy with his usual wit. Erin brought in his Vanna White cutout for *Wheel of Fortune*, which his nurses made sure he could watch every night. In another few days he would be transferred to a health care facility to continue therapy until he was ready to move back to Lake Haven.

Grandpa Dee's condition was not the only reason for Erin's elation, though. Her father, of all people, also deserved credit. Erin could hardly believe his total change of heart over the college issue. Less than a half hour earlier, when she arrived at the picnic with her parents, the first people who spotted them were the Southards—Jess and Jeremy, with Aunt Jen and Uncle Russ. Her volatile friendship with Jess had settled into equilibrium in the aftermath of the tragedy. Still, Erin knew that Jen and Russ would bring up the subject of college. ...

"So Erin," Jen said in the course of their exchange of pleasantries," what's the latest on your college plans? Virginia Tech still? Or has Princeton come calling yet?"

Erin wanted to dig a hole under the pitcher's mound and hide. She tried to think of a diplomatic reply that would not offend her dad or sound sarcastic. Suddenly, Dad rescued her in a solid voice: "Princeton won't come calling, because it's not the best place for Erin. Riverside University has called, and Erin has answered. She's going to Riverside to study forestry, or maybe elder care!" The forceful, proud words came from out of left field, not far from where they were standing, and when she looked into her father's face she saw he was staring straight into her eyes, and a moment later he whispered into her ear, "God didn't make everyone to be a doctor, right?" So he really *did* support her decision! And on that affirmation alone she beamed with delight throughout the rest of the picnic.

As for her lingering suspicion about Dad's involvement in the school's cheating culture, well, she would leave that to her parents to resolve. No matter how much she had grown up, on that question she was willing to remain a child.

The Bridgebury *Courier* was present at the picnic, though its decision-makers had wisely chosen to send a reporter other than Pete Doty, along with a photographer. Erin positioned herself to overhear an interview involving several seniors and was pleased that the journalist was not asking intrusive personal questions about the scandal. Today she had read an article about the "Riverside connection," which speculated on the role that a university research project might have played in the rise of the cheating culture. The name of Professor Don Weaver, J.J.'s father, figured prominently in the report. J.J. himself was conspicuously absent from the picnic.

Erin played a game of washers with Jess and the Straley sisters, making two straight clanging shots into the bucket but otherwise failing wretchedly, which didn't matter because the girls were not playing competitively. Then she ate a cheeseburger with lots of mustard and pickles, just the way she preferred her burgers, and allowed Tyler Batta to interview her—only after stipulating that he could not ask about Myers or the cheating scandal. Finally, she took part in a human pyramid that reached to the sixth level—21 students in all, topped by lightweight Kelly Bennett—which on the count of three collapsed amid howls of laughter and grunting.

In the absence of Tolan Myers and William LaGrange, the school board had appointed Mr. Batta to supervise the picnic, and he was doing a commendable job of keeping his oversight minimal. As long as nobody got hurt, he was willing to let the teenagers blow off their steam however they desired.

Eventually Erin wandered back to the infield and found her mom, whose business was not officially catering the picnic but was providing supplies such as paper plates and cups, napkins, and plastic tableware.

She wanted to ask Mom about Dad's change of heart, but she didn't know how.

"Mom?" she began vaguely. "You really don't mind if I go to Riverside?"

Her mom said, "Erin, your dad and I have discussed it for days. What can we say? It's no good pressuring you to go somewhere you won't belong."

Erin waited for Mom to say more.

"And what has happened in the last week has made everyone stop and take a close look at their lives. And ... well, when we heard about how you were one of the people who was still ... *clean*, I guess is the way to say it ..." Mom was struggling for words, uneasy. Her fingers fought to pull paper plates from their plastic wrap. And Erin thought of how she was anything but clean, unless you didn't count stupidity.

Then her mom set down the stack of paper plates, composed herself, locked Erin with her gaze, and said with a cracking voice and tears forming in her eyes, "You have made us very proud."

Erin hugged her mom and broke away, sobbing. She ran to the backstop, sniffling, where Matt caught her and asked what was wrong. For the first time ever it felt comfortable to be wrapped in his strong arms. She hugged him and said, "I guess everything is just hitting me now."

"Yeah, I hear you on that."

They grasped the backstop fence and shook it in unison. In the distance they saw the scaffolding that blurred the school's front entrance. Repairs on the vandalism were already in progress. In a week or two, nobody would know from looking at the beautiful pillars and canopy on the outside that something had gone terribly wrong inside.

Alone with Matt, who seemed to share her melancholy mood, or at least to understand it, she ventured to ask: "What really happened on the bridge? With Myers?" She turned to face him, and saw him swallow.

"It all happened so fast," he said, "I'm not sure if I even know, if I even remember."

It sounded practiced, rehearsed.

"That's a lie," she said, partly in fun—but the fun quickly morphed into fear. If he were lying, then the truth might be too terrible to hear.

"Not really."

"What do you remember, then?"

He leaned against the fence and looked at his shoes.

"This what I told the police. I remember Myers pulling out his gun. And McCauley was calm as a cucumber. I was really amazed by that, because I was scared to death. I don't remember anything I said, or if I said anything. I know Myers was doing a lot of talking, but I can't remember what he said. And then a car went past and its horn honked, loud and long. Next thing I knew we were wrestling with Myers, both McCauley and me. He was twisting Myers's arm to get the gun. And I just wound the cord around his neck, in self-defense, I guess. My instincts just took over, like in football. Then I saw McCauley taking a few steps toward the side and throwing the gun, I guess, over the side. And I just pushed Myers over the edge."

Erin tried to align Matt's story with what she and Mrs. Hillis had heard from their hiding spot beneath the deck.

"Why did you have a cord with you at all? Were you going to ... kill yourself?"

Matt swept his shoe over the grass. "No."

"What, then? Myers?"

"It was self-defense, Erin."

"I know. He had a gun. But ... you didn't know that ahead of time. I'm just asking why you had the bungee cord."

"I wound it around his neck during the fight, when McCauley got the gun. It was self-defense. I wound it around his neck." He sounded dull, his statement mechanical.

"You wound it around his neck." She did not try to hide her skepticism.

"Yeah."

"Four times."

"*One-two-three-four*," he said. Before she could respond, he pulled her toward the playing field, shouting "Come on!"

They joined the seniors making a human chain and dancing around the field to the tune of "Locomotion" booming from the loudspeakers. Erin wondered whether the song made Matt think of that night when he and some unnamed, unknown friend of theirs had ambushed Mr.

McCauley on the railroad tracks south of town and nearly frightened him to death. Some mysteries might never be solved.

When the dance finished, Erin stopped to catch her breath and heard Mrs. Hillis, hand in hand with her husband, calling her name and waving to her.

"I just wanted to say good-bye," Mrs. Hillis said. "We're going home. Two hours is enough excitement for me. Usually for you, too. Wouldn't you rather be off watching whirlwinds?"

"Yeah. This isn't so bad, though."

Erin reflected—that whirlwind was heavenly, but *she* was just as heavenly.

"Come and visit sometime, okay?" Mrs. Hillis asked.

"Yeah. I'll be sure. I wanted to tell you something else before you go."

"Okay."

"It's kind of private."

They walked away from the others.

"What is it?" Mrs. Hillis asked.

"I've thought of a new way to use the word *pejorative*," Erin answered. "You know, from the final exam in your class. I keep thinking of vocab words."

"I'm honored!"

"I used to think that calling somebody a One-Track was pejorative, but now I don't think so. It could be a compliment."

Mrs. Hillis looked at her with an odd expression.

"Erin," she said, "I'm a One-Track."

"You *are?*" Her heart plummeted. "Oh! I'm sorry, I hope I didn't hurt your feelings."

"Not at all. It goes with the territory."

"It does? That's weird." She looked away, trying to remember if Sally Richards or Rachel Sarks had ever said anything like that.

"Regarding your final exam," Mrs. Hillis said. "I was very impressed with what you said on the last question, your essay."

Erin beamed. The prompt had followed up on a question Mrs. Hillis had asked two or three times during the school year about how well the students were progressing toward their senior year goals. On the exam they were asked to make a final assessment.

"I loved that question," Erin said. "I felt like it was made just for me. But I would revise my answer after the last couple of weeks."

"You would? It was already a great answer."

"Thanks! But that was before what happened at the hospital, when my grandpa had his ministrokes."

She saw Mrs. Hillis's face go cloudy.

"He's okay," she quickly clarified. "But the night it happened, something wonderful happened. And when it was all over, I decided that I have learned a lot about how to live with uncertainty. I would have written that as part of my answer. Mess is okay, maybe."

Something pulled her attention to the parking lot.

Zeb returned to Robin's side. It was time for them to go.

Robin sensed some melancholy in Erin's face and asked, "Are you okay?"

Erin seemed distracted but looked into Robin's eyes and said, "Yeah. I was just thinking. Do you know what kind of triangle it is when the sides and angles are all different? Is that *isosceles*?"

"I don't know. Find Kim McGrew; he's here somewhere. Or ask Coach Batta."

"It's either *isosceles* or *scalene*."

"Why does it matter?"

"I was thinking about …" She paused, aware of Zeb's curious stare.

Robin knew, somehow. Brad McCauley was the third leg of their strange triangle.

"Zeb, would you give us another minute or two? Alone?"

"Sure, honey. I'll wait over by the fence."

Once he was out of earshot, Robin asked, "What were you thinking about?"

"Mr. McCauley."

"I thought so."

And then, as if their words had magically rubbed a genie's lamp, they heard the unmistakable revving of his motorcycle. Their hearts leapt. Their eyes turned together toward the parking lot.

McCauley gunned the engine repeatedly, and one gloved hand rose and gave a thumbs-up signal.

Robin recalled his final words from a few hours before. "I've decided to do what's right," he had said succinctly, decisively. She supposed he was referring to his dissertation. "And I couldn't have done it without you."

Robin smiled, remembering, and threw her arm around Erin's shoulder. She believed that his *you* was plural.

He would go against the current, against the tide of doing wrong that had engulfed so much of their lives.

She and Erin waved until he rode off.

"We'll never see him again," Robin said. "I wonder why he even came today?"

"I invited him," Erin said. "Well, not exactly. I called him and left a message that I wanted to say good-bye before he left town."

"Still, we'll never see him again."

"He called me back."

"Really? What did he say?"

"He said we weren't losers."

"What did he mean by that?"

"He said there was a line from a song by that singer he likes so much. I can't remember the exact words—something about winning and losing, about winners and losers, and he was a winner and had to get away from all the losers. Something like that. And he said no matter how much he wanted to think of Brookstone as being losers, he couldn't do it. He said we weren't losers."

The rumble of his motorcycle receded and died out.

"No," Robin said. "He's right about that."

Order Information

REDEMPTION
PRESS

To order additional copies of this book, please visit
www.redemption-press.com.
Also available on Amazon.com and BarnesandNoble.com
Or by calling toll free 1-844-2REDEEM.

CPSIA information can be obtained
at www.ICGtesting.com
Printed in the USA
LVOW03s1914290118
564422LV00002B/122/P